BRIDGES TO TOMORROW

Volume 2, The Best of ACLD

DATE DUE

BRIDGES

Co-edited b

an

TO TOMORROW

Selected Papers from the 17th International Conference of the
Association for Children with Learning Disabilities

WILLIAM M. CRUICKSHANK, Ph.D.

School of Public Health
University of Michigan

ARCHIE A. SILVER, M.D.

College of Medicine
University of South Florida

 SYRACUSE UNIVERSITY PRESS   1981

Library of Congress Cataloging in Publication Data
Main entry under title:

Bridges to tomorrow.

  (The Best of ACLD; v. 2)
  Bibliography: p.
  1. Learning disabilities — Addresses, essays,
lectures. I. Cruickshank, William M. II. Silver,
Archie A. III. Association for Children with
Learning Disabilities. IV. Series: Association for
Children with Learning Disabilities. Best of ACLD;
v. 2.
LC4704.B74   371.9   80-26176
ISBN 0-8156-2237-6 (pbk.)

CONTENTS

BACKGROUNDS TO EDUCATION

CONTRIBUTORS

Robert Algozzine is Associate Professor of Special Education, University of Florida, Gainsville, Florida

Donald Allen is Graduate Research Assistant, Institute for Research on Learning Disabilities, University of Minnesota, Minneapolis, Minnesota

Gordon R. Alley is Professor of Pediatrics and Research Associate, Institute for Research in Learning Disabilities, University of Kansas, Lawrence, Kansas

Jane W. Blalock is Assistant Professor, Program in Learning Disabilities, Northwestern University, Evanston, Illinois

Berttram Chiang is Assistant Professor of Special Education, University of Wisconsin at Oshkosh, Oshkosh, Wisconsin

Frances L. Clark is Research Associate, Research Institute for Learning Disabilities, Kansas Medical Center, Kansas City, Kansas

Susan L. Cohn is a medical student, University of Illinois Medical School, Chicago, Illinois

Stanley Deno is Professor of Special Education, Institute for Research on Learning Disabilities, University of Minnesota, Minneapolis, Minnesota

Donald D. Deshler is Research Coordinator at the Institute for Research in Learning Disabilities, University of Kansas, Lawrence, Kansas

Drake D. Duane is Professor of Neurology, Mayo Clinic and Mayo Foundation, Rochester, Minnesota

Susan Epps is Graduate Research Assistant, Institute for Research on Learning Disabilities, University of Minnesota, Minneapolis, Minnesota

Rosa A. Hagin is Research Professor of Psychology, New York University Medical School, New York City

Samuel A. Kirk is Professor of Special Education, University of Arizona, Tucson, Arizona

Gladys P. Knott is Associate Professor of Special Education, Kent State University, Kent, Ohio

Kathryn Kuehnle is Graduate Research Assistant, Institute for Research on Learning Disabilities, Minneapolis, Minnesota

Roger P. Larsen is Assistant Professor of Special Education, Northern Illinois University, De Kalb, Illinois

Janet W. Lerner is Professor of Special Education, Northeastern Illinois University, Chicago, Illinois

Lisa Lowry is Graduate Research Assistant, Institute for Research on Learning Disabilities, University of Minnesota, Minneapolis, Minnesota

Douglas Marston is Graduate Research Assistant, Institute for Research on Learning Disabilities, University of Minnesota, Minneapolis, Minnesota

Matthew McGue is Graduate Research Assistant, Institute for Research on Learning Disabilities, University of Minnesota, Minneapolis, Minnesota

Sandra L. McNett-McGowan is Biological Illustrator/Audio-visual Consultant, School of Pharmacy, University of the Pacific, Stockton, California

Charles Meisgeier is Professor of Education and Director of the Child Service Demonstration Center, University of Houston, Houston, Texas

Linda Menius is Training Coordinator at the Child Service Demonstration Center, University of Houston, Houston, Texas

Phyllis Mirkin is Assistant Professor of Special Education, Institute for Research on Learning Disabilities, University of Minnesota, Minneapolis, Minnesota

Stephen Poland is Graduate Research Assistant, Institute for Research and Learning Disabilities, University of Minnesota, Minneapolis, Minnesota

Margaret Potter is Graduate Research Assistant, Institute for Research and Learning Disabilities, University of Minnesota, Minneapolis, Minnesota

Richard Regan is Graduate Research Assistant, Institute for Research and Learning Disabilities, University of Minnesota, Minneapolis, Minnesota

Howell I. Runion is Professor of Physiology-Pharmacology (Electrophysiology), School of Pharmacy, University of the Pacific, Stockton, California

Jean B. Schumaker is Associate Coordinator of Research, Institute for Research in Learning Disabilities, University of Kansas, Lawrence, Kansas

Gerald M. Senf is Editor-in-Chief, *Journal of Learning Disabilities*

Mark Shinn is Graduate Research Assistant, Institute for Research on Learning Disabilities, University of Minnesota, Minneapolis, Minnesota

Archie A. Silver is Professor of Psychiatry and Chief, Division of Child and Adolescent Psychiatry, College of Medicine, University of South Florida, Tampa, Florida

Martha Thurlow is Associate Scientist, Institute for Research on Learning Disabilities, University of Minnesota, Minneapolis, Minnesota

Gerald Tindal is Graduate Assistant, Institute for Research on Learning Disabilities, University of Minnesota, Minneapolis, Minnesota

Michael M. Warner is Graduate Research Assistant, Institute for Research on Learning Disabilities, University of Minnesota, Minneapolis, Minnesota

James E. Ysseldyke is Director of the Institute for Research on Learning Disabilities, University of Minnesota, Minneapolis, Minnesota

PREFACE

O NE YEAR AGO, Volume 1 of "The Best of ACLD," *Approaches to Learning,* a collection of thirteen papers or symposia drawn from the hundreds presented at the annual ACLD meetings of 1978 and 1979, was published. Its title, of course, was, at best, presumptuous; at worst, downright untrue. However, in the judgment of the editorial board it did contain the best of the fifty or so papers which were submitted to the board for publication. As such, Volume 1 served its purpose: to prevent many excellent papers presented at the annual meetings from disappearing from sight and mind, left behind as we boarded planes to return home. Each volume, then, was to serve as a reference document of the current thinking in research and practice in the understanding and treatment of the child with a learning disability. By virtue of its very existence, too, it was intended that each volume would serve as a stimulus for excellence in the papers presented at each annual ACLD meeting.

It is our hope that Volume 2, the current volume, will also make available "The Best of ACLD," the best of papers submitted to the editors from those presented at the 1980 ACLD meeting in Milwaukee. It is a way of making interesting papers available to many at an extremely low cost. These books should also serve as further stimulus for increasing the care, thought, and documentation in the preparation of papers for ACLD annual meetings and an increasing desire to record one's thought and work in the ACLD annual. The editorial committee would be delighted to be deluged with so many papers of such excellent quality that the annual will have to be enlarged.

For the present volume, thirteen papers are presented. These range in content from a global overview of the LD scene (Kirk, Senf, and Larsen) through five papers on practical approaches to the different problem of LD in adolescence and adulthood — adolescent LD (Knott), young adult and LD (Blalock), social deficits in LD adolescents (Schumaker et al.), and emotional needs (Meisgeier and Menius); to four papers on problems of assessment and evaluation — performance on WISCR (Ysseldyke et al.), decision-making (Ysseldyke et al.), bias in placements (Ysseldyke et al.), research on an evaluation system for LD programs (Deno et al.). In addition, there are four papers on medical backgrounds to education — the EEG (Duane), brain anatomy (Runion and McNett-McGowan), pediatricians (Lerner and Cohn), and a critique of the prevention of reading failure (Silver and Hagin).

This is quite a heady fare. We hope the diet is agreeable, and that the reader will ask for more! The editorial committee appreciates your comments and suggestions.

For the Editorial Committee
Archie A. Silver, M.D.

BRIDGES TO TOMORROW

Volume 2, The Best of ACLD

1

Current Issues in Learning Disabilities

Samuel A. Kirk, Gerald M. Senf, and Roger P. Larsen

A N issue is defined as a point of discussion, debate, or dispute. In the field of learning disabilities we certainly do not lack points for discussion and debate.

It is not surprising that we have problems in definition, problems in delineating the characteristics of learning disabled children, problems in clarifying multiple etiologies, and problems in determining valid taxonomies.

All scientific fields go through such controversies and disputes. The social sciences, including education, are the latest to develop their own identity. Because of the complexities of human behavior these fields include more controversies and disputes than do the physical sciences. The area of learning disabilities is one of the newer fields. It is to be expected that numerous issues, disagreements, and misunderstandings will evolve. Our task currently is to define the major issues and to search for solutions to these debates and controversies.

The field of learning disabilities is interdisciplinary, requiring the expertise of a variety of professions. It is of greatest concern to three groups of people: (1) parents, who organized ACLD; (2) teachers and other school personnel, and (3) academicians and theoreticians. The latter group seem to publish most of the journal articles relating to controversies in learning disabilities. Many of the issues arise from academia rather than from parents and teachers.

Parents are primarily concerned with the welfare and education of their children. They want the child to develop normally; they want the child to achieve; they want their child to succeed in life. Their efforts have been primarily to achieve adequate diagnosis and adequate services for their children.

Teachers and other service personnel have been concerned with remediating and correcting developmental problems in children. They are constantly seeking better methods of assessment and better methods of remediation. They are the ones who are on the firing line and their major concern has been primarily to give more adequate service.

The theoretical issues are discussed primarily by academicians. The literature is replete with articles, controversies, issues, and position papers. This approach is extremely beneficial if the academicians follow up their criticisms by devising better methods of assessment, better methods of organization and service, and better methods of remediation.

In teaching graduate students, we have found it imperative to train them in critical thinking. In the beginning of such training they tend to be primarily negative in their criticisms of research and theory. They felt it their scholarly duty to tear to pieces published articles in journals. One of the authors was forced to call the students together at one time and to say to them that there is a very important role for criticism, but that the reason we find a flaw in an experiment or in a procedure or in a theory is for the purpose of doing a better job. It is incumbent upon us when we criticize to suggest a product or an experiment that avoids the flaws in the one that we are criticizing. Criticism just for ego purposes is not the function of a scholar. A scholar weighs both sides objectively and attempts to find a resolution to the problem in a better way than has been done previously. To emphasize this point we quoted an old adage: *Any fool can criticize and most fools do.*

SOME ISSUES

One of the most agonizing issues has been that of defining just what is meant by a learning disability. Some people do not think there is such a thing as a learning disability. Some do not like the use of the term "learning disability." Some think it is a modern invention to hire more teachers and spend more tax money. Some are satisified to continue placing these children in inappropriate services. As we travel around the country and read the literature we find statements such as:

1. You can't define learning disabilities, therefore it doesn't exist.
2. There is no such thing as a learning disability.
3. Learning disabilities is a kitchen sink term, a garbage can concept.
4. Learning disabilities is a political creation designed to obtain subsidies for schools.
5. All handicapped children are learning disabled.

Fred Weintraub has suggested a solution to the problem of defining learning disabilities — lock all the experts in a room and accept the definition of the one who comes out alive!

Seriously, we do have some major controversies that are causing considerable difficulties and concerns in the field. Many of these issues will be discussed later in this paper. We should, however, like to mention one that is being discussed. This is the problem of whether we should do diagnostic prescriptive teaching, that is find out the abilities and disabilities of the child so that we can find the appropriate instruction, or whether we should just do task analysis and task teaching without reference to abilities and disabilities of a child.

Most teachers of learning disabilities use a diagnostic prescriptive approach. This procedure is being challenged, for example by Arter and Jenkins in the Fall 1979 issue of the *Journal of Educational Research*. After reviewing the literature on this problem, these authors state: "The DD-PT [differential-diagnostic-prescriptive teaching] model is preferred by the vast majority of special education teachers. . . . 93% believe that their students had learned more when they modified instruction to match modality strengths" (p. 549).

Arter and Jenkins, however, decry this practice. They do not consider teachers as independent thinkers on this issue but believe that they have been brainwashed by their preparatory studies. The authors continue the above quotation: "The same survey provided data to suggest that teacher training programs were to a large degree responsible for these views and practices" (p. 550).

In other words, these authors state that more than 90 percent of the teachers are wrong in their practices and that the courses they take are also wrong. To correct the malpractice of DD-PT, Arter and Jenkins made the following recommendation: "We believe that until a substantial research base for the DD-PT model has been developed, it is imperative to call for a moratorium on advocacy of DD-PT, on classification and placement of children according to differential ability tests, on the purchase of instructional materials and programs which claim to improve these abilities, and on course work designed to train DD-PT teachers" (p. 550).

This very serious indictment has been published in a prestigious journal. It is therefore necessary that we look into this report to find out whether the authors have sufficient evidence to come to the conclusion that, according to these authors, more than 90 percent of teachers are conducting malpractice with children and that we must stop immediately. We must also close down those courses in colleges that are misleading teachers.

In reviewing this article we find three major flaws: (1) it misrepresents the practice of diagnostic prescriptive teaching; (2) it omits from the report the summaries of research and articles contrary to their belief;

and (3) it uses an unscholarly approach to the review of research by reporting secondary references.

Misrepresentation

Arter and Jenkins tend to *misrepresent* the practice of the diagnostic prescriptive teacher by saying that a task analytic approach teaches specific components of academic tasks while a diagnostic prescriptive teacher "teaches general abilities." This is contrary to what is advocated in diagnostic prescriptive teaching which tries to identify specific abilities which the child can utilize in performing school tasks. In making this differentiation these authors ignore the statements of writers such as Quay (1973), Raschke and Young (1976), and Kirk (1977). These authors and others refer to the interaction between the task and the specific abilities and disabilities of the child. Quay refers to this as "interactive"; Reschke and Young discuss "didactic teaching"; we have called it "process-task training." Kephart (1960) referred to this as "perceptual — motor training," while Cruickshank (1977) continues to speak of this approach as the "psychoeducational match." All these writers apparently were ignored by Arter and Jenkins. All of these writers stated in effect that diagnostic prescriptive teachers use task training and ability training at the same time. If a child has a marked visual discrimination problem, the diagnostic prescriptive teacher teaches visual discrimination of letters and words in the task itself. If the child is unable to remember words he or she sees or has a visual memory problem, the diagnostic prescriptive teacher uses a procedure that will train the memory of words and sentences such as is used by the Fernald kinesthetic method. To state that a diagnostic prescriptive teacher trains attention in the abstract or discrimination in the abstract is a misrepresentation of the theory and practice of diagnostic prescriptive teaching.

Our point here is that when one fails to refer to articles in a reveiw of the literature that are contrary to the conclusions made, it is less than scholarly. To disagree with a point of view is legitimate. To ignore contrary points of view in a so-called comprehensive review is not legitimate.

Was the Review Comprehensive?

Another question one might ask was whether the review was comprehensive or a biased selection of articles to correspond with the authors' previous assumptions. They used some secondary references that agreed with their point of view and ignored other secondary references that disagreed with their point of view.

It is unfortunate that Arter and Jenkins did not review all of the literature even though the article is presented as "a comprehensive review of research related to each assumption." In this review there is the heavy reliance on articles which have already been exposed as scientifically questionable. No references were made to criticisms of these articles, nor did the unscientific nature of the research have any influence on the authors' conclusions. One such report is the research presented by Hammill and Larsen (1978) which concluded that "psycholinguistic training constructs can be trained by existing techniques remains unvalidated." They failed to report that Lund, Foster, and Perez (1978) have reanalyzed the data and have come to opposite conclusions. They also failed to report the critical article by Minskoff (1976) which showed that Hammill and Larsen's study made an apples and pears comparison which invalidated their conclusions. It is necessary for a comprehensive report to include such studies even though they may not agree.

Another deletion is their acceptance of the studies of reporting of a study by Hammill, Parker, and Newcomer (1975) and Newcomer (1975) in which they administered every other item of the ITPA to nine-and-a-half-year-old children in the fourth grade, gave them the Metropolitan Achievement Test, and ran correlations. They concluded that the ITPA does not predict academic achievement. They failed to report the article by McLeod (1976) in which he pointed out that the children of this study averaged nine years old, reaching the top of the norms. This condition produces a restricted range, thus reducing the correlations. McLeod also pointed out the fallacy in stating that the ITPA was designed to predict reading in the fourth grade and stated that the study is striking down a straw man. Maggiore (1978), in a study of the short form of the ITPA, compared the short form with the long form and concluded that the short form was not a substitute for the long form. Kirk and Kirk (1978), in an examination of the reports of Newcomer (1975) stated that the ITPA was an intraindividual test constructed primarily for preschool children and not a test for predicting reading in the third or fourth grade.

The heavy reliance of Arter and Jenkins on studies which support their hypothesis, and the deletion of opposing studies and points of view, is less than scholarly. It is their privilege to agree with these people, but scientific and scholarly integrity require that they also include other points of view and other research whether or not they agree with the opposing points of view. Many secondary references were used, especially if the conclusions agreed with their own point of view. In scholarly work we do not accept secondary references. We expect an author to delve into the original sources if he or she is going to make an intelligent, comprehensive review. The authors justify their approach of secondary references by saying: "The literature on various aspects of the DD-PT is so extensive that a comprehensive review of primary sources would be prohibitive." In addition, they say: "It would be unwise to ignore the unique and valuable contributions of a number of scholars to the analysis of the DD-PT literature" (p. 521).

In spite of this statement and as has been shown earlier, we find that there is an extensive array of literature not supporting their point of view that was neither reviewed nor mentioned. We should not, therefore, take seriously their recommendation that we declare a moratorium on differential diagnostic prescriptive teaching.

A STUDY OF ISSUES

In the fall of 1978 we sent letters to fifty professors in colleges and universities and asked them to state the three most crucial issues in the field of learning disabilities that ought to be studied. On the basis of these replies and on the basis of a review of literature, Paul Berry, in Australia, helped us construct a questionnaire. We felt that we ought to work on those issues of concern primarily to teachers, parents, and other professional personnel. We were not so concerned with the theoretical opinions of professors who are not on the firing line. We were interested in different opinions among teachers, psychologists, administrators, and academic personnel.

At the ACLD meeting in February of 1979 we distributed the questionnaire, obtained approximately 125 replies, analyzed the data, and arrived at several conclusions regarding the major issues of concern to teachers and parents.

To obtain a large sample of teachers, administrators, parents, psychologists, and academic personnel, Gerald Senf, Editor of the *Journal of Learning Disabilities*, suggested that we revise the questionnaire again and print it in the *Journal of Learning Disabilities* with the request that readers complete the questionnaire and send them to the *Journal*. The *Journal* has obtained approximately 1,500 replies to this questionnaire. A part of the data has been analyzed by Gerald Senf and his colleagues. We will now report on some of the major issues that were delineated by teachers, psychologists, administrators, academic personnel, and others.

RESPONDENT CHARACTERISTICS

The respondents in the present sample were 71 percent female. Geographically 43 percent of the respondents resided in the eastern portion of the country, 35 percent in the Midwest, and 15 percent in the West.

As would be expected, the group has high academic credentials; 15 percent have bachelor's degrees, 93 percent of these with some kind of educational certification; 66 percent have master's degrees, 77 percent of which have certification; 18 percent have doctoral degrees, 56 percent of which have certification.

Also, as might be anticipated, 97 percent of the respondents are Caucasian, the other 3 percent being comprised of Native Americans (.9 percent), black (.7 percent), Hispanic (.4 percent), and Oriental (.4 percent).

Experience in working with LD children varied considerably, 4 percent had no work experience and 5 percent had more than twenty years of teaching experience with LD children. Those with three years or less experience comprised 24 percent of the respondents, those with four to ten years comprised 51 percent, and those with more than ten years 25 percent.

Nearly half of the sample (609) belong to ACLD, 531 belong to CEC, of which 355 belong to DCLD. Other groups to which respondents belong in large numbers included the National Education Association (319), the International Reading Association (180), the Orton Society (177), and the American Psychological Association (98). Eight other organizations or divisions of major organizations were represented by 25 or more respondents.

The primary role of the most populous group of respondents was teachers of LD pupils (499), with 162 psychologists practitioners, 134 administrators, and 110 teacher trainers. Only two other roles, that of teacher of other special education pupils (73) and remedial reading specialists (59) received a significant number of nominations.

Two-thirds of the sample were involved primarily with elementary school children, 16 percent with secondary level LD students, 11 percent with preschool, and 7 percent with college. The 7 percent college figure may be inflated as some teacher trainers may have interpreted the question to mean their own educational level, although the question specified "involvement with pupils."

Of the 810 respondents indicating "the setting in which you work most" with LD children, 57 percent worked in a resource room, 20 percent in a self-contained room, 14 percent were itinerant, and 9 percent worked in a regular classroom.

In general, there are no surprises in the make-up of the sample; it generally represented a microcosm of the learning disability community. However, conspicuously absent are responses from parents. We have been working to increase the small sample of 28 parents of LD children. These data will be reported in subsequent papers.

METHOD OF REPORTING DATA

Because the *Journal of Learning Disabilities* questionnaire is too long to report in one paper, we have elected to report selected data pertaining to (1) the concept, and (2) the definition of learning disabilities. The data are in the form of histograms which utilize only those items of an agree-disagree format. Each of the histograms notes the percent of respondents in each of six response classes: "strongly agree," "agree," "neutral," "disagree," "strongly disagree," and "no opinion." The no-opinion-response option was provided to distinguish those respondents whose attitude was neutral with respect to the question from those who wished simply not to voice an opinion. Thus, though some items may lack the full 1,266 respondents, any difference in total responses to each item is insignificant and is not reported. The numbers represent the percent expressing the associated opinion rounded to the nearest whole percent. The sum of the strongly agree and agree and the sum of the disagree and strongly disagree response categories are utilized so that the reader can readily grasp the dispersion of opinion.

THE CONCEPT OF LEARNING DISABILITIES

There was a very even distribution between persons who believe that "learning disabilities, if correctly diagnosed, are due to neurological impairments" or not. Thirty-seven percent agree with this statement, 40 percent disagree, with 10 percent of each group either strongly agreeing or strongly disagreeing. It is worth noting that a full 21 percent are neutral on this issue, perhaps reflecting the often-heard belief that neurological status is unimportant since educational intervention must be rendered in either case — the underlying assumption, which may be false, being that neurological status is not relevant to the selection of specific educational strategies.

Somewhat more consensus was achieved on the item, "Learning disabilities are a finite group of disorders, not just children with unique problems." The question was motivated by the often-heard opinion that all LD children are different and that each remedial program must be individually tailored. While the IEP mandates just such an approach, it can certainly be argued that there are only so many kinds of problems we can conceive of and a limited number of remedial strategies available to us. Matching the most appropriate strategies to disordered learning which we have recognized previously need not necessarily deny the child's individuality any more than a physician's bedside manner cannot be unique to each patient even though two or more of his or her patients may have the same disease. While slightly more than half of the respondents agree with the statement, some variation does occur between persons having different roles in the educational system. While 15 percent overall strongly agreed that "learning disabilities are a finite group of disorders, 23 percent of the administrators and 12 percent of LD teachers strongly agreed. This suggests that those in administrative positions are more apt to look to broader categories of disorders while those working individually with the children may see greater interindividual differences. The notion that there exist *types* of learning disabilities is supported in a later question (not reported here) in which "identification of the major types of LD" is ranked highly among research priorities.

Both the literature on hyperactivity and the treatment of hyperactive behavior in schools frequently fail to distinguish the hyperactive child from the learning disabled. When asked directly, respondents indicated that they disagreed that "hyperactivity is one of the learning disabilities, even if the child performs adequately academically" (59 percent). However, a full third of the respondents endorsed the statement, bearing witness to the disagreement surrounding the inclusion of hyperactivity as a sufficient characteristic for labeling a child learning disabled.

While historically old, the issue of whether "learning disabilities is essentially synonymous with middle class retardation," such thinking still does crop up in the popular press so we thought we would ask the question directly in the hope of putting the issue to rest. Ninety-two percent of the respondents disagree with the assertion. It will be interesting in further analysis to determine the background characteristics — role, memberships, etc. — of those 4 percent who agree with the statement. Though 4 percent seems small, we are talking about 50 respondents, 25 of whom *strongly* agree learning disabilities is essentially synonymous with middle class retardation!

While the identity of learning disabilities as middle class retardation was clearly denied, distinguishing the learning disabled from the slow learner was less uniformly accepted by the respondents. While 81 percent of the respondents do agree (37 percent strongly so) that an LD child can be distinguished from a slow learner, one must wonder who the remaining 19 percent are, more than half of whom (11 percent of the total) disagree that the distinction can be made. Given that this sample is heavily comprised of persons who work in public school special education settings, the fact that one in ten refuses the LD–slow learner distinction has tremendous ramifications. More detailed analysis found that this attitude is not disproportionate among LD teachers, administrators, school psychologists, or teacher trainers; consequently we can only conclude that a meaningfully large segment of the population concerned with LD children do not distinguish attributes of LD children from those of children with normal intelligence.

A related item was thought to imply that LD was a nonspecific category utilized primarily as an umbrella term to provide the individual education needed by nonretarded children. While it may be the case that the term LD is occasionally used in any given school to provide a nonretarded child with individual teaching — even though more specific LD "symptoms" may not be manifest — the fact that 31 percent of the respondents agree that LD represents just such an administrative mechanism is surprising. Apparently, not only is the term "learning disabilities" utilized *occasionally* to provide "individual teaching" but is in the minds of many respondents an essential feature of LD. Those who would support a more restrictive definition to the term can find in these data both an understanding of the large prevalence estimates and of the tendency to serve the milder cases in preference to what they might call "severe LD."

A related item, "There is really no difference between a learning disability and a learning problem/learning difficulty," further supports the conclusion that those in front-line positions do not have a firm fix on how the alleged "true LD" case can be distinguished. Though 65 percent disagree that there is *no* difference between a learning disability and a learning problem/learning difficulty, the fact that a full third either are neutral or believe that there is really no difference helps us further to understand the definitional confusion in practice. Interestingly, while 20 percent strongly disagree there is no difference, it is the administrators (29 percent) and teacher trainers (35 percent) who disproportionately strongly disagree, while only 17 percent of the LD teachers strongly disagree with the statement. This internal analysis suggests that those who deal with the children more closely (the LD teacher) are least willing to make the distinction between a learning disability and a learning problem/learning difficulty. Those in administrative positions and those in the university make the distinction more readily — but may do so through administrative need without reference to truly distinguishing characteristics or out of theoretical distinctions which are not noticed by the front-line practitioner.

It is not surprising that a sizeable majority disagree that "a sure way to determine if a learning disability is present is to use a formula to measure the difference between mental age and academic performance." People do not simply question the psychometric power of the formula; a sizeable minority appears to be questioning their conceptual grounds. Many administrators may not wish to be told by a formula which of many needy children they legitimately may serve with special education funds. Similarly, psychologist practitioners and others involved in psychoeducational testing may look to broader child concerns in assigning diagnosis, knowing that only a few can receive additional assistance. While operationally cleaner, the formula necessarily takes from the profession the judgment which the professional may wish to keep for him or herself.

THE DEFINITION OF LEARNING DISABILITIES

Because we sensed considerable disagreements as to who should or should not be labeled LD, we sought to determine whether the differences were conceptual or related merely to the application of an accepted definition to individual cases. Thus, we asked respondents to indicate "for each of the following characteristics, do you agree or disagree that each *must* be present to diagnose a child as LD?" We asked this question for those characteristics noted in the federal definition of learning disabilities and in the regulations pertaining to identification. You will recall that the federal definition, only slightly amended from the National Advisory Committee's definition (1968), states, "Specific learning disability means a disorder in one or more of the basic psychological processes involved in understanding or in using language, spoken or written, which may manifest itself in an imperfect ability to listen, think, speak, read, write, spell, or to do mathematical calculations. The term includes such conditions as perceptual handicaps, brain injury, minimal brain dysfunction, dyslexia, and developmental aphasia. The term does not include children who have learning problems which are primarily the result of visual, hearing, or motor handicaps, of mental retardation, or of economic, cultural, or economic disadvantage" (Federal Register, 42, p. 42478).

The hallmark of this definition clearly is "a disorder in one or more of the basic psychological processes." Yet, only 59 percent of the respondents agreed that psychological process deficits must be present, with 25 percent disagreeing and 15 percent being neutral. We shall see in a later series of questions that the explanation for this finding is *not* that psychological processes are considered unimportant for either understanding LD or in planning remedial programs. Rather, it appears more related to the attitude that the slow learner and learning disorder/ difficulty child cannot be distinguished from a learning disabled child, these latter groupings of children presumably not having specific psychological process deficits. Further statistical work not yet accomplished will attempt to verify this speculation. In any case, it is most important to recognize that only 59 percent of the respondents agree with the cornerstone concept of the learning disabilities definition — at least the federal definition.

While the definition does not require physiological/neurological irregularities, the inclusion of references such as "perceptual handicaps, brain injury, minimal brain dysfunction, dyslexia, and developmental aphasia" tend to imply neurophysiological involvement. However, respondents were about evenly divided as to whether such characteristics were necessary, with a full 21 percent indicating that they were neutral on this issue. The pattern of these data is identical to that which asked, "Learning disabilities, if correctly diagnosed, are due to neurological impairments." Though the cross tabulation has not yet been accomplished, one would presume that there exists a subset of respondents who believe that learning disabilities have a neurological base and that only conditions that have a neurological base are truly learning disabilities.

While the definition requires intact senses and while two-thirds of the respondents agreed that the child's senses must be intact in order to utilize the term "learning disabilities," a quarter disagree. Either there is substantial disagreement with the federal definition or persons are saying that learning disability can exist in the absence of intact senses as would be the case were a blind child to have a learning disability. Note that the federal definition states that the learning disability must not be "primarily the result of visual, hearing, or motor handicaps," but does not rule out the possibility that children with such handicaps could be learning disabled due to a process disorder.

The data regarding mental retardation are similar, but more respondents feel that no mental retardation should be present (74 percent). Eighteen percent do not agree that mental retardation must be absent. The same explanation as with intact senses may be operative — that learning disability *may occur in consort with* mental retardation but not be primarily *caused by* the retardation.

The data on adequate cultural environment and on opportunity to learn — as an amalgam of "environmental and economic disadvantage" — present vastly different pictures. Though opinion is spread, respondents do not feel that an adequate cultural environment is necessary. While it is clear that historically this exclusory clause was aimed at disadvantaged-environment children, it is not clear whether our present respondents are responding to the pejorative implication that disadvantaged environments are necessarily inadequate or whether they are simply affirming that learning disabilities can occur among any cultural group.

Opportunity to learn is thought to be a necessary characteristic by 81 percent of the respondents. Whether the lack of opportunity to learn is due to absenteeism or poor teaching, the respondents overwhelmingly support the notion that learning opportunity should have been present if a child is to be labeled learning disabled.

Agreement was obtained, curiously enough, in an area that had no relationship to the definition — namely the performance-potential discrepancy. With only 6 percent dissenting and 5 percent neutral, 89 percent of the respondents believe that a performance-potential discrepancy must be present to diagnose a child as LD. It should be recalled that the performance-potential discrepancy is the hallmark of the *regulations* for diagnosing LD (Federal Register, December 29, 1977) — minus the formula, which had been proposed in the initial regulations. Thus, though the definition which derives from neurological, psychological, and neuropsychological thought over the past century makes no reference to the performance-potential discrepancy except through the implicit notion of deficit or damage, it is the single most agreed upon benchmark of LD today. It does not necessarily follow that the "performance-potential discrepancy" is considered by respondents as based on the difference between mental age and measured achievement as recommended in the federal regulations. Rather, respondents may be conceiving of the difference between specific behavioral inadequacies in the face of greater general competence. As has been discussed elsewhere (Senf 1978), it would be most costly to lose the thinking and research heritage of our neuropsychological history.

PROCESS TRAINING

While much has been said about process training in the literature, one may consider it remarkable that so many persons appear to persist in teaching children as though they believed in process-related concepts. The data indicate that 83 percent of the people believe that "Teaching learning processes such as attention, memory, and discrimination are a necessary part of teaching skills such as reading, writing, etc." The moratorium called for by Arter and Jenkins (1979) which would scrap process training in favor of task training may force a false dichotomy. There is often little difference, except in the degree to which recording procedures are formalized, between instruction with an underlying process-task orientation (Kirk 1977) and that with a task orientation. Often, it would appear that it is only the less formal record-keeping of the process trainer which distinguishes him or her from the task trainer. Further, the behaviorist's claim to "objectivity" may be illusory as the behaviorist typically does not enunciate the substantive theory upon which the specific behavioral methods employed are based. For example, the analysis of a task into subtasks cannot be done without some theory of the task involved, whether or not one wishes to make one's theory public or proceed as though there were only one theory — the one implicitly being used. Consequently, the data likely indicate that persons involved with the learning disabled, however defined, wish to understand their children and formulate a remedial program which makes sense in terms of that understanding.

In two follow-up questions we asked whether concern with learning processes was still necessary if one used "a task analysis approach" or "behavior modification." It is clear that 80 to 90 percent of the respondents still believe that attention to learning processes such as memory, attention, and discrimination are necessary. It may be the case as Arter and Jenkins (1979) suggest that teacher trainers have indoctrinated the people who have responded to this questionnaire into believing in the necessity of process thinking. To accept such a thesis, we would have to believe that so diverse a population as has answered this questionnaire has been successfully duped by mentors from a very wide range of specialties. Furthermore, we would have to believe that they continue to be duped, failing to let their experience correct their practices. We would also have to believe that the relatively dull blade of evaluation research is sharper than the clinician's eye and that as a result scientific dictates must take precedence until a sharper blade can prove the clinician right (or wrong). It is our observation that research outcomes do not change policy or opinions so much as policy and opinions change what is researched. In this regard, the final figure is reassuring. In as dramatic a consensus of any question in the survey, 91 percent of the people agree with the statement that "Research concerning basic learning processes is essential in evolving new remedial strategies." While some readably criticizable outcome research may not have shown the value of process thinking, an overwhelming majority of persons playing a whole host of roles in this broad field of learning disabilities seem to know what got them where they are and that further knowledge of the same kind will be needed to make them more successful in the future.

REFERENCES

Arter, J. A., and Jenkins, J. R. "Differential Diagnosis — Prescriptive Teaching: A Critical Appraisal." *Review of Educational Research* 49, 4 (Fall 1979): 517–55.

Cruickshank, W. M. *Learning isabilities in Home, School, and Community.* Syracuse: Syracuse University Press, 1977.

Hammill, D. D., and Larsen, S. C. "The Effectiveness of Psycholinguistic Training." *Exceptional Children* 41 (1974): 5–14.

Hammill, D. D., Parker, R., and Newcomer, P. "Psycholinguistic Correlates of Academic Achievement." *Journal of School Psychology* 13 (1975): 18.

Kephart, N. C. *The Slow Learner in the Classroom.* Columbus, Ohio: Merrill, 1960.

Kirk, S. "Specific Learning Disabilities." *Journal of Clinical Child Psychology* (Winter 1977): 23–26.

Kirk, S. A., and Kirk, W. D. "Uses and Abuses of the ITPA." *Journal of Speech and Hearing Disorders* 43, 1 (February 1978).

Kirk, S. A., Berry, P. B., Senf, G. M., Larsen, R. P., and Luick, A. H. "A Survey of Attitudes concerning Learning Disabilities." *Journal of Learning Disabilities* 12 (1979): 239–45.

Lund, K. A., Foster, G. E., and Perez, F. C. "The Effectiveness of Psycholinguistic Training, a Reevaluation." *Exceptional Children* (February 1978): 310–19.

Newcomer, P., and Hammill, D. "ITPA and Academic Achievement: A Survey." *Reading Teacher* 28 (1975): 731–41.

McLeod, J. "A Reaction to Psycholinguistics in the Schools." In *Psycholinguistics in the Schools,* edited by P. Newcomer and D. Hammill. Columbus: Merrill, 1976, pp. 128–43.

Minskoff, E. "Research on the Efficacy of Remediating Psycholinguistic Disabilities: Critique and Recommendations." In *Psycholinguistics in the Schools,* edited by P. Newcomer and D. Hammill. Columbus: Merrill, 1976, pp. 103–27.

Quay, H. C. "Special Education: Assumptions, Techniques, and Evaluation Criteria." *Exceptional Children* 40 (1973): 165–70.

Reschke, D., and Young, A. 1976a. "A Comparative Analysis of the Diagnostic-Prescriptive and Behavioral-Analysis Models in Preparation for the Development of a Dialectic Pedagogical System." *Education and Training of the Mentally Retarded* 11 (April): 135–45.

———. 1976b. "The Dialectic Teaching System: A Comprehensive Model Derived from Two Educational Approaches." *Education and Training of the Mentally Retarded* 11 (October): 232–46.

Senf, G. M. "Implications of the Final Procedures for Evaluating Specific Learning Disabilities." *Journal of Learning Disabilities* 11 (1978): 124–26.

ADOLESCENCE, COLLEGE AGE, AND ADULTHOOD

2

Adolescent Learning Disabilities: Beyond Phonics, Punctuation, and Popularity

Gladys P. Knott

O F THE ACADEMIC ACHIEVEMENT DIFFICULTIES learning disabled adolescents experience, reading comprehension and written language seem to be the most debilitating. These areas appear to be of greatest concern to classroom teachers, regardless of subject content. One of my purposes is to review recent research on learning disabled adolescents' communication abilities. Language reception, expression, and use, nonverbal communication, reading comprehension, and written language are included in the present context. Another purpose is to propose a model for educational programming of learning disabled adolescents in regular high school environments. A final purpose is to suggest materials which my associates and I have found to be amenable to learning disabled adolescents' psychosocial maturity and yet conducive to fostering improved communication. The reader needs to be aware of certain premises or underpinnings which influence this contribution, including the assessment-intervention procedures and the selection of suggested materials which follow the review of research.

PREMISES

Traditionally, communication ability is discussed in terms of language arts at the elementary school level and as English at the secondary level. Further, language arts — listening, speaking, reading, and writing — are often segmented at the elementary level while literature, usage, and composition are segmented in the secondary English curriculum. A major premise of this discussion is that the various components of communication ability are interrelated, not separate, and that development in one component facilitates understanding and use of another. The perspective on communication ability is global and inclusive.

Another common tradition in fostering communication ability is to focus almost totally on verbal behavior. This practice is a misrepresentation of what actually occurs in all social interactions. Verbal and nonverbal communication are shared whenever two or more individuals send and receive meaningful messages. Therefore, a second major premise of the discussion is that improvement of learning disabled adolescents' communication ability requires consideration of these students' development of verbal and nonverbal communication, their awareness of the functions of the channels as separate entities, and relationships between the modes of communication.

On a surface level, many learning disabled adolescents appear to have internalized control of communicative behaviors for social purposes. Often the observation obscures teachers' perception and recognition of these students' underlying problems in academic achievement. In turn, a final premise of this discussion is that communication ability of many learning disabled adolescents is not fully developed, that systematic observation in naturalistic or simulated environments is necessary to determine specific difficulties, and that direct intervention is often a correlate.

This discussion continues with a review of pertinent research on learning disabled adolescents' communicative behavior, reading comprehension, and written language. Although the writer has suggested that components of communication ability are interrelated, the reader will note that researchers conventionally separate the components. An assumption is that it is done for investigative purposes. In this regard, the first section of the review is an examination of verbal communication.

REVIEW OF RESEARCH

Language Reception, Expression, and Use

Researchers have contributed few empirically based studies of learning disabled adolescents' capacities to comprehend and express ideas and information through oral communication. Even less attention has been focused on these students' behaviors in using linguistic competence to achieve personal and social goals. However, these circumstances have not obviated some classroom teachers' and researchers' observations that many learning disabled adolescents manifest oral communication problems. These students present difficulties in interpreting and relating spoken language to their internalized thoughts (Gow 1974); they experience specific academic failure as a result of language processing impairments (de Hirsch 1963; Wiig and Semel 1976).

Although comprehensive data-based studies of learning disabled adolescents' linguistic competencies do not exist, some progress has been made recently in understanding specific phonological, morphological, syntactic, and semantic behavior of these students. Researchers have described characteristics of language impairment and discussed psychological processes underlying select aspects of linguistic behavior.

In particular, one case study of a language-delayed adolescent, Art (CA:16; WAIS results: Verbal Scale IQ 77, Performance Scale IQ 92), indicates that young children may continue to exhibit communication difficulties as they become adults. Weiner (1974) reports "alternation between well-formed and poorly formed constructions in Art's use of base structure and morphological rules" (p. 207) and transformational expressions. Also reported are faulty phonological productions and use of semantic generalizations in formal language sampling and spontaneous social communication.

The nature and extent of learning disabled adolescents' difficulties in language processing and language production have been investigated via a communication processing model (Wiig and Semel 1974, 1975, 1976; Wiig 1976). It features perceptual, linguistic, and cognitive-semantic processes and relationships among them. Utilizing a variety of standardized tests and specifically designed informal measures of language processing and production, learning disabled adolescents are found to manifest "difficulties in the retrieval of associated concepts and semantic units from long term memory" (1976, p. 220). They present inefficient associative clustering strategies, reductions in word retrieval and definition, formulation and syntax, and cognition of semantic elements. Certainly, most academic efforts are affected.

Learning disabled adolescents' use of linguistic behavior in various social contexts to achieve personal goals is the present concern. However, educators' interest and concern about pragmatic aspects of language acquisition and development are quite recent. Studies of pragmatic behavior, as defined by Halliday (1975), Bates (1976), Wood (1977) and others, in learning disabled children and adolescents remain to be conducted. Certain inferences can be drawn about this aspect of language in research on nonverbal communication, the next section topic of this discussion.

In summary, the literature indicates a variety of general and specific problems learning disabled adolescents experience in their linguistic behavior. Similarly, various secondary language learning programs have been developed and implemented. However, as different philosophical or theoretical bases underly investigations of these students' linguistic competence, evidence of this concern is missing in language intervention programs. Basic language skills (Drake and Cavanaugh 1970; Herbert 1974), language therapy to assist reading improvement (Ansara 1972), and development of compensatory language facility to meet secondary academic demands (Wepman et al. 1975) characterize program recommendations and offerings for learning disabled adolescents. Clearly, the need to construct theoretically based as well as functional approaches to language intervention is well established in the literature.

Nonverbal Communication

Interrelated with verbal communication are abilities in understanding, expressing, and appropriately using nonverbal communication. Given that learning disabled adolescents present a variety of difficulties in major components of linguistic behavior, a seeming conjecture is that problems exist in nonverbal communication behavior. This approximation is weighted positively when research on young and older learning disabled children's performances in this communication channel is examined (cf. Johnson and Myklebust 1967; Bryan 1976, 1978; Knott 1974, 1979). The evidence suggests that learning disabled children exhibit moderate to severe problems in comprehending and expressing nonverbal communication through the major channels. These include proxemics (perception and use of space or distance), paralanguage (voice quality, pitch, prosodic features), and kinesics (gestures, facial expressions, and body movement). Social interaction, status, and establishing of interpersonal relations are adversely affected. Although these findings are related to young and older learning disabled children, a general assumption is that they continue to manifest difficulties as adolescents, and perhaps through adulthood. One research study supports the assumption.

Learning disabled adolescents' ability to identify six affective states — anger, fear, embarrassment, frustration, joy, and love — is compared with a normal peer group (Wiig and Harris 1974). Learning disabled adolescents identified fewer conventional affective states than their peers. In contrast to their peers, learning disabled adolescents made more substitutions in labeling emotional states; they confused emotional states such as joy and embarrassment. This study suggests a need for direct training with learning disabled students to foster improved recognition and use of nonverbal communication in interpersonal interactions in various situational contexts.

However, educational intervention models, materials and teaching strategies for learning disabled adolescents remain to be developed. The reader is advised that materials and strategies suggested for elementary school learning disabled children (Johnson and Myklebust 1967) may be inappropriate for many secondary students. Psychosocial maturity, experiential background and learning strategies of older learning disabled students reflect a need to approach intervention through real and simulated life experiences. The goal is to enable learning disabled adolescents to cognize nonverbal communication not as a superficial structure aimed at winning popularity contests but rather as an important medium in relating and presenting self to others in interpersonal situations.

Reading Comprehension

Obtaining meaning through printed messages and expressing ideas in written form are perhaps the most pervasive difficulties secondary learning disabled students experience. Unfortunately, researchers have not devoted much attention to improving our understanding of the nature of these students' difficulties. Nor have adequate instructional programs based on general characteristics of secondary learning disabled students' problems come forth. Models of normal reading processes and discussions of reading problems among the learning disabled center primarily on young and older elementary school children. With few exceptions, the literature is sparse with respect to learning disabled and/or dyslexic adolescents.

Johnson and Myklebust (1965) studied a group of dyslexic students, aged seven to eighteen, to formulate specific diagnosis and remediation procedures. Of the sixty subjects in the study, approximately twenty-four were of secondary school age. Defining dyslexia as a basic language disability which affects allied academic areas, the authors report that memory, left-right orientation, body image and body concept impairments, written language disorders, mathematics difficulties, and below average social maturity are behaviors observed in the subjects. In regard to remediation, Johnson and Myklebust caution that "the teacher of these children should not become method-oriented, but rather child and problem oriented." A "sight vocabulary and a language approach to reading" are recommended for the auditory dyslexic; an "analytic ap-

proach" (Gillingham and Stillman 1940) is suggested for the visual
dyslexic, while auditory-visual sequence is stressed with the student
presenting "integrative problems" (p. 283).

Wiig and Semel (1974) compare thirty randomly selected children
in grade six with thirty learning disabled adolescents, sixth to ninth
grade, age approximately twelve to sixteen years, on ability to comprehend material read orally to the subjects. Fifty "logico-grammatical"
sentences consisting of comparative, familial, passive, spatial, and temporal relationships were read. Learning disabled adolescents in this
study were less able than sixth graders in comprehending the select
sentences. The researchers concluded that the adolescents demonstrated difficulties in auditory verbal comprehension, logical processing, and coding of semantic elements.

In summary, this brief review of literature on secondary learning
disabled adolescents' reading achievement suggests a dire need for
additional research. It is not enough to offer that if a younger learning
disabled child presents reading problems in elementary school, the same
will be manifested at the secondary level. The cumulative educational
development of secondary learning disabled students warrants intensive
study to provide well-planned instruction. Language and information
processing studies with learning disabled adolescents are needed.

Written Language

Systematic study and analysis of learning disabled adolescents'
difficulties in written language are less presented in the literature when
compared to other verbal channels. De Hirsch (1963) and Myklebust
(1973) report careful investigations of problems and learning processes
encountered by many secondary learning disabled students.

De Hirsch (1963) attributes spelling disabilities in these students to
deficient visual and auditory memory and discrimination ability. Learning disabled adolescents are unable to retain visual configurations of
morphemes and revisualize them for later use. De Hirsch (1974) reiter-
ates that these adolescents may compensate for reading difficulties but
continue to manifest problems in spelling and written expression.

Myklebust (1973) describes the Picture Story Language Test and
studies written language of adolescents categorized as learning disabled
and dyslexic. From urban public schools, the author selected sixty-six
seven- to eighteen-year-olds and compared their performance with a
group of normal peers. Syntactical expressions and length of produc-

tions pose difficulties for learning disabled students according to Myk-lebust. In addition, processing of auditory verbal behavior and written language appear to be positively correlated.

In reviewing the research cited in the previous section, the reader readily deduces that not much has been systematically learned about learning disabled adolescents' communication difficulties during the past decade. Several implications are unavoidable. More research is indicated in all areas of learning disabled adolescents' communicative behavior. If these students are to benefit from "least restrictive environments" as legislated by PL 94-142, the Education of All Handicapped Children's Act (1975), then professionals in the field of learning disabilities are obliged to provide assistance to regular classroom teachers. Assessment-intervention strategies appropriate for regular classroom implementation must be developed to assure that these students' idiosyncratic learning processes and intervention procedures are matched. This latter concern is addressed in the following section of this discussion.

COMMUNICATION ASSESSMENT-INTERVENTION

There are many variables involved in educating language disabled adolescents, for example, learning style, motivational factors, previous educational experiences, value of standardized tests, teacher preparation, family support, etc. The list could be extended; the point is that educating learning disabled adolescents is an individual teacher-student, decision-making matter. In this regard, I have proposed a seven-step on-going assessment-intervention model for assisting learning disabled adolescents achieve success in academic efforts and interpersonal interactions.

1. *Naturalistic assessment.* Conducting naturalistic assessment is not a compex process. However, it does require knowledge of verbal and nonverbal communication processes, including language comprehension, expression, and pragmatics; nonverbal symbolic behavior; reading and written language processes. General knowledge of classroom observation techniques is also required. In regard to various frameworks for conducting observations, Lister (1969) explains several factors that influence the value of data obtained: "(1) the accuracy with which observations are made and recorded; (2) the extent to which conditions under which observations occur are noted and considered in

interpreting observational data; (3) the degree to which observations focus on important aspects of the child's behavior; and (4) the extent to which the child's behavior is not influenced by the observation procedures. When these conditions are met, the teacher has data which can be useful in assessing the child's level of effectiveness" (p. 184).

The previous statement of factors pertaining to observation is applicable in the present context. In addition, different observation settings are necessary to obtain reliable data. The process is continual rather than using a single session to determine educational needs and progress.

To make systematic naturalistic assessment of learning disabled adolescents' communicative behaviors, teachers need some type of structure to record and analyze data. I have considered these students' developmental learning characteristics, educational needs, social maturity, and affective states in constructing a checklist of behaviors to be observed in naturalistic or simulated life situations. These behaviors are presented in Figure 2.1.

As shown, not all learning and social behaviors and needs are included. However, the checklist is suggestive of pertinent variables affecting learning disabled adolescents' communicative development and improvement in school environments. Research and theoretical contributions of several authors are represented in the synthesis. Particularly, the reader will observe categories of reading behavior from Goodman and Burke (1972). These authors, too, have designed a naturalistic framework for qualifying reading comprehension problems, and their program is incorporated in the communication assessment-intervention model.

In regard to simulated environments, school related activities such as cafeteria periods, extra curricular organization meetings and formal and informal social events may be utilized. In any given situation, the communicative context must be shared mutually by the participants, including learning disabled adolescents. That is, the teacher has to consider *who* is participating, *what* is being discussed, and *when* and *where* the discussions take place. Communication outcomes can be affected by any one or more of these variables.

2. *Language description.* Verbal and nonverbal language, reading comprehension, and written language are included. Tape recording of a student's verbal behavior facilitates analysis of the various linguistic components. Observations of a student's nonverbal communication are made unobtrusively. Both occur during peer-peer, student-stranger, student-authority person, student-parent or other interpersonal interactions. The objective is to record adequate data to facilitate a description

COMMUNICATIVE COMPETENCE PROFILE
SECONDARY LEVEL

ME	EXAMINER (1)	DATE (1)
NTEXT (1)	EXAMINER (2)	DATE (2)
NTEXT (2)	DESIGNATORS:	D Behavior Demonstrated
		N Behavior Not Demonstrated
		M Behavior Minimally Demonstrated
		O Behavior Not Examined

INFORMATION PROCESSING	1	2	N2 KINESICS	1	2	N3 PROXEMICS	1	2	N4 PARALANGUAGE	1	2	N5 INTERACTIVE STRATEGIES	1	2
areness/Perception			Gestures			Encroachment			Nonlanguage, e.g. Muttering, whining			Respects Others		
mory			Facial Expressions			Territorial Spacing:						Cooperative		
ociation			Posture			Social			Voice Quality, e.g. Pitch, rhythm			Bossy/Hostile		
Spatialization			Body Movements			Personal						Considerate		
nverbal Decoding						Public			Non-Words, e.g. "uh-huh", "ah", "er"			Pretentious		
nverbal Encoding						Prefers Isolation						Ethnic Variation		

INFORMATION PROCESSING	1	2	A2 PHONOLOGY	1	2	A3 MORPHOLOGY	1	2	A4 SYNTAX	1	2	A5 SEMANTICS	1	2
ditory Perception			Phoneme Discrimination			Verb Tense			Soc. Reg. Variation			Sequential Events		
ditory Memory						Mood and Aspect			Complex Sentence			Comparative Relations		
mbolization			"Tone of Voice"			Semantic Units, e.g. noun, adj., adv., etc.			Com-Complex Sent.			Temporal Relations		
nceptualization									Relative Clause			Cause and Effect		
straction									Indirect Discourse			Implications		
									Passive Transform			Inferences		

INFORMATION PROCESSING	1	2	O2 PHONOLOGY & MORPHOLOGY	1	2	O3 FORMULATION	1	2	O4 CONVERGENT PRODUCTION	1	2	O5 DIVERGENT PRODUCTION	1	2
rception			Articulation			Aud.-Motor Integration			Vocabulary			Lexical Variety		
mory/Retrieval			Progressive			Agrammatic			Word-Finding			Sentence Variety		
mbolization			Tense			Word-Order			Dysnomia			Verbal Elaboration		
nceptualization			Possessive			Incomplete Sentence			Synthesis			Figurative Language		
straction			Inflection			Circumlocutions			Minimal Content			Analogies		
			Plural			Dialect Variation			Basic Sent. Structure					

NFORMATION PROCESSING	1	2	P2 CONTROLLING	1	2	P3 FEELING	1	2	P4 INFORMING	1	2	P5 RITUALIZING	1	2	P6 IMAGINING	1	2
rception			Commands			Expresses Emotion, Attitudes			Explains			Demonstrates			Creative Behavior		
mory			Suggests						Demonstrates			Cultural Amenities			Role Plays		
mbolization			Rejects			Agrees/Disagrees			Questions			Facilitates Social Interaction			Dramatizes		
sociation			Acknowledges			Taunts			States Information						Simulates Experience		
nceptualization			Argues			Tale-Tells			Justifies			Observes Speaker: Takes Turns					
			Persuades			Signifies											
			Justifies			Agrees											
						Pretends											

NFORMATION PROCESSING	1	2	R2 PSYCHOLOGICAL FACTORS *	1	2	R3 SPECIFIC READING SKILLS	1	2	R4 ORAL READING MISCUES	1	2	R5 COMPREHENSION STRATEGIES	1	2
rception: Auditory & Visual			Purpose			Phonemic Analysis			Intonation			Relating Oral & Written Language		
mory: Auditory & Visual			Informative			Structural Analysis			Dialect Influence					
			Identification			Context Clues			Graphic Similarity			Use of Relational & Lexical Meaning		
mbolization			Reality Speculation			Dictionary Usage			Sound Similarity					
ociation			Recreation			Rate			Gramm. Function			Using Context Clues		
nceptualization			Health Problem			Study Skills			Miscue Correction			Anticipating Theme, Plot, Events		
rsensory Learning			Failure			Scanning			Gramm. Acceptability					
			Attitude:			Skimming			Sem. Acceptability			Interpretation: Literal/Inferential		
						Questioning			Meaning Change					
			Affective Response:			Reviewing						Critical/Applied		
												Application		
												Self-Evaluation		

INFORMATION PROCESSING	1	2	W2 PSYCHOMOTOR	1	2	W3 PSYCHOLOGICAL FACTORS *	1	2	W4 CRAFT	1	2	W5 CONTENT	1	2
rception			Dysgraphia						Mechanics			Personal View		
mory			Handwriting:						Organization			World Reflection		
mbolization						Oral Tradition			Note Taking			Descriptive:		
nceptualization						Mature Writing			Paraphrasing			Concrete		
sualization			Adequate Copying			Failure			Summarizing			Abstract		
alysis			Prefers Typing			Attitude & Motivation			Proofreading			Imaginative:		
nthesis												Concrete		
ersensory Learning						Socially Adjusted						Abstract		

RCES:
dman and Burke, 1972; Wood, B. (ed.)., 1977; Johnson and Myklebust, 1967; Knott, 1974, 1980.
me of these factors may require professional psychological evaluation.

of the student's understanding and application of rules governing functional use of linguistic and nonlinguistic behavior. A more comprehensive discussion of this step in the communication assessment-intervention model is reported by Knott (1980).

To make a thorough analysis of learning disabled students' reading behavior from a language perspective, the reader is referred to Goodman and Burke (1972). Continuity is established in the initial assessment process by having students read material for the Reading Miscue Inventory which they have discussed during the assessment of auditory verbal behavior. Seemingly, frustrations and anxiety of learning disabled adolescents are relieved through this procedure. On completion of this step, the teacher has data to relate to students' auditory verbal behavior. For example, are there similarities and differences between a student's use of graphophonic, syntactic and semantic information in auditory verbal and reading comprehension behaviors?

Following the "retelling" of the story or passage in the Reading Miscue Inventory procedure, I have asked adolescents to continue their communication experience by expressing the same ideas in written form. Again, the effect seems to be that frustration and fear of failure are reduced, and students have specific ideas to which they can relate. This sample of written language is studied in regard to fundamentals suggested on the communicative competence profile. Throughout this step, listening, speaking, reading, and written expression are related. Obviously, students' confidence and capacities to discern relationships among the forms of communication are fostered.

In summary, these data are utilized to formulate a comprehensive description of the learning disabled adolescent's communicative competence. The description is based on functional communication interactions and suggests what the student's strengths and needs for improvement are. When naturalistic assessment is conducted in different situational contexts, the descriptions are compared and more reliable data are available to structure ongoing assessment-intervention strategies.

3. *Task and learner analysis.* Specifically, task and learner analysis provide additional diagnostic information for formulating behavioral objectives. Frameworks for conducting these procedures are adequately discussed by Johnson (1967), Bateman (1974), and Lerner (1976). The mainstay of task and learner analysis is that there should be congruence between the cognitive and affective states of the student and materials and intervention strategies.

4. *Formulating objectives.* Behavioral objectives serve to structure intervention. They include a concept or task to be learned by the student; they specify what the student will demonstrate to illustrate

acquisition of a concept or completion of a task. For example, the teacher may state "to distinguish between cause and effect in interpersonal relations" or "to identify warranted and unwarranted criticism of a personality figure" as behavioral objectives. A complete guide to formulating behavioral objectives is beyond the scope of this discussion. The interested reader is referred to authors such as Gronlund (1970) and Thiagarajan (1980).

5. *Materials selection.* Materials are tools to be used to help learning disabled students learn, and classroom teachers need to be aware that not all materials used with normal learners are appropriate for learning disabled students, especially adolescents. Criteria such as those proposed by Hasazi (1979), Goodman and Mann (1976), and Van Etten and Van Etten (1980) are recommended in making selections to meet individual needs. Collectively, the criteria have been applied in the selection of materials suggested at the conclusion of this section.

6. *Instruction and evaluation.* To establish agreement or a match between a student's educational needs and instructional programming, clinical teaching is recommended. Johnson and Myklebust (1967) summarize implications of this dynamic approach: "Clinical Teaching implies that the teacher is fully aware of the child's disability, ... strengths and deficits, ... efforts are to bring about a balance between [the child's] tolerance levels and the stimulation provided. [The teacher] considers [the child's] problem in multidimensional, not in unitary terms, and recognizes the need for controlling certain behavioral variables while activating or manipulating others. ... Included is the inference that to prevent the integrities from becoming developed out of proportion to the deficits, it is necessary to hold the high points of ability while properly developing the low points" (p. 64).

Evaluation is an integral part of clinical teaching and serves as a feedback mechanism to the teacher and student. Results from the teacher's instruction or the student's use of materials to learn will depend largely on the teacher's accuracy in earlier steps of the assessment-intervention cycle. For example, if the behavioral objective and selected materials match the learner's cognitive and affective characteristics and form an appropriate lesson, then the student should demonstrate acquisition of knowledge or behavior. When learning does not occur, an investigation and intervention related to other factors which may impede progress are suggested. This section brings the discussion to the final step in a single communication assessment-intervention cycle.

7. *Modification of goals.* Learning disabled adolescents' needs change with exposure to appropriate learning experiences. These experiences include appropriate teaching strategies, materials and be-

havior management techniques which promote growth and development. More important perhaps, learning disabled students' needs change as they become able to communicate effectively in various situational contexts. As students demonstrate progress in achieving competence with respect to certain goals of communicative development, teachers will find it necessary to modify or select new goals. Progress in communicative development may also suggest the need to supplement, alter, or select different teaching strategies and materials as well. Likewise, lack of progress may suggest modification of an immediate goal, perhaps to an earlier prerequisite. The process is continuous and logical; modification of communication learning goals is made to relate to what the student knows and needs to learn with respect to the components of communicative competence.

This section concludes the discussion of the proposed communication assessment-intervention model. In the next section select materials are suggested. The list is not exhaustive, rather it is consistent with learning disabled adolescents' psychosocial development, emotional maturity, and educational needs. Materials followed by an asterisk are intended for teacher use.

SELECT MATERIALS

Austin, M. *Raining Cats and Dogs* and *Holding Your Horses*. Beaverton, Ore.: Dormac, 1978. The two selections assist students in understanding idioms frequently expressed in social interactions.

Forsdale, L. *Nonverbal Communication* (part of Making Contact series). New York: Harcourt Brace Jovanovich, 1974. Appropriate for student-teacher discussion of nonverbal communication.

Goodman, Y., and Burke, C. *Reading Strategies: Focus on Comprehension*. New York: Holt, Rinehart and Winston, 1980.* An excellent model for developing comprehension-centered reading activities for learning disabled adolescents. Modifications in some context may be necessary.

Heyman, M. *Simulation Games for the Classroom*. Bloomington, In.: Phi Delta Kappa Educational Foundation, 1975.* Assists teachers in constructing simulations which relate classroom activities to the real world. Many sources for simulations are listed.

McCarr, D. *Vocabulary Building Exercises for the Young Adult*. Beaverton, Ore.: Dormac, 1977. Books A, B, C. Assists students in comprehending and using terms frequently expressed in newspapers, magazines, and everyday living.

McCarr, J. *Lessons in Syntax.* Beaverton, Ore.: Dormac, 1973. Assists the student in understanding standard English structures and semantic-syntactic relationships. Teacher manual and student workbooks are available.

Morris, K., and Cinnamon, K. *A Handbook of Nonverbal Group Exercises.* Kansas City, Mo.: CMA, 1975.* "Subsidiary goals" in this volume are excellent for teachers to consider in designing nonverbal communication intervention strategies.

Thompson, J. *Using Role Playing in the Classroom.* Bloomington, In.: Phi Delta Kappa Educational Foundation, 1978.* A concise overview of role playing as an instructional activity; guidelines and activities for classroom use are suggested.

Wood, B., ed. *Development of Functional Communication Competencies: Grades 7–12.* Falls Church, Va.: Speech Communication Association, 1977.* Selections assist students in becoming aware of uses of language in various communicative contexts.

REFERENCES

Ansara, A. "Language Therapy to Salvage the College Potential of Dyslexic Adolescents." *Bulletin of the Orton Society* 22 (1972):123–39.

Bates, E. *Language and Context: The Acquisition of Pragmatics.* New York: Academic Press, 1976.

Bateman, B. "Educational Implications of Minimal Brain Dysfunction." *Reading Teacher* 27 (1974):662–68.

Bryan, T. "Peer Popularity of Learning Disabled Children: A Replication." *Journal of Learning Disabilities* 9 (1976):307–11.

———. "Verbal Interactions and Social Relationships of Learning Disabled Children." *Journal of Learning Disabilities* 11, 2 (1978):107–115.

———. *Learning Disabilities: The Struggle from Adolescence toward Adulthood.* Syracuse: Syracuse University Press, 1980.

De Hirsch, K. "Two Categories of Learning Difficulties in Adolescents." *American Journal of Orthopsychiatry* 33 (1963):87–91.

———. "Learning Disabilities: An Overview." *Bulletin of the New York Academy of Medicine* 50 (1974):459–79.

Drake, C., and Cavanaugh, J. "Teaching the High School Dyslexic." In *Helping the Adolescent with the Hidden Handicap,* edited by L. Anderson. New York: Academic Therapy, 1970.

Gillingham, A., and Stillman, B. *Remedial Training for Children with Specific Disability in Reading, Spelling, and Penmanship.* New York: Sackett and Wilhelms, 1940.

Goodman, Y., and Burke, C. *Reading Miscue Inventory.* New York: Macmillan, 1972.

Gow, D. "Dyslexic Adolescent Boys: Classroom Remediation is Not Enough." *Bulletin of the Orton Society* 24 (1974):154–63.

Gronlund, N. *Stating Behavioral Objectives for Classroom Instruction.* New York: Macmillan, 1970.

Halliday, M. *Explorations in the Functions of Language.* London: Edward Arnold, 1973.

Hasazi, S. "Evaluating Special Education Materials." *Early Years* 8 (1979): 31–33.

Herbert, J. "Specific Language Disability in Secondary Schools." *Bulletin of the Orton Society* 24 (1974):135–40.

Johnson, D. "Educational Principles for Children with Learning Disabilities." *Rehabilitation Literature* 28 (1967):317–22.

Johnson, D., and Myklebust, H. "Dyslexia in Childhood." *Learning Disorders* (Vol. 1), edited by J. Hellmuth. Seattle: Special Child Publications, 1965.

———. *Learning Disabilities: Educational Principles and Practices.* New York: Grune & Stratton, 1967.

Knott, G. "A Study of Gesture as Nonverbal Communication in Preschool Language Disabled and Preschool Normal Children." Doctoral Dissertation, Northwestern University, 1974.

———. "Nonverbal Communication During Early Childhood." *Theory into Practice* 18, 4 (1979):226–33.

———. "Communication Competence and Secondary Learning Disabled Students." *The Directive Teacher* 2, 3 (Winter 1980):22–24.

Lerner, J. *Children with Learning Disabilities.* 2nd Ed. Houghton Mifflin, 1976.

Lister, J. "Personal-Emotional-Social Skills." In *Teacher Diagnosis of Educational Difficulties,* edited by R. Smith. Columbus, Ohio: Merrill, 1969.

Myklebust, H. R. *Development and Disorders of Written Language,* Vol. II. New York: Grune & Stratton, 1973.

———, ed. *Progress in Learning Disabilities,* Vol. IV. New York: Grune & Stratton, 1978.

Thiagarajan, S. "Individualizing Instructional Objectives." *Teaching Exceptional Children* 12, 3 (1980):126–27.

Van Etten, C., and Van Etten, G. "A Working Model for Developing Instructional Materials for the Learning Disabled." *Learning Disabilities Quarterly* 1, 2 (1978).

Weiner, P. "A Language-Delayed Child at Adolescence." *Journal of Speech and Hearing Disorders* 39 (1974):204–12.

Wepman, J.; Cruickshank, W.; Deutch, M.; Morency, A.; and Strother, C. "Learning Disabilities." In *Issues in the Classification of Children*, Vol. 1, edited by N. Hobbs. San Francisco: Jossey-Bass, 1975.

Wiig, E. "Language Disabilities of Adolescents: Implications for Diagnosis and Remediation." *British Journal of Disorders of Communication* 11, 2 (1976):135–43.

Wiig, E., and Harris, S. "Perception and Interpretation of Nonverbally Expressed Emotions by Adolescents with Learning Disabilities." *Perceptual and Motor Skills* 38 (1974):239–45.

Wiig, E., and Semel, E. "Logico-Grammatical Sentence Comprehension by Adolescents with Learning Disabilities." *Perceptual Motor Skills* 38 (1974):1331–34.

———. "A Preliminary Study of Productive Language Abilities in Learning Disabled Adolescents." *Journal of Learning Disabilities* 8 (1975):578–86.

———. *Language Disabilities in Children and Adolescents*. Columbus, Ohio: Merrill, 1976.

3

Persistent Problems and Concerns of Young Adults with Learning Disabilities

Jane W. Blalock

THE RECENT EMPHASIS ON THE PROBLEMS AND NEEDS of the learning disabled adolescent has resulted in an increase in the development of educational and vocational programming in secondary schools. Researchers and educators are attempting to determine what problems persist and what types of programs will be most effective. To plan effective programs it is essential to understand what problems face learning disabled young people, both in and out of school. Perhaps the best people to provide information about persistent learning disabilities are learning disabled adults. Information about persistent academic, social, and vocational problems should be used in planning programs in secondary schools as well as programs for young adults with persistent problems.

There is growing evidence that learning disabilities do not disappear when learning disabled children successfully (or unsuccessfully) leave the public school system. The belief that learning disabilities are primarily academic problems and will make little difference once the people are placed in jobs that fit their strengths is being disproven. Educators, vocational counselors, and employers as well as the learning disabled young adults and their families are becoming increasingly concerned with the persistent learning problems which interfere with functioning in higher education, vocations, and social situations. In recent years we have received hundreds of requests for evaluation and remedial services from young adults who continue to have difficulty learning in higher education, on the job, and in developing social skills.

The Learning Disabilities Center at Northwestern University has provided services for adults for many years, but in 1975, a small program was started especially for adults. In addition to providing services to this group, the purposes of the program were: (1) to study the nature of persistent learning disabilities; (2) to find out how these problems interfere vocationally, educationally, socially, and in developing independent

living skills; (3) to determine what support systems were most helpful; and (4) to determine the effectiveness of individual remediation
with adults.

The purpose of this paper is to report some of the preliminary
findings and raise some questions about the nature of learning disabilities and programming needs for learning disabled individuals of all
ages. The nature of persistent problems, how these problems interfere,
what services have been helpful, and some issues regarding services for
young adults will be discussed. Before discussing these findings it is
important to point out that the group of young adults studied at the
Learning Disabilities Center is a biased one and cannot be considered a
representative sample of the learning disabled adult population.

The people seen for evaluation and remediation must request the
evaluation themselves in writing. They are asked to send a handwritten,
uncorrected letter describing their problems and stating why they would
like the evaluation. They are also asked to send any additional available
information. Letters have varied from a string of difficult-to-read words
to twelve pages describing what it is like to have a learning disability.
This procedure, in addition to a waiting period of more than one year,
results in our seeing very persistent, highly motivated young adults.

EVALUATION PROCEDURE

After letters and other available information are received, evaluations
are scheduled. People are seen one evening a week for five or six weeks
or for one and one-half day evaluations. We use the same frames of
reference for studying adults that we use in studying children (Johnson
and Myklebust 1967). Basically the same combinations of formal and
informal testing, trial teaching, and case history information are used.
Evaluations consist of lengthy interviews, intelligence testing, hearing
screening, and assessment (formal and informal) in each of the following
areas: oral language, reading written language, arithmetic, nonverbal
abilities, and thinking and reasoning.

Results of the evaluation are discussed with the person at the
conclusion of the evaluation. Frequently we obtain additional information at this time when relationships between specific processing deficits
and real-life problems are discussed. At that time decisions are made
about whether or not remediation should follow. This decision is based
on their reasons for requesting the evaluation, their goals, and their
schedules.

DESCRIPTION OF THE GROUP

The records of 38 of approximately 70 young adults seen in our Clinic were reviewed for this paper. This group consisted of 28 men and 10 women ranging in age from 17 to 37 years. Six were aged 17–19; eleven 20–22; seven 23–25; two 26–28; five 29–31; four 32–34; and three 35–37. No students currently enrolled in high school were included in this group. Of the total group only three had not completed high school. Several had attempted college and dropped out or failed out before completing one year. Thirteen were enrolled in a college or junior college at the time of the evaluation. Seven were unemployed at the time they were tested; thirteen were students; six were laborers; four were clerks or stockboys; three were salespersons or waitresses; one each was a supervisor, mechanic, security guard, artist/photographer, and nurse.

Only young adults who were diagnosed as being learning disabled were included in the group described in this paper. With two exceptions, they all demonstrated at least average ability on one or both Scales of the *Wechsler Adult Intelligence Scale*. These two had one or both scores (Verbal/Performance) within the Low Average range.

Designation of severity of diagnosed problems was somewhat arbitrary and based on levels of achievement rather than impact of the problem on functioning in society. These designations do not, in fact, have much relationship to the individuals' success in his or her current situation. Many people whose problems were classified as being "mild" (grade 8 and up — fifteen) described much more frustration and failure than some whose problems were said to be "severe" (grade 4 and under — thirteen). For this reason the severity designation cannot be taken as an indication of the actual or perceived severity of the problems in terms of impact on the peoples' lives. It should be pointed out that nineteen of the group were self-supporting and others were functioning quite well in their college settings.

PERSISTENT PROBLEMS

Almost every letter described some academically related problem. Most frequently mentioned were reading and written language. A very different picture emerged in the interview. It seemed as if they did not see relationships between problems related to academics and problems in their daily lives. When questioned, they gave excellent descriptions of their problems and their strategies for avoiding failure or difficult situations. In many instances their reading and writing difficulties were not the problems that concerned them most.

One of the most common complaints that cut across problem areas was that of the effort that went into avoiding or hiding the problem. Husbands took reports home for wives to write, dictionaries were stashed in every possible location, friends were called to spell a word, secretaries asked to "make a note of this, I'm in a hurry," etc. Specific types of situations, both business and social, were avoided, resulting in an amazing amount of energy and time being spent in hiding problems.

Types of residual problems will be discussed by area. Table 3.1 shows the number of people complaining about problems in each area and the actual number of problems diagnosed by area.

TABLE 3.1

Number of Complaints and Diagnosed Problems by Area

	Complaints	Diagnosed
Oral Language	3	18
Reading	25	28
Written Language	30	36
Arithmetic	5	15
Nonverbal Abilities*	0	13

*This does not include those six who had mild-moderate social perception problems with primarily verbal deficits.

Oral Language

Oral language problems were not reported in the application letters often, but problems were reported in the interviews and were evident in the testing. With only one exception, oral language problems did not obviously interfere with communication during the evaluation. These problems were interfering in several areas of functioning, however.

Residual receptive problems included difficulty in listening, auditory perception, auditory comprehension, and auditory memory. Listening problems were typically part of a larger attention problem, but several reported real problems of listening and understanding in noise.

While only two people reported auditory perceptual problems (previously diagnosed), residual auditory discrimination problems were diagnosed in at least twelve of the group. These problems were not always evident on discrimination tests (although seven scored at least one standard deviation below the mean for eight year olds on the Wepman *Auditory Discrimination Test*), but did show up on other tests and in conversation. The auditory discrimination problems were particularly troublesome to people whose jobs involved telephoning. They had problems with messages, especially names and unfamiliar terminology. Noise made these problems worse for most people. These people also frequently had difficulty pronouncing and spelling multisyllabic words.

Comprehension problems were rarely mentioned in letters or the interviews. Two people did complain of not understanding jokes and conversations in social groups. Problems in this area were seen during testing in difficulty with multiple word meanings and in explaining idioms and proverbs. Ten scored very low on a task of judging grammaticality of sentences read to them. These subtle comprehension problems were underlying many reading comprehension problems which were frequently mentioned.

Memory problems were reported by four people and diagnosed in eight. Problems were seen in both span and sequence. The reported problems included difficulty remembering directions, order of steps in a task, and telephone numbers. They said they frequently forgot errands or some task at work, creating discord on the job and at home.

Expressively, problems were seen in word retrieval, sequencing, pronunciation, and formation, with problems most obvious on metalinguistic tasks. With one exception, all of the young adults were readily intelligible in conversational speech. Several had mild residual articulation problems.

Retrieval problems were not mentioned in letters, but were diagnosed in five adults. Others had mild problems that did not seem to be seriously interfering with communication. These problems were evident in confrontation naming and in conversation.

Several problems interfered with the pronunciation of unfamiliar (real and nonsense) and multisyllabic words. As mentioned above, auditory discrimination problems interfered. In addition, auditory memory for sequence of syllables and sounds in words and residual apraxia affected pronunciation. These pronunciation problems were embarrassing to the six with the most severe problems.

Very few had noticeable problems in syntax and morphology. Auditory discrimination problems caused a few problems in word endings, particularly past-tense markers. *Knowledge* about sounds, words, and syntax, however, was poor in more than half of the group. They had great difficulty on abstract, less automatic tasks such as sentence building, segmenting, rhyming, and applying grammatical rules to nonsense words. These problems were viewed as being metalinguistic or metacognitive in nature and interfered with written language more than oral.

Organization and formulation of ideas was a problem reported frequently in written language, but not in oral language. Four had difficulty conveying information clearly and concisely. They tended to ramble, mis-sequence ideas, and had numerous reformulations. Even more had difficulty selecting the most relevant information to convey and often gave too much in response to questions allowing the listener to select what she liked.

In summary, residual oral language deficits *were* seen. These involved auditory perception; higher levels of comprehension, particularly abstract language; pronunciation problems resulting from difficulty in discrimination, memory for sequence, and/or residual apraxia; and formulation problems. By far the most significant problems were seen on metalinguistic tasks — those involving manipulation of sounds in words, nonsense words, sentence building with function words. This appeared to be reflected in written more than oral expression. Many of these people did not have *knowledge* about language, even though they had adequate oral expression.

Reading Problems

Fifteen of the thirty complained about reading problems. It was found that few were reading at a level commensurate with their ability and educational levels.

Of those found to have decoding problems, many of the complaints pertained to reading rate, particularly the people continuing in school. Evaluation revealed that the actual problem was in poor decoding. These people did not have automatic decoding skills. Their efforts to decode, then re-read for meaning made reading a laborious, time-consuming task. Usually they were reading at a sixth or seventh grade level, which is not adequate for a college student. Many of them were amazingly adept at using context and scored much lower when reading single words. Those with lower level skills usually reported decoding problems rather than problems of rate.

Comprehension problems were found in many with adequate decoding skills. Their complaints involved rate and remembering as well as understanding. Problems were very much related to content, and there was considerable variation of performance both within and across tests. Several types of questions seemed to be missed more frequently by those with reading comprehension problems. They had difficulty with main ideas, titles, reasons, and inferences, and with determining specific word meanings from context.

Several observations were made about both groups with reading problems. Information brought to the selection significantly affected decoding and comprehension. This use of information with resulting variation of performance seemed much more dramatic in the adults than in school-aged youngsters. In addition, several had great difficulty with the cloze procedure, which may have been a reflection of their metalinguistic problems.

Assessment of processes related to reading revealed problems of auditory discrimination and auditory analysis. Of the twenty-six who were given a test of segmenting by syllables, only eleven gave the correct number of syllables in twelve words ranging from two to five syllables in length. Only five were able to say what each syllable was. Sixteen of the group had some difficulty rhyming. These problems might be regarded as metalinguistic in nature since the tasks required some reflection on and manipulation of words and sounds.

Many made errors suggestive of visual discrimination problems when reading. Few had difficulty matching words and letters. It seemed that the overload of reading aloud caused a breakdown that was not evident on pure discrimination tasks. This is supported by the fact that the problems were most evident when they were reading lists of unfamiliar single words. On these lists there was no context or expectancy to help them decode.

Assessment of phonics skills was done on eighteen of the thirty-eight. Of that group not one gave the correct sounds for all single consonants. Four missed only one sound. Only three correctly gave all of the short vowel sounds. Several were unable to complete the task. (Reading levels on the *Wide Range Achievement Test* for the 18 ranged from 4.8 to 15.0.)

Perhaps the most prevalent problem was that of automaticity. Many of the group were much better on isolated skills tasks than in actual reading. They did not automatically recognize a large number of words and when they attempted to decode did not have systematic, automatic word attach skills. The process of reading appeared to be a series of steps as opposed to a single fluid process.

Written Language

Eighty to 90 percent of the group reported and were found to have problems in one or more aspects of written language.

Handwriting problems of a severe nature were reported and diagnosed in two of the groups. Others had less severe problems that were not of primary concern to them. While the two with severe handwriting problems were most concerned about their handwriting, both of them were found to have nonverbal problems as well.

Spelling problems were the number-one complaint. These problems resulted from deficits in visual memory, auditory discrimination, auditory analysis, problems with phonics, rule problems, and monitoring difficulties. Many did somewhat better on dictated spelling tests than in spontaneous spelling.

Many problems in *syntax and morphology* were felt to be the residuals of oral language problems. Thirty of the group completed a written sentence-building task. Only four correctly used all of the target words in complete, grammatically acceptable sentences. The most difficult words for the group were *an, for,* and *because.* Many did not write in complete sentences, and monitoring was a problem for several.

Even group members with adequate scores on most reading, spelling, and written language tasks reported serious problems in *connected writing formulation.* Numerous written samples were obtained from these individuals, and problems were seen in organization and sequencing of ideas. Many could not outline or select main ideas and topic sentences. These problems interfered most in the lives of college students and those whose jobs involved written reports. These problems frequently *were not* specific to writing papers, but involved organizing in a much broader sense. Problems were evident in taking notes, organizing tasks on the job, planning a project, scheduling, and developing priorities. The problems were present in varying degrees of severity. Some could not organize sentences within a paragraph, while others did well until the project became more complicated, such as term papers.

Problems with *mechanics* were present in most written samples. These ranged from little to no knowledge of punctuation and capitalization rules to a lack of monitoring. Many could correct errors when asked to do so. Varying degrees of cueing were necessary.

Mathematics

Only five of the thirty-eight reported problems in arithmetic. This area was perhaps the most difficult to assess in the adults because of the tremendous differences in instruction in the use of math skills. Only seventeen scored at or above eighth grade level on the screening calculation test. Some of those scoring below the eighth grade level were very bright college students. Two scoring above this level had severe conceptual problems. Fifteen were diagnosed as having learning disabilities in this area.

One sub-group had considerable difficulty with many nonverbal abilities and concepts. They did not comprehend part-whole relationships and consequently failed on many application tasks involving fractions and measurement. While they could work division problems, they could not consistently tell whether the answer to an oral or written problem would be larger or smaller than either of the numbers in the problem. The specific areas they scored lowest in were decimals, fractions, and percentages. The larger, more basic problem was apparent when they were asked to estimate or explain answers. Several of this group had great difficulty with class inclusion and conservation tasks.

Calculation

While the first group had numerous errors in calculation, there was a group whose concepts were good, but they simply could not calculate accurately. Frequently they could not remember basic facts and sequences of steps. Monitoring was often a problem in this group.

Language-Related Problems

Poor reading interfered with performance on some arithmetic tests. Problems in auditory memory could have affected the oral arithmetic scores of several individuals.

It was difficult to say how many people had actual deficits in arithmetic. It was evident that many more than the five who complained had problems severe enough to interfere with adequate functioning in daily life.

Nonverbal Abilities

This area was one of the least mentioned in letters. Nonverbal problems appeared to have the biggest impact on independence and daily living. Those with severe reading problems were frequently functioning in society much better than those with far less severe nonverbal problems

Orientation

Two people complained specifically about problems of spatial orientation. Six were diagnosed as having difficulties in this area. These problems manifested themselves in different ways. The person with the most severe problem got lost frequently, could not find her way to our Center after six trips, could not read maps, and had problems imitating movements. The problems of some were not evident in two-dimensional functioning (paper and pencil tasks) but seriously interfered with three-dimensional tasks. Others had more difficulty with two-dimensional space. Time orientation was not a reported problem. Three had difficulty arriving at the appropriate hour. Two always arrived 20–30 minutes late and one at least one hour early each week. Eight scored 15 or more points lower than their intelligence levels on a time orientation test, but none reported significant time problems. Since organization and scheduling presented problems to so many of the group in their jobs, time orientation may have been more of a problem than they thought.

Visual-Motor Problems

Significant nonverbal visual perceptual and visual-motor problems were found in five of the group. They had difficulty with daily living skills such as tying ties and shoes, folding paper, packing, putting keys in the keyholes, hanging up clothes, etc. Several had handwriting problems as well.

Social Perception

Social perception problems did not appear to be specific to those with nonverbal problems although the most obvious problems were seen in those with nonverbal problems. Three of the group had severe problems in social perception, while about half were judged to have mild to moderate problems. These were evident in reports of few friends, inappropriate comments, inappropriate use of personal space, and social behavior. Questioning during the interview and the final conference usually supported observation.

THINKING AND REASONING SKILLS

High-level thinking and organizational problems were seen in many with relatively mild problems. Difficulties with outlining, selecting main ideas, and identifying relevant material were evident. Organizational problems were complained about very frequently and interfered most with writing papers and performing adequately on the job. More serious thinking and conceptual problems were seen in the people with verbal comprehension difficulties and those with severe nonverbal problems.

SUMMARY OF PROBLEMS REPORTED AND DIAGNOSED

Reading and written language problems were most frequently complained about and most often diagnosed. Additional problems were often present and many times the chief concern was not related to the academic underachievement. Processing deficits seemed to be less severe, but still problematic, especially on complex tasks. Vocational problems were of the greatest concern. Written language, especially spelling, was the academic problem most frequently reported to be troublesome on the job while reading and written language interfered most educationally.

The learning disabilities did indeed persist into adulthood. It seems that the type of learning may change with different demands, but the inability to profit from experience remains a problem even when a "curriculum" is no longer an obstacle. Many of these people might be viewed as special education "successes" because of their skill levels, but they continue to experience difficulty learning and fulfilling their potentials and goals.

HOW THE PROBLEMS INTERFERE

Daily Living

Problems frequently interfered with daily functioning, especially nonverbal deficits. Those with orientation disturbances had serious problems getting around in their communities. They got lost very frequently and usually could not read maps. Evidence of these problems was seen at the clinic when the people attempted to find us for the first few appointments. Typically, maps are sent out with appointment letters. In many instances landmarks had to be given orally and even then many missed the first appointments. One person consistently walked the wrong way after getting off the train and usually did not recognize the fact for several blocks.

Other less obvious problems associated with nonverbal deficits were in setting alarm clocks (until digital alarms, one stated that she always had to get up on the hour), fixing things, packing boxes, hanging up clothes, tying ties, and folding letters. Individuals with language as well as nonverbal problems had difficulty learning how to function in new situations like laundromats and grocery stores, cooking, following written directions, measuring, hanging pictures, planning schedules, and other tasks often taken for granted by those without problems. These people reported that as a result of these problems their lives were often more rigid and routinized to avoid new and unfamiliar activities and situations. As one young woman stated, "Your learning disability is in your head, is always there, and has to be considered all the time. If you can't organize inside your head, you have to do it externally."

Those with reading and writing difficulties reported great anxiety about having to fill out forms and applications, write checks, and/or leave messages. They frequently took great pains to escape the situation to fill out forms. Adequate skills were said to break down under pressure, and they could not read and write "on the spot."

Social Problems

At least half of the group reported some social problems, with many stating that they had few close friends. Problems related to academic difficulties involved not being able to participate in many games played by their peers, such as word games or card games. Oral language deficits seriously interfered with the social interactions of several. Some could not follow the rapid verbal interactions of their friends, did not understand jokes, and could not follow conversations that rapidly shifted topics. Word retrieval and pronunciation problems made them less confident in speaking. A few reported that people made fun of them because of pronunciation problems.

The nonverbal problems created the most severe problems socially. Some of these people reported an inability to learn dance steps which was felt to be a serious problem by several. They had difficulty finding their way around and were teased. Perhaps the biggest problem for many of the group was social imperception. These problems were rarely reported and often not obvious in a testing situation. Prolonged interaction during the testing and later revealed social perception difficulties that needed remediation. Those with social perception problems did not use space appropriately, said very inappropriate things in a group, often did not look at people, and/or did not respond to nonverbal cues that they should leave, stop talking, or were interrupting something. This group in particular reported feeling somewhat "alone" and had few friends. Many were unaware of their problems and what they were doing to "turn people off."

Vocational Problems

Society is becoming *much* more aware of the vocational problems of the learning disabled adult. This increasing awareness is probably the result of several things: (1) the early groups of "diagnosed" children having job-related problems as adults; (2) implementation of the laws regarding handicapped individuals; and (3) the inability of "typical" vocational training and vocational counselling programs to deal effectively with this group. The problem is of concern not only to the learning disabled individual and his or her family but to vocational counsellors and employers.

The concern of employers is reflected in the increasing number of referrals from this group. Young adults with a history of many job failures often reported the confusion of employers: "You are bright and have the skills and abilities to handle the job, but things are not working out."

A part of the information obtained during our evaluation pertains to job history. Several of the older adults (27–37 years) reported numerous job problems and changes. One very bright, talented young man with mild problems had had twelve jobs in eight years. They often seemed uncertain about what had gone wrong. During the course of our contact with these people we have seen numerous job changes and an increase in the number who are unemployed. Job-related problems reported by the adults vary according to the nature of their processing deficits and jobs. Auditory processing deficits in those whose jobs involved telephone work and/or communicating in noisy environments were a significant factor in creating problems. Efforts to hide problems in reading and written language took considerable energy and time. Many reported having to "fake it" much of the time. Organizational problems often resulted in unfinished projects or forgotten and neglected tasks. Social interaction problems also interfered.

Many of the adults we worked with were very bright, talented individuals. Some made very good first impressions and frequently found themselves in jobs they could not handle. They seemed unable to anticipate problems that might arise in these jobs. If some analysis of the problem was not given to them, they often made the same mistakes in selecting the next job.

Educational Problems

Problems of all kinds and severity have interfered with college careers and some vocational training programs. Problems range from the inability to write papers described above to difficulty listening to and following lectures. An eighth grade reading level is not sufficient for college work, and many college students were reading at levels below that. One of the best solutions for many has been to take a reduced load. This frequently was enough to enable the student to succeed. Quite a few young people have been refused permission to take less than a full load in some colleges and universities, however. Another problem faced by many learning disabled college students was the foreign language requirement. In most instances this can be waived for students who have diagnosed learning disabilities.

In days of declining enrollments in colleges and universities, it is possible for students without the skills and/or abilities necessary for successful college work to be admitted. Several of those in the group were in programs they could not handle, even with reduced loads and supplementary help.

For quite a few of the group, a college education was a perfectly realistic and reasonable goal. Their decisions needed to be made keeping in mind the amount of effort it would require to complete college. Some had decided that it was worth it, others that it was not. The few who were going to college because it was "the thing to do" were having the most problems deciding on majors.

Goals

Goals, skills, and abilities were often incompatible in the group we saw. Many, however, did have goals that were realistic, even though not immediately within reach. One subgroup had goals and ambitions that were unrealistic in light of their overall abilities and skills. For example, several expressed a desire to graduate from college in areas that required good quantitative abilities when they had severe problems in that area. Unrealistic goals often were seen in individuals who had little understanding of their learning disabilities. It is important to note that several were very uncertain of what they wanted to do and seemed to change goals frequently. External pressures and expectancies of others often played a role in the expressed goals of the uncertain and unrealistic people.

WHAT HAS HELPED MOST AND LEAST?

Eight of the thirty-eight cases reviewed here had had learning disabilities help in the past. Most had received some tutoring in difficult subjects. At least eighteen had received psychological counselling or therapy since completing high school. Two had been in programs for the behaviorally disordered or emotionally disturbed at some point during their school careers. When asked what had helped most, several reported that the learning disabilities help was beneficial. Several stated than an occasional teacher who understood and helped had been the most help. Tutoring was reported to have been of very little help by many. Adult education classes and speed reading courses were also said to be of no help.

Counselling and psychotherapy was frequently said to have been of help in dealing with frustrations and "other problems" by many of those who received it. Those who entered therapy with hopes of solving the problems in learning usually commented that it was of little value. These people concluded that they did not generally recommend counselling or psychotherapy to all learning disabled adults, only those with "other problems."

Some of the young adults expressed a need to know about and talk with others who were experiencing the same problems. They viewed this type of group interaction as most beneficial, but did not see it as being a long-term interaction. These conclusions were confirmed by a member of a group for learning disabled adults who stated that frequently people attended several meetings, reported that it had been very beneficial to meet with others having similar problems, and did not continue because their needs had been met.

We have been very interested in the types of family support viewed as most beneficial. The responses have been somewhat mixed suggesting that there is no "best way" of dealing with a learning disabled child. Many stated that their interactions with their families had been somewhat stormy, *but* they would not be where they were "if they hadn't pushed." Several reported that "realistic expectancy" would be ideal. This was described as not expecting the impossible, but *"knowing* that you could do it." Individuals who were included in the "what helped most?" answers included parents, teachers, and/or friends who "understood and helped."

The most frequently reported thing that "helped least" and, in fact, was viewed as most damaging was being told that they were "lazy" or "unmotivated" and that they could do better if they "tried harder." The people who reported this were frequently those with mild and moderate problems. Those with severe problems usually had had some form of help.

A few of the group had been in classes or schools for the emotionally disturbed or behaviorally disordered as youngsters. These people were very outspoken in stating that this was damaging to them at the time and that they continued to have bad feelings about that placement.

ATTITUDES

No description of this group would be complete without a discussion of the attitudes and feelings about their problems expressed in the interviews. All of the people seen were aware that there was some type of problem. Many did not know what a learning disability was but knew that something was the matter. Most of the group viewed the problems as something that was interfering with reaching goals. They appeared to see themselves as individuals with an "uphill struggle" to function in life the way they would like. This undoubtedly reflects the nature of this particular highly motivated, persistent group.

They were asked to describe their reactions (current and retrospective) to their problems and experiences. Many reported a feeling of confusion about why things were always so difficult for them. Many said that they knew they were not "dumb" because everyone told them that, but they could not discover how to "try harder." Frustration was frequently reported. This was because of the inability to perform at levels expected by themselves as well as others. *Impatience* with themselves about their inability to "overcome the problems" was also mentioned by many. Some mentioned feeling guilty because they did not do better in school. These feelings were reported in the interviews and also in optional group sessions conducted by a social worker at our Center (Rosenblum 1977).

Observations of the individuals in this group suggested that they had strong egos, were well-defended, and had developed amazing strategies for avoiding, hiding, and dealing with problems. They seemed relieved to have someone to talk with about their learning problems and to find out that others had similar difficulties. Anger was seen in several of this group. It was often directed toward systems that did not recognize their problems and provide appropriate teaching. These were frequently people with undiagnosed problems. The single descriptive term that described most of them best is *persistent*.

In several instances, the learning disabled adults viewed their problems as more severe than they appeared in the evaluation. Two explanations were given when they were asked about this: "Well, no one ever believed I had a problem so I was making certain you listened," and "You just don't know what I'm going through to avoid the problem." One other observation was made in a few cases. Several were apparently unaware of the difficulties people without learning disabilities have in writing, operating under pressure, etc., and blamed every difficult situation on the learning disability.

When asked what they wanted from the Learning Disabilities Center, they usually said they wanted help in understanding their problems and, most of all, they wanted help in learning so they could move ahead vocationally or educationally.

IMPRESSIONS AND ISSUES

What is a Learning Disability in an Adult?

Specific learning disabilities in adults are like those in preschoolers, school age children, and adolescents. Their processing deficits are quite similar, but the things they are called upon to learn and the situations in which they must function differ. The similarities across age groups suggest that to view a learning disability as an academic problem is a mistake that can result in programming across age groups that is too narrow. This point was aptly made by the parent of an adolescent who gently said, "The problem with you special educators is that you spend too much time telling me how my child is doing learning to read and write. I know that's a problem, but I care more about how he's going to learn things like getting along in life socially and vocationally."

What is the Nature of Persistent Problems?

While similar processing deficits are seen, in children and adults, these problems are very frequently much more subtle and are seen less blatantly. Most of the learning disabled adults described here are leading productive, successful lives. Their residual problems are frequently frustrating to them by interfering with higher education and vocational goals. As has been reported by others, the problems seen most often are at the levels of metacognitive abilities and automaticity in integrative use of skills. Although their problems are subtle, in many instances, learning and performing in job situations is a very real problem that must be dealt with by a large group of people.

Can Remediation be Effective with
Older Learning Disabled Individuals?

We have not done extensive re-evaluations to date. Indications are that definite improvement can be made in the young adult group. That age is not the determining factor in the ability to profit from remediation is supported by the finding of several investigators (Zigmond 1978; Johnson, Blalock, and Nesbitt 1978).

What are the Problems and Issues in Dealing
with Learning Disabled Adults?

Educational

Many of the problems and issues pertaining to educational programming for young adults are like those discussed in relation to adolescents (Johnson, Blalock, and Nesbitt 1978). Problems also arise regarding higher education. While many learning disabled young adults are very capable of successfully completing undergraduate and graduate programs, some are not. Determining who should be admitted and who should not is a major problem facing colleges and universities. How many and what kind of adjustments in entrance and graduation requirements should be made?

The problems facing the learning disabled young adult and his or her family are also significant. How does one evaluate the nature of college programs for the learning disabled? What kind, if any, adjustments in requirements need to be made? What support is needed? Is college even a realistic goal? Identified learning disabled students admitted to college and university programs need careful advising both prior to and after admittance. Advising should include some discussion of the amount of effort and time required on their parts as well as what modifications can and will be made by the institution. Decisions about whether or not that kind of effort is worth it need to be made by the individual, not by well-meaning friends and relatives. Many times goals and priorities need to be re-evaluated periodically.

Many learning disabled young adults with mild to moderate residual problems are admitted to college without the college officials ever being aware of their problems. Some with mild problems do not discover the problems themselves until they are in college. Many of these students do well without modifications, but a tremendous amount of energy and effort is usually required. The same decisions need to be made about investing that amount of effort.

Vocational Counselling and Training

We have found that vocational aptitude and interest tests are often not as beneficial to the learning disabled group as to others. Interests and skills may be incompatible or specific deficits may interfere with aspects of functioning not directly related to the abilities and interests used to make recommendations.

The vocational counsellor needs information about required abilities and skills for types of jobs, what is involved in training for these fields, and how the specific problems of the individual might interfere. This is difficult because of the assumptions of certain underlying abilities and skills in most descriptions of jobs and the variety of patterns of abilities and disabilities in the learning disabled population.

Even when skills, interests, abilities, and problems are compatible with a selected job-type, problems can arise. The specific conditions and requirements of the particular placement must be considered in relation to the individual person's problems. For example, job success might be affected by the following: Where the work is done (noisy or quiet location); pressures of the particular job; the amount of self-organization and planning required in the position.

Another area of consideration needs to be that of job-getting and job-keeping behaviors. Even subtle, mild social perception problems may interfere with interview behavior, relationships with fellow workers, and interaction with customers, clients, or the public. Analysis of specific problems and teaching in this area may be needed. Many of the individuals with these problems are unaware of them and do not know why they have difficulty on the job.

Related to this is the problem of not understanding the specific nature and extent of one's own learning deficits. This would help the individual anticipate problems that might arise. While most of the people we evaluated were aware of specific problem areas, few understood the relationships between their different problems. An understanding of the underlying problems and how they interfere across areas of functioning might aid in anticipating problems. Focus on areas of academic under-achievement and subskill building during school years does not provide the child or his family with this understanding that might help in anticipating future non-academic problems.

Other Needs

Young adults frequently need remediation after their public school educations are completed. Changing priorities and goal and social problems, as well as changes in types of available employment, make this necessary. When faced with learning new tasks or improving skills, it seems that specialized teaching is again needed.

Equally important is the need for researchers to carefully examine the nature and impact of residual learning deficits in young adults and the effectiveness of remediation with adults. The implementation of PL 94-142 is causing changes in programming for learning disabled children and adolescents. The programs developed might be much more effective if they are based on the needs and problems in learning being experienced by young adults in society. The preliminary findings reported here suggest that viewing a learning disability as an academic problem is inaccurate and results in providing services that are too narrow.

REFERENCES

Johnson, D.; Blalock, J.; and Nesbitt, J. "Adolescents with Learning Disabilities: Perspectives from an Educational Clinic." *Learning Disability Quarterly* 4 (1978):24–36.

Johnson, D., and Myklebust, H. *Learning Disabilities: Educational Principles and Practices.* New York: Grune & Stratton, 1967.

Rosenblum, L. "Adolescents with Learning Disabilities." Presentation to Northwestern University Learning Disabilities Conference. Evanston, Ill., May 1977.

Zigmond, N. "A Prototype of Comprehensive Services for Secondary Students with Learning Disabilities." *Learning Disability Quarterly* 1 (1978):39–49.

4

Social Interaction Deficits in Learning Disabled Adolescents — Another Myth?

Donald D. Deshler, Jean B. Schumaker, Gordon R. Alley,
Michael M. Warner, and Frances L. Clark

SINCE THE INCEPTION of the learning disability field in the early 1960s, emphasis for treatment and intervention has been on younger children. Only recently has attention been turned to addressing the educational and life adjustment needs of adolescents and young adults as well (Alley and Deshler 1979). A prerequisite step to developing sound instructional systems and procedures for the older learning disabled person is for the field to achieve a thorough understanding of the complex nature of the condition of learning disabilities in older populations.

Some unique problems related to adolescents which have not been adequately addressed by the research on learning disabilities in elementary populations include the following: first, the demands of the curriculum in secondary schools or job requirements in employment settings are significantly different from the demands placed on LD students in elementary settings. Thus, the manifestations of the specific learning disability may be altered. Second, there are many variables associated with the condition of learning disabilities. It would appear that the complexity and interaction of these increase as the adolescent moves from school to non-school settings and as the number and variety of his/her social groupings increase (Deshler 1978). Thirdly, there is very little knowledge about the conditions confronting the LD adolescent and young adult in non-school settings and the degree to which these individuals can cope with these circumstances.

The complex nature of the condition of learning disabilities and the unique features of the conditions and the environment facing the LD adolescent and young adult demonstrate the need for systematic research on this population. Therefore, the purpose of a major line of research conducted by The University of Kansas Institute for Research in Learning Disabilities has been to collect a broad array of data to form an epidemiological data base on older LD populations. Data have been collected from the environmental setting of the LD adolescent which pertain to interventions applied on behalf of the student, conditions under which he or she operates, and support systems available for the student's use. These data have been considered in relation to data on specific learner characteristics in order to gain a more complete profile of the older LD individual.

In the past several years there has been a great deal of interest shown by practitioners and researchers in the social interactions and activities of mildly handicapped individuals. Zigmond (1980) cited several reasons for this increased emphasis on social skills: (1) by the time students reach adolescence, training in academic skills has limited pay off (Drake and Cavanaugh 1970); (2) ameliorating social deficits may allow students to profit more from other educational experiences (Zigmond 1978); (3) training in social skills can facilitate student placement in mainstreamed settings (Laurie, Buchwach, Silverman, and Zigmond 1978); and (4) improvement in social skills is likely to increase student's employability (Irvine, Goodman, and Mann 1978; Mathews, Whang, and Fawcett 1980).

Most research on social interactions and activities with learning disabled populations is available on elementary aged students. This research has documented the hypothesis that LD children are likely to be the objects of their peers' social rejection. Bryan (1974), for example, found that LD white females were likely to be rejected by their classmates when rejection was assessed with sociometric measures. Similarly, Siperstein, Bopp, and Bak (1977) and Bruininks (1978) also found learning disabled students to be rejected by their peers. Bryan and Bryan (1978) have delineated specific factors that may account for the rejection experienced by the learning disabled students. Specifically, communications to and from learning disabled students tended to be nastier in rejection categories. Most of these research efforts, however, have compared LD populations with normal populations, not other handicapped or low-achieving populations.

Contrary to literature contributions on elementary LD populations, most writings on social skills for LD adolescents are not data based. A common *assumption* underlying most of these writings is that a major, distinguishing characteristic of older-aged LD populations is a broad array of deficient social skills such as social rejection, isolation, and ineptitude. Furthermore, these writings often assume that addressing such deficits through intervention programs is central to impacting not only the life adjustment but academic success of LD adolescents. An essential prerequisite step to designing social skill intervention procedures for LD adolescents is to determine if this population is in fact deficit on salient characteristics that would be the basis of social skill interventions.

"Social skills" is a generic term used to mean the composite of abilities necessary for interpersonal functioning. This article will report on several studies conducted by the University of Kansas Institute for Research in Learning Disabilities designed to study various dimensions and indices of social skills of LD adolescents.

A major research priority of the institute has been to study LD adolescents in relation to low-achieving peers as well as normal achieving peers. The specification of factors that differentiate LD students from other students in a school setting who are experiencing academic adjustment problems is central to resolution on the definitional issue facing the field. Three groups of adolescents, their parents, and their teachers participated in most of the studies reported below. The adolescents included LD students, low-achieving students, and normal-achieving students in grades 7, 8, 9, 10, 11, and 12. LD students were those currently being served in programs for learning disabled students and validated by the IRLD Validation Team. Low-achieving (LA) students were students who had recently received one or more failing grades in required subjects, scored below the 33rd percentile on group administered achievement tests, and who were not receiving special educational services. Normal-achieving (NA) students were those who had passing grades, scored above the 33rd percentile in achievement, and who were not receiving special educational services.

MAJOR FINDINGS

Peer Relationships and Extracurricular Involvement

Deshler, Schumaker, Warner, Alley, and Clark (1980) studied two sets of variables related to social skill interactions of LD adolescents: peer relationships and involvement in extracurricular activities. Data were gathered from students' self-reports and from parent and teacher reports. Fifteen variables relating to peer relationships were studied, and only two were found to differentiate LD and LA adolescents. The two variables were: "Going somewhere with a friend who asks you" and "Asking other students to go somewhere." In each instance the LD students reported less frequent involvement in these behaviors than LAs. Significant differences were found on three variables that differentiated LD and LA students from their NA peers (hanging around the neighborhood, just hanging around with friends, and having friends over to their house). On each variable LD and LA students reported greater frequency of involvement in these behaviors than their NA peers. The variables in which no differences were found between the groups are interesting to note in that they indicate normal behavior along several dimensions of social interaction. Among these variables were the following: playing games with friends, receiving phone calls from friends, number of close friends you can talk to about important things, and calling friends on phone just to talk. In terms of extracurricular activity involvement only one variable (of fifteen) was found to differentiate LD and LA students (sports spectating with friends). LD students reported significantly less involvement in sports spectating with friends than their LA and NA peers. Ten variables, however, were significant in differentiating the NA group from the LD and LA groups. These data show a general trend for LD and LA adolescents to engage in a limited number of extracurricular school activities. LD and LA students reported participating in such activities less than once per month, whereas NA students participate in such activities on a weekly basis. NA students spend almost three times as many hours per week in extracurricular activities than LA and LD students.

Interactions with Peers

An observational study of the social behavior of LD adolescents in regular class settings was conducted by Schumaker, Sheldon-Wildgen, and Sherman (1980). The results of the social behavior comparisons indicate that LD junior high students are not social isolates in the classroom. They were found to talk to as many different peers as the non-LD students and spend slightly more time engaged in conversations with peers than the non-LD students. Peers were not found to ignore their initiations much more often than they ignore the non-LD students' initiations. The LD students, however, initiated 5 percent more of their interactions than the non-LD students.

Regular Class Teacher Perception

Regular class teachers and parents of LD and NA adolescents were asked to report on their perceptions of the behavioral and social skills of these students in a study conducted by Alley, Warner, Schumaker, Deshler, and Clark (1980). Teachers perceived the LD junior high school adolescents as more positive than their LA peers on the following social behaviors: speaks courteously to teacher, brings materials to class, pays attention to lecture or discussion, completes in-class assignments, completes homework assignments, hands in assignments on time, asks for help when appropriate, starts work when instructed, follows instructions, gets along well with authority figures, tries hard to improve when criticized, is appreciative of praise, and meets task deadlines with satisfactory products. Teacher perceptions of these behaviors ranged from "sometimes" to "often." The extremes of these behaviors ("never" and "always"), however, are not attributed to the LD junior high school student. The superiority of LD junior high school students confirmed at the senior high school level. It may well be that the demands of the senior high school are at a level that the LD adolescent cannot attain irrespective of efforts.

Skrtic (1980) conducted a study to analyze the regular classroom interactions of LD adolescents and their regular class teachers. His research was conducted at the senior high school level in twenty-nine classrooms. Skrtic's major findings were the following: (1) teachers interacted with LD and non-LD students with comparable frequency; (2) teachers did not rate LD and non-LD students differently on level of hyperactivity, defiance, or dependency; (3) teachers called on LD students as frequently as on non-LD students; (4) teachers offered assistance to LD and non-LD students with the same frequency; (5) the majority of interactions between students and teachers were academic rather than social in nature — most of the academic interactions were positive; (6) a greater proportion of academic interactions between teachers and students were directed toward LD students. Even though observational data indicated that if any differences existed in the treatment of LD and non-LD students they were in favor of LD students, LD students perceived their teachers as directing significantly less approval and somewhat more disapproval toward them than did non-LD students. These results may suggest that LD students misperceived the interactions that took place between themselves and their teachers.

Social Skills Related to Occupational Success

Another study which examined the social skills of LD adolescents was that of Mathews, Whang, and Fawcett (1980). Their analysis of social skills was done in the context of studying critical behaviors related to obtaining and retaining a job. Of the thirteen behaviors, several were social variables (accepting criticism from an employer, providing constructive criticism to a co-worker, accepting a compliment from a co-worker). The overall mean percentage of social interactions performed by LD adolescents (32 percent) was not significantly different from the non-LD students (35 percent). The two groups were differentiated, however, on cognitive and academically related skills (accuracy of filling out job applications, completion of résumés, and writing letters of inquiry about a job).

Social Skills in Young Adult Populations

A retrospective study was conducted by White, Schumaker, Warner, Alley, and Deshler (1980) for the purpose of examining, among LD and NA young adults, a broad array of factors suspected to be indicative of personal, social, and vocational success. The young adult samples for this study had an average age of 20.5 years (range 18–25). Data were gathered through self-report instruments completed by the young adults. Variables on making friends and taking part in activities were seen as being related to the social/personal adjustment of this population. Both groups reported approximately the same number of friends they could "talk to about things that are very important" to them (LD $\bar{x}$ = 4.45; NLD $\bar{x}$ = 4.96). However, the NLD group reported having more friends they could go places with or share activities with (LD $\bar{x}$ = 9.13; NLD $\bar{x}$ = 14.08). While this result is statistically significant, it is questionable whether there is a practical difference in having 14 as compared to 9 friends. The groups also differed with respect to their involvement in different types of activities. Neither group was involved in church or religious activities, politics, community service, professional organizations, or labor union activities. The NLD group was more active in social or fraternal activities (p < .01) and recreational activities (p < .05) than the LD sample. The NLD group also reported belonging to more community clubs and groups than the LD groups (p < .01).

Training Social Skills

Finally, a study currently in progress by Hazel, Schumaker, Sherman, and Sheldon-Wildgen is developing a social skills and problem-solving program for use in school and juvenile justice settings. A set of social skills have been taught to LD, non-LD, and non-LD juvenile delinquent samples in the areas of giving positive feedback, giving negative feedback, accepting negative feedback, resisting peer pressure, problem solving, and negotiation. Generally, all groups have shown the same pre-training skill levels and all groups learned the social skills to the same levels. The LD students, however, did not learn the problem solving skill to the same level as the other two groups. These data suggest that LD youths do not differ from non-LD youths in terms of social-interaction skills, but they do differ in the acquisition of more cognitive-type skills. The preliminary data also indicate that LD youths are as poor as other youths (such as JD groups) in resisting peer pressure.

SUMMARY

The picture that is beginning to emerge from our research on the social skills and interactions of LD adolescents is a different one than presented in much of the literature on this population. In essence, LD adolescents do not appear to be social isolates in school situations. To the contrary, LD students were found to have friends, to enjoy positive interactions with them as well as teachers and to participate in social related activities. On the other hand, the findings reported above may not be presenting the entire picture on the social status of LD adolescents. While LD students were found on many measures to be comparable to their LA or NA peers, strong conclusions cannot be drawn about LD adolescents' social behaviors until more specific measures of exactly what they say and do in social interactions with peers can be taken. Schumaker et al. (1980) concluded: "It is possible that by adolescence they 'catch-up' with their peers in the social realm. It is also possible, however, that even though they interact as frequently as non-LD peers, the quality of those interactions are not comparable" (p. 28). Thus, a high research priority of our Institute in subsequent years will be to determine the specific nature of the social skills, status, and interactions of LD adolescents. These current data, however, should serve as a caution of those who would divert extensive amounts of instructional time from cognitive/academic areas to training social skills. The need for a continued critical examination of assumptions related to the population characteristics of older-aged LD populations is warranted before interventions are developed.

REFERENCES

Alley, G. R., and Deshler, D. D. *Teaching the Learning Disabled Adolescent: Strategies and Methods.* Denver: Love, 1979.

Alley, G. R.; Warner, M. M.; Schumaker, J. B.; and Deshler, D. D. *An Epidemiology Study of Learning Disabled Adolescents in Secondary Schools: Behavioral and Emotional Status from the Perspective of Parents and Teachers.* Research Report No. 16. Lawrence: University of Kansas Institute for Research in Learning Disabilities, 1980.

Bruininks, V. L. "Actual and Perceived Peer Status of Learning Disabled Students in Mainstream Programs." *The Journal of Special Education* 12 (1978):51–58.

Bryan, T. "Peer Popularity of Learning Disabled Children." *Journal of Learning Disabilities* 7 (1974):261–68.

Bryan, T. H., and Bryan, J. H. "Social Interactions of Learning Disabled Children." *Learning Disability Quarterly* 1 (1978):33–38.

Deshler, D. D. "Psychoeducational Aspects of Learning Disabled Adolescents." In *Teaching the Learning Disabled Adolescent,* edited by L. Mann, L. Goodman, and J. L. Wiederholt. Boston: Houghton-Mifflin, 1978.

Deshler, D. D.; Schumaker, J. B.; Warner, M. M.; Alley, G. R.; and Clark, F. L. *An Epidemiology Study of Learning Disabled Adolescents in Secondary Schools: Social Status, Peer Relationships, Time Use and Activities In and Out of School.* Research Report No. 18. Lawrence: University of Kansas Institute for Research in Learning Disabilities, 1980.

Drake, C., and Cavanaugh, J. A. "Teaching the High School Dyslexic." In *Helping the Adolescent with the Hidden Handicap,* edited by L. E. Anderson. Belmont, Calif.: Fearon, 1970.

Matthews, R. M.; Whang, P. L.; and Fawcett, S. B. *Behavioral Assessment of Occupational Skills of Learning Disabled Adolescents.* Research Report No. 5. Lawrence: University of Kansas Institute for Research in Learning Disabilities, 1980.

Schumaker, J. B.; Sheldon-Wildgen, J.; and Sherman, J. A. *An Observational Study of the Academic and Social Behaviors of Learning Disabled Adolescents in the Regular Classroom.* Research Report No. 22. Lawrence: University of Kansas Institute for Research in Learning Disabilities, 1980.

Siperstein, G. N.; Bopp, M. J.; and Bak, J. J. *Social Status of Learning Disabled Children.* RIEP-Print No. 100. Cambridge, Mass.: Research Institute for Educational Problems, 1977.

Skrtic, T. M. *The Regular Classroom Interactions of Learning Disabled Adolescents and their Teachers.* Research Report No. 8. Lawrence: University of Kansas Institute for Research in Learning Disabilities, 1980.

White, W. J.; Schumaker, J. B.; Warner, M. M.; Alley, G. R.; and Deshler, D. D. *The Current Status of Young Adults Identified as Learning Disabled during their School Career.* Research Report No. 21. Lawrence: University of Kansas Institute for Research in Learning Disabilities.

Zigmond, N. "A Prototype of Comprehensive Services for Secondary Students with Learning Disabilities." *Learning Disability Quarterly* 1 (1978):39–49.

Zigmond, N., and Brownlee, J. "Social Skills Training for Adolescents with Learning Disabilities." *Exceptional Educational Quarterly* 1 (1980):87–93.

5

Meeting the Emotional Needs of the Mildly Handicapped: A New Social/Behavioral Program for the Adolescent Student with Learning Disabilities

Charles Meisgeier and Linda Menius

THE PROBLEM OF DESIGNING appropriate instruction for the adolescent learning disabled student is very complex. The student's poor academic performance is frequently compounded by social skill deficits and emotional instability. Some articles have been published describing the LD adolescent's poor self-concept, inadequate peer relationships, academic failures, and need for success. While these characteristics are accepted as substantial problems for the student, few authors have proposed methods for dealing with their combined ramifications. There continues to be confusion, differences of opinion, and perplexity regarding the content, methods, and strategies to be used in educating the LD adolescent.

Many good programs have been developed which attempt to remediate a student's academic skill performance with the hope that self-confidence will increase as skill levels increase. A few pilot programs focus on modification of the student's self-image or self-concept, with the hope that academic performance will likewise improve if the student can develop a positive view of self and others. However, no either-or approach to the problem seems to be sufficient.

To achieve substantial student change at this age, it seems that both academic and affective needs must be addressed and interventions must simultaneously impact a student's skill deficits and his affective problems. Meisgeier's (1977) concept of "synergistic education" attempts to reconcile the need for such a dual approach. Synergy is used to illustrate the concept that a combination of affective and skill interventions will create a greater effect than either intervention would produce in isolation. The synergistic concept has been put into operation in middle and senior high schools of a medium-sized school district in Houston, Texas.

The total Synergistic Education program includes: (1) the High Intensity Learning Center (HILC), (2) Parent Support Group (for parents of students enrolled in the program), (3) a Content Mastery program to support the success of the LD student in the regular classroom, and (4) an Essential Skills program to provide limited follow-up skill instruction after a student completes the HILC. The synergistic response of the total program comes from combined emphasis on the student in regular and special classes, the parent, and teachers. Within itself each component is also designed to achieve synergistic learning. The affective needs of the LD adolescent are addressed throughout the total program and most specifically in the Social/Behavioral Component of the High Intensity Learning Center.

THE HIGH INTENSITY LEARNING EXPERIENCE

The High Intensity Learning Center provides structured activities in reading and related skills and in affective instruction. The purposes of the HILC are: (1) to improve student's basic academic skills, primarily reading; (2) to make diagnostic prescriptions for the student's future education; and (3) to encourage the student's personal/social development.

The instructional program is structured to give students success experiences in both academics and interpersonal relationships, creating an atmosphere of growth and achievement. The HILC operates the first twelve or eighteen weeks of the school year for three consecutive hours each day. Students who have received special services in elementary school are assigned to the HILC when they enter junior or senior high school; students who are initially placed in special programs during their junior high school career also attend the HILC at some point.

The HILC has been designed to be an atypical learning environment, organized to modify developed patterns of academic failure and inappropriate behavior. These patterns may be perpetuated indefinitely if students continue to receive instruction in typical settings. By placing students in a different learning experience, it is hoped that old, inappropriate behaviors will be "unfrozen" and that the new academic and interpersonal skills practiced in the HILC will be "refrozen." The small group, high involvement, concentrated time setting also provides the group familiarity and cohesiveness necessary for students and teachers to practice the interpersonal skills presented, to receive feedback on their use of these skills, and to adapt the skills to personal weaknesses and needs.

ADDRESSING THE STUDENT'S SOCIAL/BEHAVIORAL NEEDS

Rationale

The learning disabled adolescent brings to his educational experiences not only academic failures, but also a poor self-concept and a lack of interpersonal skills. Achieving success in academic areas may be one way to reverse a negative self-image. However, by the time a student reaches junior or senior high school, the promise of success in academics, particularly reading and writing, is not likely to have much power. The relationship between self-concept and academic achievement has been well documented, although the relative contribution of self-concept to achievement is not known. Combs and Kelly (reported in Leviton and Kiraly 1979) believe that learning performance is limited by a low self-concept as well as by biological factors. They state that while little can be done about biological factors, there is something which can be done about non-biological factors such as self-concept. A number of strategies have been devised in an attempt to "do something about self-concept." Four of these strategies — affective programs, racial studies programs, tutoring programs (where the tutor is profiting), and competency programs (where the student client is profiting) — have been identified as effective in improving the self-concepts of participants (Leviton and Kiraly 1979). The High Intensity Learning Center employs an affective program strategy to provide specific structured experiences which lead to self-awareness and acceptance of one's abilities and limitations.

Smith (1975) states that self-concept is determined by what one would ideally like to be and how one views himself in relation to other people. A person's self-concept grows out of his interactions with others and is a reflection of the way others view a person. Using such a definition of self-concept, it is apparent that a student's interactions with family, teacher, and peers are extremely important. Bryan and Bryan (1978) report a number of studies which emphasize the fact that parents, teachers, and peers view the learning disabled student negatively. Together, these studies suggest that parents see their LD children as unable to control impulses, as less considerate than others, as exhibiting poor judgment; teachers view the LD child as less cooperative, less accepting of responsibility, less socially acceptable than non-disabled and as being aggressive; peers view them as less popular than normal students. The learning disabled adolescent receives daily messages of rejection from these individuals. In order to reverse these negative messages and perceived traits, he must learn new behaviors to alter the way others view him.

Learning disabled students are often unaware of their impact on others; they do not act on incidental cues which influence a normal student's actions. Wiig and Harris (reported in Bryan and Bryan 1978) studied learning disabled students' ability to identify nonverbal expressions of a female model in videotapes. They found that the learning disabled students more frequently mislabeled the emotion than did normal students and that the mislabelings were occasionally extreme (such as labeling a person happy when he was angry). Gordon (1970) states that educators must devise training methods that compensate for this deficit, rather than leave the youth to anticipate or misread the effect of his behavior on others. With guided practice and experience in ways to interact with others, the learning disabled student's behavior may change such that other people view him in more positive ways.

The student who feels he is a failure, who sees himself as a nobody, is likely to be rejected by his peers. However, peer groups are an important socializing agent for adolescents. Without the opportunity to engage in group activities and to learn from his peers, a student's self-concept can be further undermined (White 1975). The student who is receiving instruction in the regular classroom must be given skills which help him to be acceptable to both his teacher and his peers. He must be given a fair chance at inclusion in the classroom activities as well as in social activities.

Most teachers and parents are aware that social/behavioral variables are a major factor influencing student success. It is not the handicap itself which will limit the disabled adolescent in the long run. It is his attitude about himself that will determine whether he goes ahead successfully or not (Gordon 1970). The social/behavioral program has been developed to help students understand their handicap, to improve their personal relationships, and to help them present themselves as competent individuals.

Social/Behavioral Curriculum

Variables associated with personal maturity have been identified by Torgenson (1977) as (1) increased independence, (2) accepting responsibility for personal behavior, (3) awareness of unique individuality, and (4) realistic appraisal of personal strengths and weaknesses. Meisgeier's consultations with experts from the fields of business, education, human relations, and psychology identified similar variables for consideration as the course content of the social/behavioral program. The variables identified were synthesized by Meisgeier into four major concept or skill areas that became the base for the Social/Behavioral Curriculum. The areas and their student oriented definitions are:

1. *self-responsibility:* Owning up to (admitting) your own behavior, statements, and actions and actively finding positive ways to handle everyday stress and problems.
2. *communication:* Any verbal or non-verbal way of getting across a message, feeling, or thought to another person.
3. *assertiveness:* Positive verbal and nonverbal ways of standing up for your own rights, ideas, and opinions.
4. *problem solving:* Actively working through or following a set of steps to find a good, workable answer to a problem.

The program is a structured, educational experience involving group and individual activities. It is not a group encounter session or a counseling session. The program involves one hour daily of the three hour HILC block. Students are introduced to the component as though it were a psychology course. Grades are given, but are based on participation and effort only. Twelve units containing sixty lessons have been developed. The lessons are sequenced so that skills introduced early in the course are reinforced in later lessons and more complex skills presented later in the sequence are built upon earlier learned skills. There are twenty-four self-responsibility lessons, eleven communication lessons, eight assertiveness lessons, five problem solving lessons, and twelve individual goal lessons. In these individual sessions, each student works on a personal goal relevant to one of the areas. Table 5.1 shows the sequence of lessons by area and topic.

GROUP LESSON FORMAT

Each lesson follows a standard format. The fifty-minute lesson is divided in the following manner:

5 minutes	Deep Breath/Relaxation Exercises
5 minutes	Introduction to Activity
35 minutes	Activity (Skill to be Learned)
5 minutes	Ego Trip/Journal

TABLE 5.1

Sequence of Affective Lessons

1. Introduction
2. Communication: *A Discussion Model*
3. Responsibility: *Responsible Statements*
4. Responsibility: *Assuming Responsibility*
5. Responsibility: *Dealing with Persons in Authority*
6. Self Concept: *Having a LD*
7. Student Conferences: *LD and Goals*
8. Student Conferences: *LD and Goals*
9. Communication: *Two Way Communication*
10. Communication: *Verbal Communication*
11. Nonverbal Communication: *Eye Contact*
12. Nonverbal Communication: *Body Language*
13. Individual Sessions
14. Assertiveness: *Aggressive Behavior*
15. Assertiveness: *Passive Behavior*
16. Assertiveness: *Assertive Behavior*
17. Assertiveness: *Assertive Overview*
18. Individual Sessions
19. Assertiveness: *Society's Stereotypes*
20. Communication: *Positive Strokes*
21. Communication: *Your Stroke Support System*
22. Communication: *Negative Strokes*
23. Individual Sessions
24. Communication: *Negative Stroke Rejection*
25. Communication: *Compliments and Conversations*
26. Communication: *Making Requests*
27. Communication: *Refusing Requests*
28. Individual Sessions
29. Assertiveness: *Denial of Rights and Expressing Opinions*
30. Assertiveness: *Coping with Anger*
31. Assertiveness: *Expressing Anger*
32. Responsibility: *Winners and Nonwinners*
33. Individual Sessions
34. Responsibility: *Feelings are a Choice*
35. Responsibility: *Making the Choice*
36. Responsibility: *Meeting Physical Needs*
37. Responsibility: *Basic Emotion Needs Identified*
38. Individual Sessions
39. Responsibility: *Emotional Needs: Ways to Meet Them*
40. Responsibility: *Taking Risks*
41. Responsibility: *Risks and Stress*
42. Responsibility: *Stress Coping*

TABLE 5.1 (cont'd.)

43. Responsibility: *Stress Coping*   4 day module
44. Responsibility: *Stress Coping*
45. Responsibility: *Stress Coping*
46. Responsibility: *You and Group Pressure*
47. Responsibility: *Trust and Friends*
48. Individual Sessions
49. Responsibility: *Trust Walk*
50. Problem Solving: *Introduction*
51. Problem Solving: *You and Regular Class*
52. Problem Solving: *You and Regular Class*
53. Problem Solving: *Practice 1*
54. Problem Solving: *Practice 2*
55. Student Conferences
56. Student Conferences
57. Post-Test
58. Post-Test
59. Pre- and Post-Test Comparisons
60. Succeeding in Regular Classes

Relaxation Exercises

The deep breath/relaxation exercises have three primary purposes. First, students who have encountered frustration during any of the academic sessions may need to be relaxed and "un-frustrated" before they can participate in and learn from the day's activity. Secondly, many of the activities undertaken during the hour produce anxiety and stress within the student. Problems which the student has chosen to ignore or hide from may be discussed. Because of this it is beneficial for all students to be as relaxed as possible before the lesson begins. Thirdly, it is anticipated that students who have practiced relaxation exercises regularly in class will be able to transfer this skill to other stressful situations in school, at home, or with friends.

The relaxation method used is a simple, muscle relaxing activity led by the teacher. Students are instructed to inhale and exhale for a series of counts, to tighten their leg and thigh muscles for a series of counts, to clinch their fists for a series of counts, and to contact their facial muscles for a series of counts.

Introduction to Activity

Following the relaxation exercises, the teacher moves into the introduction in order (1) to review ideas presented in earlier lessons which are incorporated into the next activity; (2) to give the purpose of the lesson, and (3) to create within the student a need to discuss or become skilled in this particular topic.

Activities

The activities related to each topic take many forms. Role plays, discussions, activities based on video or audio tapes, labeling behaviors, practice exercises, and synopsis are frequent methods used. On a typical day, two or three activities are planned which relate directly to the topic. For example, representative activities from the twenty-four lessons on self-responsibility include:

1. a group game in which students experience external control over simple physical actions; the game is followed by a discussion of how it feels to be told what to do and how it feels to do the controlling;
2. an exercise with cartoon strips which present adolescents in situations where they experience external control (on the job, at home, etc.); students solve problems about how to control their mental outlook when faced with such everyday situations;
3. a mini-lecture explaining and demonstrating the concept that each individual makes a choice in assigning meaning and feelings to certain situations;
4. a workbook activity in which students graph their daily schedule (sleep, eat, recreation, work) and identify how they could better meet their physical needs;
5. a discussion in which students identify a stressful situation for them, their usual behavior in this situation, and a possible alternative way to cope with the stress.

Discussions are frequently built into the daily activities. These discussions are used to increase student skills in the affective behavior being addressed and in the art of discussion. A good discussion extends a student's understanding of activities by eliciting other students' ideas and opinions. The discussion also develops a student's skill in participation and expression of ideas. Because discussions are often held in content classrooms, the affective discussions have been structured to cue each student about his participation, his interruptions, and his off-task remarks. Thus, the affective curriculum should have carry-over into academic classes in classroom skills as well as student self-concept.

Ego Trip/Journal

The final activity of each lesson is an exercise titled "Ego Trip/Journal." At this time students are handed a mimeographed sheet for their personal journal. Printed at the top of the sheet is the "ego trip" message. The statement reads:

"I am an important person."
"I am a worthwhile person."
"I like myself and I feel good today because..."

Students and teachers recite this message in unison. As a person comes to the blank after "because" he fills in a statement which relates something he has done that day which made him feel good. Examples from student journals include:

"I like myself and I feel good today because I am ignoring some of the people who are being silly."
"I like myself and feel good today because I read 164 words in a minute."
"I like myself and feel good today because I learned that I am not dumb."

The student completes a statement which says "Today I learned..." and writes either a summary of the day's lesson or some entry about the way he felt during the lesson. The journal pages are accumulated in each student's journal notebook.

The "Ego Trip/Journal" serves several purposes in the program. First, it forces each student to verbalize daily that he has value as a person. The act of saying these words impresses on the student that they apply to him. Secondly, the "ego trip" requires that the student specify and acknowledge at least one thing which he did well that day. Thirdly, writing a summary of the day's activity makes the topic for that day more personally relevant to the student.

The structure of the social/behavioral group lessons is summarized in Table 5.2.

TABLE 5.2

Social/Behavioral Lesson Format

Lesson Structure	Instructional Arrangement	Activities	Time
1. Relaxation Exercise	Group	Muscle relaxation	5 min.
2. Introduction to activity	Group	Mini-lecture discussion	5 min.
3. Activities	Group, partners, individual	Mini-lecture, discussion, role play, simulations, games, filmstrips, etc.	35 min.
4. Ego Trip/Journal	Group, individual	Oral affirmation statement Journal Sheet	5 min.
			50 min.

THE GROWTH GOALS INVENTORY

Learning disabled students at the secondary level tend to deny that they have a problem. Anxiety, self-anger, depression, passivity, passive aggressive, or aggressive acting out behavior begin to manifest as never before. The realities of a learning disability weigh heavily on adolescent shoulders and they are immature in personality development (Torgensen 1977). These factors coupled with cognitive delays create a mushrooming effect on the failure/frustration/confusion that is already present. The way a child perceives his disability has been identified by Anderson (1970) as an important component of learning disabilities in addition to physical factors such as maturational lags, perceptual problems, and minimal neurological dysfunction identified by many specialists in the field.

Rosenthal (1973) reported that initially, young dyslexic children are not emotionally disturbed nor do they resist conventional methods of instruction. They generally do have these problems by adolescence. In Rosenthal's study of asthmatic, normal, and dyslexic children, the dyslexic child appeared to have significantly lower self-esteem as measured by a modified Coopersmith Self-Esteem Inventory than a matched normal or asthmatic control group. However, teacher behavior reports showed no significant differences for the three groups. Although the asthmatic and the dyslexic students both had a handicap, it would appear that the dyslexic child's problem, manifested by academic deficiencies, impeded the development of a positive self-concept more so than the asthmatic child. Rosenthal points out that the inability to read in a culture which places such high value on academic performance magnifies poor performance and may tend to increase the dyslexic's feeling of unworthiness, self-anger, depression or anxiety (in Kraus and McKeever 1977).

Students with learning disabilities have a great deal of difficulty making accurate assessments of their own behavior or performance in setting realistic goals. Robbins and Harway (1977) explored the manner in which the child's sense of competency or adequacy reflected his ability to set realistic goals. They reported that LD children with a long history of failure characteristically set goals much higher or much lower than is warranted by their previous performances. Further, both LD and normal children tend to raise their estimates of future performances in comparison with their previous performance level.

In an effort to facilitate student growth in self-acceptance, in appropriate behavior, and in realistic goal setting, a Growth Goals Inventory was developed to help the student and teacher (Observer/ Guide) identify specific student goals for personal improvement.

Inventory Items

The Growth Goals Inventory allows the student to make his own self-estimation of where he thinks he is or how he currently behaves in specific situations related to the four curriculum areas of (1) responsibility, (2) communication skills, (3) assertiveness, and (4) problem solving. The student also indicates where he would like to be in respect to this behavior. There are twenty-seven items on the inventory (see Figure 5.1).

Action Plan

Initially, the student examines his own self-estimation on all (or groups) of attitudes and behavior items selected from the HILC social/

behavioral curriculum. Then with the teacher's help, the student selects a specific goal each week from the inventory items and develops an action plan for improving his behavior. The action plan is designed to focus the student's attention on specific and positive ways to change.

During the development of the action plan, the observer/guide (usually the teacher) makes an independent assessment of the student's

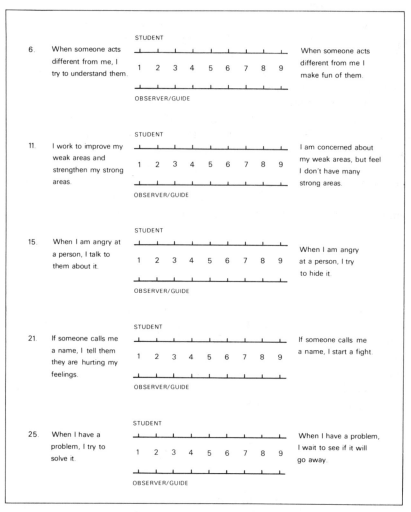

FIGURE 5.1. Inventory examples

behavior, helps him develop realistic goals, and helps develop a workable behaviorally oriented action plan. The teacher serves as observer/ guide in a short personal conference with each student. The action plan structure guides students to identify behaviors or feelings which may hinder and help the reaching of the goal, to identify specifically the behavior to increase and to decrease, and to establish a series of steps for bringing about the desired behavior. The action plan format is illustrated in Figure 5.2.

The student's progress is jointly evaluated each week by the student and teacher in the individual conference. If the student feels he has made significant progress on his goal, he moves on to a new goal and a new action plan. If the teacher and student feel that the goal has not been met, a discussion is held to pinpoint what has hindered the student in reaching the goal. Teacher and student then alter the original one or draw up a new plan and make a commitment to work on the goal one more week. The teacher provides realistic and positive feedback.

Individual action plan cards contain space for transferring goal items so that students will have a ready reference about their goal and so that the original inventory can be placed in a folder and used as a post test at the completion of the social/behavioral program.

PARENT INVOLVEMENT

The success of the social/behavioral program is linked very strongly with the degree to which students are called upon to practice the skills in their typical behavior. The student must be made aware that he practices certain behaviors, that he can change these behaviors, and that he has been given the skills necessary to change them.

The student who begins to use skills presented in the affective program may change his behavior at home as well as at school. Parents need to be aware of the program goals and need to offer support and reinforcement for the student's efforts to change. So that they can meet these needs, parents of students enrolled in HILC are encouraged to participate in a High Intensity Parent Group. This group acquaints parents with the skills the students are learning and allows parents to practice the same skills. Information sharing and support are other purposes of the parent group.

ACTION PLAN

Student: _____   Date: _____

Observer/Guide: _____

GOAL: _____

_____

STUDENT

1   2   3   4   5   6   7   8   9

OBSERVER/GUIDE

BLOCKS: Self: _____

             Others: _____

HELPS: Self: _____

             Others: _____

ACTION PLAN

    DO (behavior to increase): _____

    DO NOT (behavior to decrease): _____

    PLAN: _____

            _____

            _____

EVALUATION: I will know I have reached my goal when _____

_____

Be Specific - identify specific behaviors and plans. Record progress on reverse side.

FIGURE 5.2. Growth goals inventory

REFERENCES

Anderson, R. P. *The Child with Learning Disabilities.* Boston: Houghton Mifflin, 1970.

Bryan, T. H., and Bryan, J. H. *Understanding Learning Disabilities,* 2nd ed. California: Alfred, 1978.

Gordon, S. "Reversing a Negative Self-Image." In *Helping the Adolescent with the Hidden Handicap,* edited by L. Anderson. California: Calif. Assn. for Neurologically Handicapped Children, 1970.

Kraus, W., and McKeever, C. "Rational-Emotive Education with Learning Disabled Children." *Journal of Learning Disabilities* 10 (1977):16–19.

Leviton, H., and Kiraly, J. "Intervention Strategies for Promoting Self-Concept Development." *Academic Therapy* 14, 5 (May 1979):535–45.

Meisgeier, C. H. "The Synergistic Classroom Model: A Model Demonstration Center for Children with Specific Learning Disabilities," Continuation Proposal for Federal Assistance (USOE-BEH), 1977.

Robbins, R., and Harway, H. "Goal Setting and Reactions to Success and Failure in Children with Learning Disabilities." *Journal of Learning Disabilities* 10 (1977):356–62.

Rosenthal, J. H. "Self-Esteem in Dyslexic Children." *Academic Therapy* 9 (1973):27–38.

Smith, M. E. "The Development of the Adolescent Self-Concept." In *Educational Considerations for the Learning Disabled Adolescent: Selected Papers,* edited by E. Ensminger and L. Smiley. Georgia: Georgia State University, 1975.

Torgensen, J. K. "The Role of Non-Specific Factors in the Task Performance of Learning Disabled Children: A Theoretical Assessment." *Journal of Learning Disabilities* 1 (1977):27–34.

White, M. M. "Peer Group Effect on Adolescent Development." In *Educational Considerations for the Learning Disabled Adolescent: Selected Papers,* edited by E. Ensminger and L. Smiley. Georgia: Georgia State University, 1975.

ASSESSMENT AND EVALUATION

6

Performance of Learning Disabled and Low-Achieving Students on the Wechsler Intelligence Scale for Children, Revised, and the Tests of Cognitive Abilities from the Woodcock-Johnson Psycho-Educational Battery

James Ysseldyke, Mark Shinn, Matthew McGue, and Susan Epps

W ITH THE PASSING OF THE Education for All Handicapped Children Act of 1975 (Public Law 94-142), the legitimacy of the classification of exceptional children was reinforced. And, for the first time, one of the amendments to the bill added the category of "learning disabled," enabling a new type of child to be protected by the law. The chief symptom of a learning disability is said to be lack of achievement. Yet a student who is not achieving is not viewed as automatically being learning disabled. Special educators have maintained that qualitative differences exist between the learning disabled and slow learners.

The identification of learning disabilities involves a process of differential diagnosis from slow learners, one that Shepard (1975) has argued is difficult to make. Wepman, Cruickshank, Deutsch, Morency, and Strothers (1975) have also addressed the similarities between these two populations and strongly state that educational personnel *must* be able to recognize the differences between low achievers and the learning disabled.

This study compared a sample of school identified learning disabled students with a sample of low-achieving students using the WISCR on the variables of Full Scale, Verbal Scale, and Performance Scale IQs, Verbal-Performance discrepancies, subtest scaled scores, and subtest scatter. Additionally, the same samples were compared on

The research was supported by Contract #300-77-0491 between the Bureau of Education for the Handicapped and the University of Minnesota Institute for Research on Learning Disabilities.

the Tests of Cognitive Abilities from the Woodcock-Johnson Psycho-Educational Battery, a recent and increasingly popular device used in the assessment of the learning disabled.

METHOD

Subjects

The LD sample consisted of fifty fourth-grade children from metropolitan Minneapolis and St. Paul schools. They were identified as learning disabled by placement teams in the school districts they attended. The average achievement level for this group, obtained from the Peabody Individual Achievement Test (PIAT) total score, was 91.9 (S = 8.78) and indicated low achievement. The low-achieving sample consisted of forty-nine fourth-grade children from the same metropolitan area. They had not been identified as LD by their school districts, but scored at or below the 25th percentile on the Iowa Tests of Basic Skills administered during the fall of the current school year.

The LD sample was selected for participation in the present study within six months of their identification as learning disabled. This restriction in subject selection was used in order to reduce the effect of the intervention. Similarly, the low-achieving sample had been group tested within six months of their selection for participation. Selected demographic information is presented in Table 6.1; no statistical differences were indicated between the two groups on any of these variables (i.e., Chi square and t tests were not significant, p > .05).

TABLE 6.1

Description of Subjects on Selected Demographic Variables

	Sex of Child		Parental Marital Status		Age of Child (in months)		Father's SES*		Mother's SES*		Family Income	
	Male	Female	Married	Unmarried	X	SD	X	SD	X	SD	X	SD
LD	40	10	26	9	121.04	5.04	58.32	25.84	47.56	24.16	$21,423	$10,472
Non-LD	35	14	28	8	121.06	4.04	51.44	27.57	46.35	18.07	$22,852	$11,02⁷

*SES was determined using Otis Dudley Duncan's Occupational Socioeconomic Index, "A Socioeconomic Index for All Occupations," In *Occupations and Social Status,* edited by A. J. Reiss, Jr. New York: Free Press of Glencoe, 1961.

Procedure

In addition to the WISCR and the Woodcock-Johnson Tests of Cognitive Abilities, data from other standardized tests (Peabody Individual Achievement Test, Stanford Achievement Test — mathematics computation and mathematics concepts subtests, seven of the 10 W-J Achievement subtests — Letter-Word Identification, Word Attack, Passage Comprehension, Calculation, Applied Problems, Dictation, and Proofing, Bender Visual Motor Gestalt Test, and Developmental Test of Visual-Motor Integration) were collected concurrently as part of a larger study. All testing was completed by qualified psychometricians and occurred during approximately the same period of time (January to May). Subjects were tested in either three or four, one and one-half hour sessions. Demographic information was collected from the parent(s) of the children, and a behavior rating scale was completed by their current teacher.

RESULTS

A comparison of the WISCR test performance for the learning disabled and low-achieving samples is reported in Table 6.2. Included in the table

TABLE 6.2

Comparison of the WISCR Test Performance of Learning Disabled and Low-Achieving Students

WISCR	Low Achievers (N = 49) Mean	SD	LD (N = 50) Mean	SD	Mean Difference	t	Identical Scores*	Percentage Overlap
Full Scale IQ	102.63	9.50	100.04	12.45	2.59	1.16	28	97
Verbal IQ†	101.27	9.33	96.78	12.66	4.49	2.00	27	97
Performance IQ	103.90	11.27	104.12	13.74	−.22	−.09	22	97
Information*	101.02	9.30	96.20	11.59	4.82	2.28	36	100
Similarities	101.33	13.91	97.90	16.69	3.43	1.11	35	96
Arithmetic	95.10	10.97	92.70	10.75	2.40	1.10	42	100
Vocabulary*	102.55	11.14	97.00	14.57	5.55	2.13	33	93
Comprehension	106.22	12.35	103.16	15.02	3.06	1.10	35	98
Picture Completion	104.29	13.46	102.70	13.10	1.59	.59	38	99
Picture Arrangement	106.63	12.72	107.20	15.88	−.57	−.20	38	96
Block Design	98.78	17.58	101.80	13.32	−3.02	−.97	38	95
Object Assembly	105.51	14.62	106.43	16.27	−.92	−.29	38	98
Coding	99.90	12.93	97.86	12.54	2.04	.79	41	95
Verbal Performance Discrepancy	−2.63	11.15	−7.34	13.41	4.71	1.90		

*Number of identical scores possible was 49.
†Difference between means significant (p < .05).

are the subgroup means and standard deviations for the Full Scale, Verbal, and Performance IQs along with the ten WISCR subtests and the discrepancy scores for the difference between the Verbal and Performance IQs. The table also presents the number of identical scores and the percentage overlap of the distributions. The reported t statistics can be used to test the significance of the observed mean differences. In general, the low-achieving children attained higher scores on the WISCR, with the possible exception of the slight, and non-significant, advantage enjoyed by the learning disabled children on three of the Performance subtests. There was great similarity in the groups as evidenced by the number of identical scores and the percent of overlap.

A similar comparison is made for the Woodcock-Johnson Psycho-Educational Battery clusters and subtests in Table 6.3. Again,

TABLE 6.3

Comparison of Woodcock-Johnson Test Performance of Learning Disabled and Low-Achieving Students

Woodcock-Johnson	Low Achievers (N = 49) Mean	SD	LD (N = 50) Mean	SD	Mean Difference	t	Identical Scores*	Percentage Overlap
Broad Cognitive Ability								
Full Scale†	98.33	8.75	92.36	11.37	5.97	2.92	26	94
Cognitive Factor Clusters								
Verbal Ability†	103.27	9.84	92.70	12.81	10.57	4.59	22	79
Reasoning†	94.65	12.89	101.68	17.77	−7.03	−2.25	22	99
Perceptual Speed†	98.14	10.11	93.38	12.53	4.76	2.08	23	98
Memory†	101.57	15.80	92.18	15.44	9.39	2.99	18	91
Scholastic Aptitude Clusters								
Reading†	100.08	10.08	90.90	13.35	9.18	3.86	22	98
Mathematics†	96.35	8.96	90.30	11.63	6.05	2.89	28	95
Written Language†	97.90	9.68	88.68	11.48	9.22	4.32	24	86
Knowledge†	98.39	10.17	88.32	12.01	10.07	4.50	22	92
Subtests								
Picture Vocabulary†	18.33	1.99	17.22	2.74	1.11	2.30	36	96
Spatial Relations	39.49	4.73	38.48	5.63	1.01	.97	37	97
Memory for Sentences†	13.29	1.99	11.62	2.69	1.67	3.49	31	95
Visual-Auditory Learning	114.88	7.96	114.50	8.24	.38	.23	27	95
Blending	16.78	2.90	15.66	2.82	1.12	1.94	35	97
Quantitative Concepts†	21.98	2.56	20.72	3.00	1.26	2.25	36	96
Visual Matching	16.76	1.79	16.00	2.34	.76	1.80	38	97
Antonyms-Synonyms†	20.57	2.72	17.46	4.53	3.11	4.13	29	97
Analysis-Synthesis	17.39	3.52	18.02	3.74	−.63	−.87	33	97
Numbers Reversed	7.02	2.31	6.24	1.95	.78	1.81	40	94
Concept Formation	16.22	3.97	16.12	6.53	.10	.10	35	94
Analogies	15.29	3.64	15.48	3.42	−.19	−.27	36	97

*Number of identical scores possible was 49.
†Difference between means significant (p < .05)

we find that, in general, the low-achieving children outperform the learning disabled children, with eight of the nine clusters demonstrating a significantly larger mean level of performance for the low-achieving children. However, again there is great similarity of the individuals' scores. Of special interest is the Reasoning cluster, where we find that the learning disabled children performed significantly *better* than the low achieving children. Inspection of the t statistics for the subtests again demonstrates in a more consistent manner the superior performance of the low-achieving children.

It has been hypothesized that it is the subtest scatter or variability rather than the overall profile level that differentiates learning disabled children from their low-achieving peers. To assess this hypothesis, we computed the variance of the subtest performance for each individual separately, and then averaged these variances for each of the two groups (the larger this variance, the greater the subtest scatter). For the WISCR the average subtest scatter for the learning disabled children was 136.3 as compared to the average for the low-achieving students of 138.7, a difference that is both trivial and in the opposite direction of the hypothesized difference. For the Woodcock-Johnson, the average cluster scatter for the learning disabled children was 102.9 as compared to the average of the low-achieving children of 83.5. Although the difference here is in the hypothesized direction, it is not significant (p = .18), and could probably be attributed to the relative superiority of the learning disabled children on the Reasoning cluster as compared to their general poor performance on the battery.

DISCUSSION

An inspection of the mean differences of the two groups' performances on the tests administered could lead to erroneous conclusions. This section attempts (1) to explain the difference in performance of the groups on the WISCR and WJTCA and (2) to discuss the implications of the results in terms of their ramifications for individual daignosis.

As has been noted, the low-achieving group performed significantly better on the Information and Vocabulary subtests of the WISCR. We believe the obtained results fit the perceptions of tested intelligence formulated by Newland (1971) and Cattell (1963). Both Newland and Cattell argue that intelligence test items range along a continuum from those that sample predominantly what has been learned (measures of crystallized intelligence or product) to those that sample primarily those processes necessary to learning (measures of fluid intelligence or process-dominant measures). The Information and Vocabulary subtests are product-dominant measures, assessing primarily what has been learned. Thus, what is witnessed is the learning disabled students' lack of achievement in these areas. The significance of the Verbal IQ mean difference between the groups is also a direct function of the differences on these subtests, since the Verbal IQ score is in essence a sum of the Verbal subtests.

An explanation of the differences on the WJTCA is more complex. For a number of reasons (see McGue, Shinn, and Ysseldyke 1979), the validity of the clusters of the WJTCA is suspect with these populations. While there are significant differences in the means on all the clusters, when examining actual mean differences on the subtests, only four of the eleven (Picture Vocabulary, Memory for Sentences, Quantitative Concepts, and Antonyms-Synonyms) account for these differences. This is due to the substantial overlap of the subtests in the clusters. For example, the Antonyms-Synonyms subtest is included in the Verbal Ability, Reasoning, Reading Aptitude, Mathematics Aptitude, Written Language Aptitude, and Knowledge Aptitude Clusters. Thus, a significantly poorer performance on this subtest results in significantly poorer performances on these clusters. In fact, each cluster has in its composition at least one subtest on which the groups differed significantly. Of particular interest is the cluster of Reasoning on which the learning disabled sample performed significantly better. A superficial examination could have resulted in the interpretation that learning disabled students are better reasoners. An examination of the cluster's composition *and* the test's construction procedures showed that the groups differed, as has been discussed, on the Antonyms-Synonyms subtest which in this case was negatively weighted. Therefore, the *poorer* a learning disabled student performed on Antonyms-Synonyms, the *higher* was his/her Reasoning Score.

In light of the misleading conclusions that could possibly be derived from interpreting the differences between the groups using the WJTCA clusters, a comparison of the groups by subtests is offered instead. Similar to the WISCR subtest differences explanation, viewing the four WJTCA subtests as measuring product or crystallized intelligence, i.e., achievement, offers the best explanation of these differences. For example, Picture Vocabulary measures what names a subject has learned for pictures. Antonyms-Synonyms measures word knowledge.

Finally, the utility of these results in individual diagnosis or identification must be questioned. It must be remembered that these data are group means. To classify individuals on the basis of five point differences on some of these means is an impossible task. This is best exemplified by looking at the distribution of individual scores. As demonstrated by Figures 6.1 and 6.2, there exists considerable overlap between the groups and the distributions are remarkably similar. A comparison of the number of identical scores on each of the subtests shows that for each subtest more than half of each groups' members have someone in the other group who has the same score.

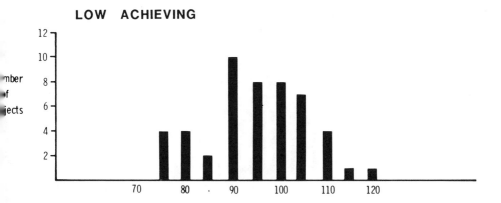

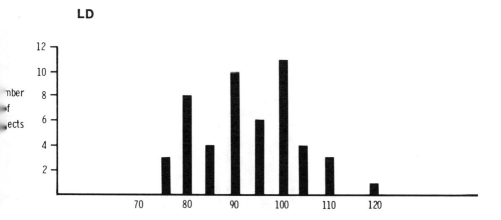

FIGURE 6.1. Distribution of standard scores on WISCR Arithmetic Subtest for low-achieving and LD subjects

REFERENCES

Cattell, R. B. "Theory of Fluid and Crystallized Intelligence. A Critical Experiment." *Journal of Educational Psychology* 54 (1963):1–22.

McGue, M.; Shinn, M.; and Ysseldyke, J. *Validity of the Woodcock-Johnson Psycho-Educational Battery with Learning Disabled Students* (Research Report No. 15). Minneapolis: University of Minnesota, Institute for Research on Learning Disabilities, 1979.

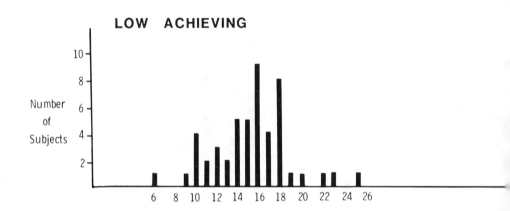

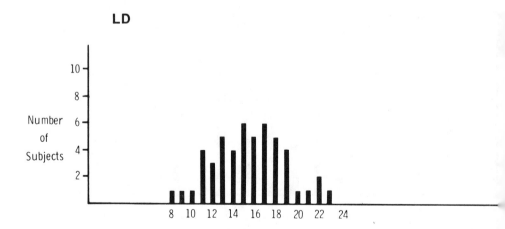

FIGURE 6.2. Distribution of raw scores on Woodcock-Johnson Analogies Subtest for low-achieving and LD subjects

Newland, T. E. "Psychological Assessment of Exceptional Children and Youth." In *Psychology of Exceptional Children and Youth*, edited by William M. Cruickshank. Englewood Cliffs, N.J.: Prentice-Hall, 1971.

Rugel, R. P. "WISC Subtest Scores of Disabled Readers: A Review with Respect to Bannatyne's Recategorization." *Journal of Learning Disabilities* 7 (1974):57–64.

Shepard, M. J. "'LD' or Slow Learner?" *School Psychology Digest* 5, 1 (1975):32–35.

Wepman, J. M.; Cruickshank, W. M.; Deutsch, C. P.; Morency, A.; and Strothers, C. R. "Learning Disabilities." In N. Hobbs, ed., *Issues in the Classification of Children*, Vol. 1. San Francisco: Jossey-Bass, 1975.

7

Current Assessment and Decision-Making Practices

James Ysseldyke, Phyllis Murkin, Martha Thurlow,
Stephen Poland, and Donald Allen

ASSESSMENT and decision making are common activities in today's educational environment. Public Law 94-142 mandated the need for assessment and decision-making practices that will identify all handicapped children and ensure that their special needs are met. Following the enactment of the Education for All Handicapped Children Act, researchers began to study in greater depth some of the issues involved in educational assessment and decision making. The National Education Association (1978) has reported that decisions frequently are made before parents are involved or before the IEP meeting. In general, studies have not looked at the assessment and decision-making process in its entirety.

The present investigation was conducted in order to describe assessment and decision-making practices from a broad perspective, with data from several sources and with information on several aspects of the process.

METHOD

Subjects

Data were obtained from three subject groups: special education directors (N = 100), Child Service Demonstration Centers (N = 44), and school decision-making teams (N = 23). The special education directors were located in 49 states, and included individuals in both large and small school districts, from urban, suburban, and rural locations. The Child Service Demonstration Centers (CSDCs) were ones funded by

The research was supported by Contract #300-77-0491 between the Bureau of Education for the Handicapped and the University of Minnesota Institute for Research on Learning Disabilities.

BEH during 1978–79 to provide quality educational services for learning disabled youngsters. The CSDCs were located in twenty-six states. The school teams were from Minnesota schools agreeing to have meetings videotaped for research purposes. In some cases data were obtained from two or three meetings within one school district; eight school districts were represented in the sample.

Materials

Questionnaires were used to obtain information from all three subject groups. In addition, observations of videotapes were used to collect data from team meetings. Commonalities in the information obtained from questionnaires and observations provided the data for the present analysis.

Procedures

Procedures for obtaining questionnaire data from directors of special education and CSDCs were similar. Potential subjects were sent the questionnaires and stamped return envelopes. Follow-up letters were sent to those who had not responded after six weeks. The return rates were 62 percent and 85 percent for the directors and CSDCs, respectively.

Questionnaire data and videotapes were obtained from team decision-making meetings. Videotapes were made of twenty-three meetings (eight screening and fifteen placement) and questionnaires were collected at the end of the meetings from 154 meeting participants. Data on specific assessment devices used, type of data discussed (academic vs. social), team membership, and amount of participation were later collected from the videotapes. Special observation forms were developed to assess the types of data discussed and the amount of participation by each team member. An interval method of recording (10 second intervals) was used for each. Interrater agreement averaged 85 percent for participation by role recording and 89 percent for type of data discussed.

RESULTS

Process Concerns

Eighty directors listed the three most significant problems their districts faced in implementing the placement team and IEP planning process. Concerns involving time and scheduling were mentioned most often (N = 44). Directors noted the difficulty in finding convenient meeting times for all persons involved, as well as the amount of time required to attend meetings, do paperwork, and write IEPs, which resulted in less time to devote to such other staff duties as teaching or preventative interventions.

The second most frequently listed area of concern was parental involvement in the process (N = 26). Some directors singled out lack of parental attendance at placement meetings and, when in attendance, a lack of parental input. Related to this, problems faced by parents were mentioned: (a) insufficient or unclear information about proposed school actions and their legal rights, and (b) being overwhelmed by the large number of professionals present at the placement team meeting.

Many directors (N = 23) described lack of training and lack of certified personnel as significant problems. The classroom teacher frequently was cited as the person most in need of training. In a few instances, the type of training was specified: decision-making skills, and/or writing IEPs. Most of the directors (89 percent) indicating the need for additional qualified staff were located in rural school settings.

The IEP, especially its quality, also was seen as a significant problem (N = 15). IEPs were said to be of variable quality, lacking in backup data, or written to meet legal requirements rather than as a vehicle for educational program planning.

Team Membership

The average size of placement teams, as reported by directors and CSDCs, and as observed in actual meetings, was approximately eight individuals (Directors: $\bar{X}$ = 9.0, SD = 2.7; CSDCs: $\bar{X}$ = 8.2, SD = 2.7; Teams: $\bar{X}$ = 7.4, SD = 1.9). The largest teams involved from twelve to sixteen persons.

Table 7.1 summarizes the membership of placement teams. There was considerable agreement concerning the individuals most frequently included on teams. Among the five individuals most frequently listed by

TABLE 7.1

Membership and Participation in Placement Teams

Team Member*	Directors†	CSDCs‡	Teams§	Participation/Meeting‖
Parent	91	79	80	19.2
School administrator	89	71	100	10.7
LD specialist	62	76	93	32.6
Special education teacher	85	71	M	M
School psychologist	81	63	80	28.2
Regular classroom teacher	78	82	67	28.1
Speech/language/audiology specialist	68	55	40	16.4
Educational diagnostician	62	55	M	M

*Table includes only those members included at a level of 50 percent for at least two subject groups.

† Numbers are percentages of 99 directors listing members. Overall, 34 different members were listed by the directors.

‡ Numbers are percentages of 38 CSDCs listing members. Overall, 30 different members were listed by CSDCs.

§ Numbers are percentages of 15 meetings attended by members.

‖ Numbers are means of the percentages of meeting times (10 second intervals) during which members spoke.

each subject group, the classroom teacher, parent, and school administrator (principal) were included most often. Directors listed the parent most frequently, CSDCs listed the regular classroom teacher most frequently, and teams included a school administrator (specifically, the principal) most frequently.

Analysis of the videotapes of team meetings suggested that the amount of participation during actual meetings varied with the role of the individual. As Table 7.1 indicates, LD specialists, psychologists, and regular classroom teachers spoke most often during the team meetings. In many meetings (53 percent), a second LD specialist was present. The participation by the second LD specialist (14.1 percent) was considerably less than that of most other team members.

Directors also provided information on the membership of teams making screening and instructional planning decisions. The numbers included on screening ($\bar{X}$ = 7.6, SD = 2.8) and instructional planning ($\bar{X}$ = 6.9, SD = 2.8) teams were slightly less than included on placement teams ($\bar{X}$ = 9.0, SD = 2.7). The special education teacher was included on screening teams by less than 50 percent of the directors, yet was included on instructional planning teams by nearly 90 percent of the directors. The psychologist was noted more often as participating on screening (64 percent) and placement (81 percent) teams, and less often on instructional planning teams (48 percent). The only individual mentioned by over 70 percent of the directors as participating in all three types of meetings was the regular classroom teacher.

Process Steps

Directors and CSDCs listed major steps in the assessment and decision-making process. The percentages of directors and CSDCs mentioning steps that conformed to a 13-step model are displayed in Table 7.2.

TABLE 7.2

Percentages of Directors (N = 97) and CSDCs (N = 35) Mentioning each of the Steps in a Thirteen-Step Assessment/Decision-Making Model

Step	Directors	CSDCs
Referral/Child find	96.9	94.3
Review referral	37.1	40.0
Appoint assessment team	11.3	11.4
Parental permission to assess	46.4	40.0
Assessment	97.9	97.1
Review assessment results	20.6	45.7
Eligibility determination	18.6	14.3
Contact parent after assessment	12.4	22.8
Develop IEP	77.3	42.8
Placement decision	35.1	37.1
Parental permission for placement	27.8	11.4
Develop strategies to implement IEP	4.1	14.3
Implement program	62.9	48.6

The thirteen-step model was derived from a survey of literature dealing with the team decision-making and IEP processes (cf. Gillespie 1978; Hoff, Fenton, Yoshida, and Kaufman 1978; H. Walker 1978; J. Walker 1976) as well as from a sample of the responses to this item by directors and CSDCs. A step including periodic reassessment after program implementation was omitted from the model to conform to instructions given to respondents.

Directors and CSDCs included an average of nine steps in their descriptions (CSDCs: $\overline{X} = 9.0$, SD = 2.6; Directors: $\overline{X} = 8.9$, SD = 2.4). Coding of responses reduced the number of steps since multiple steps were often coded as a single step.

Inspection of Table 7.2 indicates that the most commonly included steps were the referral (child find) and the assessment. Comparison of the five steps mentioned most frequently by directors and CSDCs indicated agreement in four of the five: referral, assessment, development of the IEP, and program implementation. The percentages of directors and CSDCs mentioning each aspect of the process were quite similar, up to the point of assessment. Beyond this point, CSDCs placed greater emphasis on the review of assessment results, contacting parents after assessment, and developing strategies to implement the IEP; directors emphasized development of the IEP and parental permission for placement.

Nearly all directors and CSDCs agreed with the sequence presented in the model. The single notable exception was describing the placement decision as occurring before development of the IEP.

Most directors and CSDCs began their descriptions of the process with referral or child find. Only a few included attempts at modifying the classroom setting as part of the process. More than half the directors (68 percent) and CSDCs (52 percent) specified the regular classroom teacher, either alone or in combination with others, as the initiator of the referral.

The next major step in the process was assessment. In the steps linking referral and assessment, a few directors included intervention efforts preceding assessment (such as a thirty-day trial period for trying local school interventions, or within-school interventions developed by the referral team). While most directors described referral and assessment as carried out primarily by local school personnel, a few described a process in which a specialized district-level team carried out the assessment in the local school. The assessment step often was specified in more detail than any other step. Psychological assessments and observation procedures were the most frequently mentioned content areas by both directors and CSDCs. The psychologist and the regular classroom teacher were two of the three professionals most frequently mentioned in the descriptions of the assessment step.

The next major step in the directors' descriptions was development of the IEP. Where eligibility determination was mentioned as a step by the directors, it was frequently described as occurring at a meeting preceding the meeting in which the IEP was developed. Most frequently, the eligibility decision involved a team of individuals; in a few cases, a single individual such as the director of special education or the school psychologist made the decision. In some cases, eligibility decisions were made at the same meeting in which placement decisions were made and the IEP written.

Although many directors indicated the IEP was developed at a meeting with the parents present, in a few cases considerable development of the plan preceded the parent meeting (for example, one director noted that the teacher wrote the IEP before meeting with the parent).

Few directors (4.1 percent) mentioned the development of strategies to implement the IEP as a step in the process; this step was mentioned more frequently (14.3 percent) by the CSDCs. The final step that was coded in the process was implementing the program.

Factors Influencing the Team Decision

Table 7.3 shows directors' and team members' ratings of the influence of seventeen factors on the team decision about a child. A rating of one indicates no influence and a rating of five indicates a very significant influence.

The race and sex of the child were rated at least influential by both directors and team members. In fact, all characteristics of the child, including parental power, were judged as relatively unimportant in influence. The highest rating was given to socioeconomic status ($\bar{X}$ = 2.1) by directors and to "power" of the child's parents in the school system ($\bar{X}$ = 1.9) by team members.

Two factors clearly were rated as most influential by special education directors: classroom achievement and information provided by the parent or guardian. Medical, social, observational, and test score data

TABLE 7.3

Ratings* of Factors Influencing the Team Decision

Factor	Directors†	Team Members‡
Type of Data		
Teacher reports of classroom achievement	4.38 (.65)	4.40 (.79)
Information from parents/guardians	4.07 (.75)	3.74 (1.10)
Scores on achievement tests	3.93 (.78)	3.92 (1.20)
Observational data	3.65 (.73)	3.59 (1.14)
Teacher reports of social behavior	3.65 (.68)	3.59 (1.14)
Scores on intelligence tests	3.82 (.84)	3.41 (1.44)
Scores on psycholinguistic tests	3.67 (.82)	3.02 (1.46)
Scores on perceptual-motor tests	3.84 (.80)	2.74 (1.51)
Medical information	3.85 (.84)	2.03 (1.34)
Institutional/External Constraints		
Availability of services	3.22 (1.25)	3.69 (1.20)
School attendance record	3.29 (.89)	2.28 (1.37)
Teacher-child match	3.12 (1.01)	2.50 (1.35)
Child Characteristics		
Parents' power in school system	2.04 (.97)	1.91 (1.26)
Socioeconomic status	2.07 (.91)	1.64 (.99)
Physical appearance	1.80 (.82)	1.57 (.96)
Sex	1.50 (.69)	1.29 (.50)
Race	1.39 (.65)	1.19 (.50)

*1 = None, 2 = Insignificant, 3 = Moderate, 4 = Significant, 5 = Very significant
†Ratings are means and SDs based on responses of 99 directors of special education.
‡Ratings are means and SDs based on responses of 154 team members.

were rated as moderate to significant in influence. There was little difference in the perceived importance of different types of test data: mean ratings for achievement, perceptual-motor, psycholinguistic, and intelligence test data ranged from 3.7 to 3.9.

For team members, the two factors rated as most influential were teacher reports of classroom achievement and the child's scores on achievement tests. The ratings of the other types of data were more variable than those given by special education directors. Notably, medical information, scores on perceptual-motor tests, and scores on psycholinguistic tests received considerably lower ratings from team members than from special education directors.

Factors reflecting institutional and external constraints on the decision (attendance record, availability of services, teacher-child match) were rated as having moderate influence on the decision by directors. Team members were more variable in their ratings of these factors. Availability of services was given a higher rating, while the child's school attendance and the teacher-child match were given lower ratings.

Assessment Data

Table 7.4 presents the sources of data used by CSDCs and the decisions to which those data were applied. As indicated in the table,

TABLE 7.4

Percentages of CSDCs Using Different Data Sources for Different Decisions

Data Source	CSDCs using†	Decision for Which Used*				
		Screening	Placement	Instructional Programming	Pupil Evaluation	Program Evaluation
Norm-referenced tests	100.0	61.5	71.8	61.5	66.7	76.9
Criterion-referenced tests	94.8	46.2	56.4	84.6	69.2	48.7
Informal devices	89.7	53.8	41.0	79.5	64.1	25.6
Observation	89.7	69.2	74.4	66.7	66.7	33.3
Interviewing	87.2	51.3	53.8	35.9	5.9	23.1
Adaptive behavior/social data	84.6	48.7	56.4	41.0	46.2	25.6
Past records	84.6	59.0	61.5	30.8	30.8	12.8
Medical & social histories	82.0	41.0	53.8	17.9	20.5	7.7
Medical data	71.8	35.9	51.3	23.1	17.9	2.6

*Percentages reflect numbers of CDSCs using data for each purpose based on all responding CSDCs (N = 39).

†Percentages reflect numbers of 39 CSDCs indicating each data source was used for one or more of five decisions.

each data source was used by more than 70 percent of the CSDCs. Medical data were used least often, yet were still used by more than 70 percent of the CSDCs. All CSDCs used norm-referenced tests and all but two CSDCs used criterion-referenced tests. Furthermore, nearly all data sources were used for all types of decisions, ranging from screening to program evaluation. Norm-referenced tests were among the top two most frequently used sources of data in all decision areas, except in instructional programming decisions, where criterion-referenced tests, informal devices, and observation were used more often.

Analysis of the type of data discussed during actual placement team meetings revealed that academic characteristics of the referred child were discussed almost twice as much as social characteristics ($\bar{X}$ = 34.4 percent academic vs. 17.7 percent social, over nine meetings analyzed).

Assessment Instruments

More than 150 different assessment instruments were used by thirty-nine CSDCs. A total of 105 of these was used by only one CSDC. The number of devices listed varied greatly, ranging from three to 39 ($\bar{X}$ = 11.5, SD = 6.3). One CSDC noted that it used more than fifty instruments, but had listed only those seven used most frequently.

More than thirty different assessment instruments were referred to in the 15 videotaped placement meetings; only twelve of these were mentioned in more than one meeting. The number of instruments referred to during a meeting ranged from zero to twelve ($\bar{X}$ = 5.0, SD = 3.5).

The specific instruments cited in fifteen team meetings and used by five or more CSDCs are summarized in Table 7.5. Only five assessment instruments were used by more than half of the responding CSDCs — WISC/WISCR (64 percent), Key Math (59 percent), WRAT (59 percent), informal/center-developed instruments (59 percent), and PIAT (54 percent). Only the WISCR (60 percent) and PIAT (53 percent) were referred to in over half of the team meetings. Of the twenty-three CSDCs reporting the use of informal/center-developed assessment devices, seventeen used more than one such device; the number of such devices used by each CSDC ranged from one to seven ($\bar{X}$ = 2.86; SD = 1.72).

As with data sources, specific assessment instruments were used for almost all decisions by CSDCs. Overall, tests were used least frequently for program evaluation decisions. Only one instrument (Slos-

TABLE 7.5

Percentages of Different Assessment Instruments used in Decision Making

Instrument	Teams Citing†	CSDCs Using‡	Scrn.	Placmt.	Instruc. Prog.	Pupil Eval.	Prog. Eval.
WISC/WISCR	60	64	44	80	48	56	8
Key Math	33	59	30	56	78	70	35
WRAT	20	59	48	60	39	56	39
Informal	M	59	61	65	91	87	56
PIAT	53	54	52	71	36	76	48
Woodcock Reading	13	38	40	80	67	60	40
PPVT	20	33	77	38	38	46	8
Beery	M	26	50	60	40	40	10
Wepman	M	23	56	89	67	78	11
Brigance	M	20	38	75	100	62	0
Detroit	M	20	38	75	75	62	25
ITPA	M	20	25	88	75	75	12
WAIS	M	15	50	67	33	67	0
Slosson	20	15	50	67	50	50	50
Piers-Harris	M	20	25	50	50	38	38
Bender	27	13	40	80	80	60	20
Carrow	M	13	60	80	100	100	20
Spache	M	13	60	80	80	80	20
Stanford-Binet	M	13	40	80	60	60	0

Column header note: *Decision for Which Used by CSDCs**

Table includes only those instruments mentioned by five or more CSDCs; four other tests were referred to in videotaped placement meetings: SRA (40 percent), Slingerland (27 percent), Houghton-Mifflin (20 percent), Iowa (13 percent).

*Percentages reflect numbers of CSDCs using instrument for each decision based only on those listing the instrument.

†Percentages reflect numbers of teams referring to each instrument.

‡Percentages reflect numbers of CSDCs listing each instrument.

son), in addition to informal devices, was used by at least 50 percent of the centers for this decision.

Data on the commercial tests used for assessment by five or more centers (those listed in Table 7.5) were judged in terms of their technical adequacy. Technical adequacy ·was evaluated on three dimensions: norms, reliability, and validity. Tests considered to be technically inadequate were those which did not include information on a dimension and those which did not meet the criteria specified by Salvia and Ysseldyke (1978), Ysseldyke (1978), and the American Psychological Association (1972) Standards. The evaluation of the eighteen specific instruments used by five or more centers indicated that only five had technically adequate norms. Of the eighteen devices, six had reliability adequate for use in decision making, while five had technically adequate validity. The two devices used by more than 50 percent of both the CSDCs and placement teams (WISCR and PIAT) both had technically adequate norms, reliability, and validity.

DISCUSSION

The data from the questionnaire studies and the observations of videotapes of placement teams suggest that the decision-making process is a multidisciplinary one. Decision-making teams are composed of a variety of individuals. Although directors indicated team membership varied somewhat as a function of the type of decision, all data sources pointed to the importance of parents, school administrators, and regular classroom teachers as members of decision-making teams.

However, frequency of inclusion on a team did not necessarily reflect amount of participation in the team meeting. Thus, although parents frequently were included on teams, observations indicated that parents did not participate as much as some other team members. This finding supports directors' expressed concern over lack of parental participation in placement team meetings. Yet, it is encouraging to discover that the level of parental participation was as high as it was (20 percent). These data, however, do not speak to the issue of the *nature* of parental participation. According to Yoshida, Fenton, Kaufman, and Maxwell (1978) placement team members have a limited set of expectancies for parental participation in meetings (viz. presenting and gathering information). It is possible that some of the parents in the observed team meetings played a restricted role; this possibility deserves further study.

Although classroom teachers were present in only two-thirds of the observed meetings, their level of participation, relative to other team members, was quite high when they were present. This is in contrast to the finding of Yoshida, Fenton, Maxwell, and Kaufman (1978) that classroom teachers perceive their participation in the team process as low and tend to be dissatisfied with it. These authors suggest that the amount a team member participates in the process is positively related to that member's satisfaction with the process.

Analysis of the steps directors and CSDCs used to describe the assessment and decision-making process indicated general agreement in a small number of basic steps (e.g., referral and assessment). However, the two subject groups often differed in terms of the frequency with which they included some steps of the process. While CSDCs mentioned development of the IEP less often than directors, they included development of strategies to implement the IEP more often. It is possible that differences such as these reflect the training or experience of professionals in these two types of settings.

Few directors or CSDCs included in their descriptions of the process efforts that precede the referral step, such as a classroom teacher's attempts to intervene and change the classroom setting. Yet, such efforts may determine how often the referral-intervention process is initiated. Indeed, one might argue that such early efforts at intervention are a way of pre-screening student problems to help ensure that referrals, when they are made, are appropriate.

The classroom teacher was the person most frequently mentioned as the initiator of the referral. It is likely, then, that the classroom teacher plays a crucial role in the assessment and decision-making process because she or he must decide whether to initiate a referral, and, once the referral has begun, is expected to play an important role in its followup. It seems appropriate that teachers be trained in decision-making skills; however, only approximately half the directors indicated that some type of training in decision making was provided to professionals who participated on decision-making teams (Poland, Ysseldyke, Thurlow, and Mirkin 1979).

There was evidence that, in most instances, development of the IEP preceded the meeting at which the parents were present. Goldstein et al. (1980) describe parents in IEP meetings as performing a "passive" role, such as approving the already developed IEP, rather than taking an active role in the formulation of goals and objectives for the plan. The practice of writing the IEP before meeting with the parents may contribute to passive parental participation.

Directors and team members agreed that the child's race, sex, and SES have little influence on the outcome of the placement team decision. However, there is evidence from simulation studies that factors such as sex, SES, and physical appearance can affect decisions to label a child as handicapped (Ysseldyke and Algozzine 1979), and even that a child's sex is an important variable in the referral step, with considerably more boys than girls being referred for special services (Gregory 1977; Naiden 1976). Both directors and team members selected teacher reports of the child's classroom achievement as the most important factor influencing the team decision, again suggesting the importance of the classroom teacher in the process. While both groups agreed on the importance of intelligence and achievement test results on the outcome, directors attributed more importance to psycholinguistic and perceptual-motor tests than did team members.

Data from the CSDCs suggested that there was little differentiation in the application of various types of assessment data to different types of educational decisions. The greatest differentiation appeared in instructional planning decisions, where criterion-referenced devices were chosen most frequently. Otherwise, norm-referenced tests clearly were a favorite. Indeed, Salvia and Ysseldyke (1978) suggest that norm-referenced devices are more useful in making screening, placement, and program evaluation decisions than they are in making instructional planning decisions, because they compare expected versus actual performance, and that criterion-referenced devices are more suitable for instructional planning purposes since they identify specific skills to be remediated.

Observations of placement meetings indicated that considerably more emphasis was placed on academic information (e.g., norm- and criterion-referenced devices) than on social information (e.g., adaptive behavior/social data), a finding which is in general agreement with the CSDC reports of data sources. However, observations of screening meetings suggested that social behavior data were discussed *more* than academic data (Allen personal communication 1980) which is not reflected in the CSDC reports.

A wide range of assessment devices were used by the CSDCs; many of which were of questionable technical adequacy. Few devices were used in common by a majority of CSDCs, which could make between-center comparisons of student progress difficult. Two technically adequate assessment devices were used in common by a majority of the CSDCs and the placement teams.

The data collected from special education directors, CSDCs, and placement teams reveal some communalities in current assessment and decision-making practices. The average number of team members in meetings is consistent across groups; classroom teachers, parents, and school administrators are frequent participants. The basic steps in the assessment and decision-making process are fairly well agreed upon. Decision makers demonstrate considerable agreement on what factors should and should not influence the decisions they make. The classroom teacher is seen as an important participant in the entire process. Yet, there is considerable variability in the process also. Different steps in the process are given different emphasis in different settings. An inordinate number of tests is used to provide data for decision making; many of these are technically inadequate. There is minimal communality in the tests used across settings. The determination of the significance of such variations in the formulation of educational decisions requires further study.

REFERENCES

American Psychological Association. *Standards for Educational and Psychological Tests*. Washington, D.C.: American Psychological Association, 1972.

Gillespie, P. H. "A Planned Change Approach to the Implementation of the IEP Provision of PL 94-142." In *Developing Criteria for the Evaluation of Individualized Education Program Provisions*. Washington, D.C.: USOE, BEH, 1978.

Goldstein, S.; Strickland, B.; Turnbull, A. P.; and Curry, L. "An Observational Analysis of the IEP Conference." *Exceptional Children* 46 (1980):278–86.

Gregory, M. K. "Sex Bias in School Referrals." *Journal of School Psychology* 15 (1977):5–8.

Hoff, M. K.; Fenton, K. S.; Yoshida, R. K.; and Kaufman, M. J. "Notice and Consent: The School's Responsibility to Inform Parents." *Journal of School Psychology* 16 (1978):265–73.

Naiden, N. "Ratio of Boys to Girls among Disabled Readers." *Reading Teacher* 29 (1976):439–46.

National Education Association. *Education for All Handicapped Children: Consensus, Conflict, and Challenge*. Washington, D.C.: National Education Association, 1978.

Poland, S.; Ysseldyke, J.; Thurlow, M.; and Mirkin, P. *Current Assessment and Decision-Making Practices in School Settings as Reported by Directors of Special Education* (Research Report No. 14). Minneapolis: University of Minnesota, Institute for Research on Learning Disabilities, 1979.

Salvia, J., and Ysseldyke, J. E. *Assessment in Special and Remedial Education*. Boston: Houghton-Mifflin, 1978.

Walker, H. M. "The Individualized Education Plan (IEP) as a Vehicle for the Delivery of Special Education and Related Services to Handicapped Children." In *Developing Criteria for the Evaluation of Individualized Education Program Provisions*. Washington, D.C.: USOE, BEH, 1978.

Walker, J. ed. *Functions of the Placement Committee in Special Education*. Washington, D.C.: National Association of State Directors of Special Education, 1976.

Yoshida, R. K.; Fenton, K. S.; Kaufman, M. J.; and Maxwell, J. P. "Parental Involvement in the Special Education Pupil Planning Process: The School's Perspective." *Exceptional Children* 44 (1978):531–34.

Yoshida, R. K.; Fenton, K. S.; Maxwell, J. P.; and Kaufman, M. J. "Group Decision Making in the Planning Team Process: Myth or Reality?" *Journal of School Psychology* 16 (1978):237–44.

Ysseldyke, J. E. "Implementing the 'Protection in Evaluation Procedures' Provisions of PL 94-142." In *Developing Criteria for Evaluation of the Protection in Evaluation Procedures Provision of Public Law 94-142.* Washington, D.C.: USOE, BEH, 1978.

Ysseldyke, J. E., and Algozzine, R. "Perspectives on Assessment of Learning Disabled Students." *Learning Disability Quarterly* 2 (1979):3–13.

8

Bias in the Making of Placement Decisions

James Ysseldyke, Robert Algozzine, Richard Regan,
Margaret Potter

S CHOOL PERSONNEL regularly must decide who, among those students experiencing academic and/or behavioral difficulties, should be declared eligible for and receive special education services. Little is known about the extent to which specific kinds of data influence the decision-making process and its outcomes.

Professionals charged with the task of making psychoeducational decisions about students routinely administer standardized tests or use the results of pupil performance on these tests during the decision-making process. While a number of investigations have reported the frequency with which various kinds of tests are used in practice, no data exist on the extent to which decision makers perceive different kinds of test information as influencing the decisions they made.

Considerable data demonstrate that both professional-student interpersonal interactions and the assessment process are differentially affected by naturally-occurring pupil characteristics (race, sex, socioeconomic status, physical attractiveness, etc.). For example, it has been demonstrated that teachers interact differently with black and white students (Coates 1972, Rubovitz and Maehr 1973), and with girls and boys (Meyer and Thompson 1956). It has also been reported that pupil sex differentially affects the kinds of academic and social difficulties decision makers expect students to demonstrate (Algozzine and Ysseldyke 1979; Schlosser and Algozzine 1979). Jackson and Lahaderne (1967) showed that the pupil's socioeconomic status differentially affects teacher-pupil interactions; several investigators (Algozzine 1975; Berscheid and Walster 1974; Ross and Salvia 1975) demonstrated that a pupil's physical attractiveness differentially affects both interactions and diagnostic outcomes.

In the current investigation a computer simulation was employed to examine both the issues of test use and the extent to which the

The research was supported by Contract #300-77-0491 between the Bureau of Education for the Handicapped and the University of Minnesota Institute for Research on Learning Disabilities.

decision-making process and outcomes of that process were biased by referral information about the child. At the same time, information was gathered on decision makers' knowledge of assessment and the extent to which they use technically adequate tests, obtain information from test manuals, and go beyond test scores to evaluate *how* youngsters earn those scores.

RATIONALE

The psychoeducational assessment and decision-making process can be, and in fact has been, investigated using many different methodologies. In many previous studies, decision makers have been asked about aspects of the process. Recent investigations of decision making in medical and educational settings have used computer simulation to study specific aspects of the process (Elstein, Shulman, and Sprafka 1978), and simulation is being used increasingly to study psychoeducational decision making (Gil, Wagner, and Vinsonhaler 1979; Patriarca, Van Roekel, and Lezotte 1979; Shulman and Elstein 1975). Computer simulation affords the investigator the opportunity to study clinical decision making without interfering in the naturalistic process and risking potential harm to students.

RESEARCH QUESTIONS

This investigation was designed to ascertain: (1) the extent to which the assessment *process* differs as a function of differences in referral information on a student (i.e., do diagnostic personnel actually use different kinds of assessment information); (2) the extent to which different naturally occurring pupil characteristics influence the outcome decisions reached by diagnostic personnel; (3) the extent to which decision makers perceive different kinds of assessment information as influencing their outcome decisions; and (4) the extent to which decision makers perceive naturally occurring pupil characteristics as influencing their outcome decisions. The following specific research questions were addressed:

1. What specific kinds of assessment data are used as a function of referral information (pupil sex, SES, appearance, and type of problem)?
2. What specific domains (e.g., intelligence, achievement, personality) do decision makers gather data in and to what extent do they review the technical and qualitative aspects of the devices?
3. Given data indicative of normal or average test performance by a referred student, to what extent do decision makers declare the student eligible for special education services?
4. Given data indicative of average pupil performance, to what extent do decision makers classify students as learning disabled, mentally retarded, and/or emotionally disturbed?
5. To what extent do decision makers predict that students will evidence difficulties in reading, mathematics, and speech?
6. What is the variability in the kinds of placements recommended for students with comparable test scores?
7. To what extent are decision makers influenced by test scores and naturally-occurring characteristics in the decisions they make?
8. To what extent is computer simulated decision making perceived as representative of "real life" decision making?

METHOD

Subjects

Subjects were 159 educators and school psychologists in Minnesota who participated in a computer simulated decision-making program. All participants were professionals who had previously participated in at least two placement team meetings. Subjects represented a broad spectrum of disciplines and experience in providing both direct and indirect services in educational settings, and included twenty-two school psychologists, forty-four special education teachers, fifty-two regular education teachers, thirteen administrators, and thirteen support personnel (counselors, nurses, social workers, etc.).

Procedure

Each subject was asked to read a case folder description of a child and then participate in a diagnostic simulation program developed specifically for this research. The program permitted the subject to access information from an archive containing the results of a variety of assessment devices. Specifically, scores were available for intelligence, achievement, perceptual-motor, personality, and language tests; performance on adaptive behavior scales and the results of several forms of behavioral observation or behavior checklists were also included in the archive. The subject was allowed to select specific tests (e.g., WISCR, ITPA, etc.) from the seven domains until he or she indicated readiness to make a diagnostic decision; the program then presented a series of decision questions. *Regardless of the specific devices selected, the simulation program consistently provided the participants with data indicating that the pupil's test performance was within the average range.* The entire sequence of activities required approximately 45 minutes to complete and each subject was paid $10 for participating.

Referral Conditions

Prior to receiving the initial case description, each subject was randomly assigned to one of sixteen treatment conditions. The sex, socioeconomic status, type of referral problem, and attractiveness of the child described in the case description were varied in the sixteen conditions. The child's name was listed as Phyllis or William, and the problem was either academic or behavioral in nature. In eight of the sixteen conditions, the referral folder contained information indicating that the student's father was a bank vice-president and the mother a realtor (high SES condition); in the other eight conditions, the student's father was a bank janitor, and the mother a check-out clerk at a local supermarket (low SES condition). Additionally, previously judged photographs were attached to the case folders to produce an "attractive" or "unattractive" child.

Dependent Variables

After reviewing the case folder and accessing the desired assessment information, each subject answered a series of questions. All were in Likert scale format and asked the participant three diagnostic questions (to what extent do you believe the referred student is learning disabled?), three prognostic questions (to what extent do you believe the referred student will have difficulty acquiring math skills?), questions asking them to rate the perceived influence of different kinds of scores (to what extent did the pupil's scores on intelligence tests influence your decision?), and questions asking them to rate the perceived influence of pupil characteristics (to what extent did the pupil's sex influence your decision?).

RESULTS

The simulation program recorded the tests used by each participant. In fourteen of the sixteen conditions, achievement tests were the most frequently used assessment devices.

Professionals from five different roles were represented in the sample (school psychologists, special education teachers, school administrators, regular class teachers, and other school personnel). The number of times each device was used by all of the participants is presented in Table 8.1; total use and percentage of use within each category of professionals is listed also. Usage generally was similar across professional roles. However, psychologists tended to use the Stanford-Binet much less than all other professionals; they also used frequency counts or event recordings and projective tests more often.

The extent to which technically adequate, inadequate, or other devices (i.e., special condition [SC] and criterion referenced [CR]) were selected during the diagnostic simulation may be derived from Tables 8.2, 8.3, and 8.4. Presented is the number of devices selected by subjects taking into account whether they reviewed either an academic or behavioral case and the number of selections made.

Due to the structure of the simulation activity, subjects were able to sample test domains more than once during data collection. This flexibility in the review process restricted analysis to nonparametric descriptive procedures.

A review of the tables suggests that subjects initially selected devices that are adequate with regard to norms, validity, and reliability whether they were reviewing an academic or behavioral case. As subjects accessed additional devices (i.e., fourth, fifth, or sixth selection), there was a marked decline in the number of devices that are technically adequate on the three dimensions under consideration. The results indicate as subjects review more data, the number of technically adequate measures selected decreases and the number of technically inadequate devices increases.

TABLE 8.1

Usage of Various Devices by School Personnel

Device	Number of Times Used	Used by School Psychologists	Used by Special Teachers	Used by School Administrators	Used by Regular Teachers	Used by Other Personnel
CAT*	20	1 (4)†	7 (14)	2 (12)	9 (17)	1 (7)
ITBS	33	2 (8)	8 (16)	3 (18)	14 (27)	6 (40)
MAT	8	0 (0)	2 (4)	1 (6)	4 (8)	1 (7)
SAT	19	2 (8)	7 (14)	2 (12)	8 (15)	0 (0)
GMRT	10	2 (8)	3 (6)	1 (6)	3 (6)	1 (7)
PIAT	37	7 (28)	17 (34)	8 (47)	2 (4)	3 (20)
WRAT	39	9 (36)	19 (38)	3 (18)	5 (10)	3 (20)
GORT	3	0 (0)	3 (6)	0 (0)	0 (0)	0 (0)
GORLT	2	0 (0)	2 (4)	0 (0)	0 (0)	0 (0)
GMRDT	5	0 (0)	1 (2)	1 (6)	2 (4)	1 (7)
DARD	14	1 (4)	7 (14)	1 (6)	1 (2)	4 (27)
SDRT	15	1 (4)	7 (14)	1 (6)	5 (10)	1 (7)
DRS	6	1 (4)	3 (6)	1 (6)	1 (2)	0 (0)
WRMT	29	8 (32)	15 (30)	2 (12)	2 (4)	2 (13)
KMDAT	35	9 (36)	16 (32)	3 (18)	6 (12)	1 (7)
SDMT	4	0 (0)	2 (4)	0 (0)	1 (2)	1 (7)
SBIS	55	2 (8)	17 (34)	6 (35)	27 (52)	3 (20)
WISCR	106	23 (92)	40 (80)	14 (82)	17 (33)	12 (80)
SIT	7	1 (4)	1 (2)	1 (6)	4 (8)	0 (0)
MSCA	1	1 (4)	0 (0)	0 (0)	0 (0)	0 (0)
FRPVT	1	0 (0)	0 (0)	0 (0)	0 (0)	1 (7)
QKT	4	1 (4)	0 (0)	1 (6)	1 (2)	1 (7)
PPVT	16	3 (12)	5 (10)	3 (18)	4 (8)	1 (7)
GHDT	2	1 (4)	0 (0)	0 (0)	1 (2)	0 (0)
HNTMA	1	0 (0)	1 (2)	0 (0)	0 (0)	0 (0)
KAIT	0	0 (0)	0 (0)	0 (0)	0 (0)	0 (0)
OLMAT	12	0 (0)	0 (0)	0 (0)	12 (23)	0 (0)
PMAT	1	0 (0)	0 (0)	0 (0)	0 (0)	1 (7)
BVMGT	74	14 (56)	19 (38)	9 (53)	23 (44)	9 (60)
DTUP	18	0 (0)	7 (14)	2 (12)	9 (17)	0 (0)
MFDT	7	1 (4)	3 (6)	0 (0)	3 (6)	0 (0)
DTVMI	14	2 (8)	5 (10)	3 (18)	4 (8)	0 (0)
PPMS	14	0 (0)	5 (10)	3 (18)	5 (10)	1 (7)
GFTA	3	0 (0)	2 (4)	0 (0)	1 (2)	0 (0)
ADT	33	2 (8)	10 (20)	6 (35)	9 (17)	6 (40)
NSST	7	0 (0)	4 (8)	2 (12)	1 (2)	0 (0)
ITPA	42	6 (24)	23 (46)	2 (12)	7 (14)	4 (27)
ABS	8	1 (4)	2 (4)	1 (6)	2 (4)	2 (13)
ABSPS	23	2 (8)	4 (8)	2 (12)	11 (21)	4 (27)
VSMS	18	2 (8)	8 (16)	1 (6)	7 (14)	0 (0)
FCER	54	13 (52)	14 (28)	4 (24)	17 (33)	6 (40)
ITY	13	3 (12)	2 (4)	2 (12)	3 (6)	3 (20)
PPR	13	5 (20)	3 (6)	3 (18)	1 (2)	1 (7)

NOTE: †percent of group members to use device.

TABLE 8.1 (cont'd.)

Usage of Various Devices by School Personnel

Device	Number of Times Used	Used by School Psychologists	Used by Special Teachers	Used by School Administrators	Used by Regular Teachers	Used by Other Personnel
DIAM	1	0 (0)	1 (2)	0 (0)	0 (0)	0 (0)
PQBPC	59	10 (40)	17 (20)	5 (29)	23 (44)	4 (27)
PHCSCS	60	9 (36)	20 (40)	2 (12)	24 (46)	5 (33)
RIBT	16	5 (20)	3 (6)	1 (6)	3 (6)	4 (27)
SAM	19	5 (20)	2 (4)	2 (12)	8 (15)	2 (13)
TAT	16	9 (36)	2 (4)	1 (6)	3 (6)	1 (7)
		n = 25	n = 50	n = 17	n = 52	n = 15

*Exact titles of each assessment device are the following:

INTELLIGENCE TESTS

Stanford Binet Intelligence Scale (SBIS)
Wechsler Intelligence Scale for Children, Revised (WISCR)
Slosson Intelligence Test (SIT)
McCarthy Scales of Children's Abilities (MSCA)
Full Range Picture Vocabulary Test (FRPVT)
Quick Test (QKT)
Peabody Picture Vocabulary Test (PPVT)
Goodenough-Harris Drawing Test (GHDT)
Henmon-Nelson Tests of Mental Ability (HNTMA)
Kuhlmann-Anderson Intelligence Tests (KAIT)
Otis-Lennon Mental Ability Test (OLMAT)
Primary Mental Abilities Test (PMAT)

ACHIEVEMENT TESTS

California Achievement Test (CAT)
Iowa Test of Basic Skills (ITBS)
Metropolitan Achievement Test (MAT)
Stanford Achievement Test (SAT)
Gates-MacGinitie Reading Tests (GMRT)
Peabody Individual Achievement Tests (PIAT)
Wide Range Achievement Test (WRAT)
Gray Oral Reading Test (GORT)
Gilmore Oral Reading Test (GORLT)
Gates-McKillop Reading Diagnostic Tests (GMRDT)
Durrell Analyses of Reading Difficulty (DARD)
Stanford Diagnostic Reading Test (SDRT)
Diagnostic Reading Scales (DRS)
Woodcock Reading Mastery Test (WRMT)
Key Math Diagnostic Arithmetic Test (KMDAT)
Stanford Diagnostic Mathematics Test (SDMT)
Diagnosis: An Instructional Aid in Math (DIAM)

TABLE 8.1 (cont'd.)

PERCEPTUAL-MOTOR TESTS

Bender Visual-Motor Gestalt (BVMGT)
Developmental Test of Visual Perception (DTVP)
Memory for Designs Test (MFDT)
Developmental Test of Visual-Motor Integration (DTVMI)
Purdue Perceptual-Motor Survey (PPMS)

BEHAVIORAL RECORDINGS

Frequency Counting or Event Recordings (FCER)
Interval or Time Samplings (ITY)
Permanent Products (PPR)
Peterson-Quay Behavior Problem Checklist (PQBPC)

PERSONALITY TESTS

Piers-Harris Self-Concept Scale (PHCSCS)
Rorschach-Inkblot Technique (RIBT)
School Apperception Method (SAM)
Thematic Apperception Test (TAT)

ADAPTIVE BEHAVIOR SCALES

AAMD Adaptive Behavior Scale (ABS)
AAMD Adaptive Behavior Scale (School Version) (ABSPS)
Vineland Social Maturity Scale (VSMS)

LANGUAGE TESTS

Goldman-Fristoe Test of Articulation (GFTA)
Auditory Discrimination Test (ADT)
Northwestern Syntax Screening Test (NSST)
Illinois Test of Psycholinguistic Abilities (ITPA)

TABLE 8.2

Frequency of Use of Devices According to Selected Technical Characteristics: Norms

Selections	Adequate		Inadequate		Other	
	Academic	Behavioral	Academic	Behavioral	Academic	Behavioral
(1)	72 (.90)	50 (.633)	8 (.10)	14 (.177)	0 (.00)	15 (.19)
(2)	36 (.47)	36 (.462)	39 (.51)	36 (.462)	2 (.02)	6 (.076)
(3)	23 (.30)	27 (.365)	51 (.67)	39 (.527)	3 (.03)	8 (.108)
(4)	14 (.19)	11 (.153)	52 (.72)	54 (.75)	6 (.09)	7 (.097)
(5)	7 (.11)	14 (.215)	54 (.84)	44 (.677)	3 (.05)	7 (.108)
(6)	8 (.16)	11 (.19)	40 (.78)	40 (.678)	3 (.06)	8 (.132)
(7)	13 (.36)	5 (.119)	21 (.58)	31 (.738)	2 (.06)	6 (.143)
(8)	2 (.09)	5 (.185)	16 (.73)	19 (.703)	4 (.18)	3 (.112)
(9)	3 (.27)	2 (.167)	8 (.73)	9 (.75)	0 (.00)	1 (.083)
(10)	1 (.25)	0 (.00)	3 (.75)	5 (1.00)	0 (.00)	0 (.00)
(11)	1 (.50)	0 (.00)	1 (.50)	1 (1.00)	0 (.00)	0 (.00)
	12 (.245)*		32 (.658)*		5 (.102)*	

*These figures represent the number of devices available during the simulated diagnostic session and their technical characteristics relative to norms.

TABLE 8.3

Frequency of Use of Devices According to Selected Technical Characteristics: Validity

Selections	Adequate		Inadequate		Other	
	Academic	Behavioral	Academic	Behavioral	Academic	Behavioral
(1)	52 (.65)	35 (.443)	28 (.35)	29 (.367)	0 (.00)	15 (.19)
(2)	32 (.42)	28 (.360)	43 (.56)	44 (.564)	2 (.02)	6 (.076)
(3)	20 (.26)	19 (.257)	54 (.70)	47 (.635)	3 (.04)	8 (.108)
(4)	12 (.17)	10 (.138)	55 (.76)	55 (.764)	5 (.07)	7 (.098)
(5)	5 (.08)	7 (.108)	56 (.88)	51 (.784)	3 (.04)	7 (.108)
(6)	2 (.04)	9 (.153)	46 (.90)	43 (.729)	3 (.06)	7 (.118)
(7)	8 (.22)	2 (.048)	26 (.72)	34 (.809)	2 (.06)	6 (.143)
(8)	3 (.14)	3 (.111)	15 (.68)	22 (.815)	4 (.18)	2 (.074)
(9)	1 (.09)	2 (.167)	10 (.91)	9 (.75)	0 (.00)	1 (.083)
(10)	0 (.00)	0 (.00)	4 (1.00)	5 (1.00)	0 (.00)	0 (.00)
(11)	1 (.50)	0 (.00)	1 (.50)	1 (1.00)	0 (.00)	0 (.00)
	12 (.245)*		33 (.673)*		4 (.082)*	

*These figures represent the number of devices available during the simulated diagnostic session and their technical characteristics relative to validity.

TABLE 8.4

Frequency of Use of Devices According to Selected
Technical Characteristics: Reliability

Selections	Adequate		Inadequate		Other	
	Academic	Behavioral	Academic	Behavioral	Academic	Behavioral
(1)	54 (.675)	38 (.481)	26 (.325)	26 (.329)	0 (.00)	15 (.19)
(2)	46 (.613)	43 (.551)	27 (.36)	29 (.371)	2 (.027)	6 (.078)
(3)	31 (.402)	30 (.405)	43 (.558)	36 (.486)	3 (.04)	8 (.109)
(4)	17 (.236)	16 (.222)	50 (.694)	49 (.681)	5 (.07)	7 (.097)
(5)	8 (.125)	8 (.138)	53 (.828)	49 (.754)	3 (.047)	7 (.108)
(6)	3 (.06)	11 (.186)	45 (.865)	41 (.695)	3 (.075)	7 (.119)
(7)	9 (.25)	2 (.05)	25 (.69)	34 (.81)	2 (.06)	6 (.14)
(8)	3 (.14)	3 (.111)	15 (.68)	22 (.815)	4 (.18)	2 (.074)
(9)	1 (.09)	2 (.167)	10 (.91)	9 (.75)	0 (.00)	1 (.083)
(10)	0 (.00)	0 (.00)	4 (1.00)	5 (1.00)	0 (.00)	0 (.00)
(11)	1 (.50)	0 (.00)	1 (.50)	1 (1.00)	0 (.00)	0 (.00)
	16 (.327)*		29 (.592)*		4 (.082)*	

*These figures represent the number of devices available during the simulated diagnostic session and their technical characteristics relative to reliability.

Although both academic and behavioral conditions use a greater frequency of technically adequate than inadequate devices early in the data collection and review process, there was a notable difference in the relative frequencies of technically adequate measures reviewed when one addresses the selection of devices from an academic versus behavioral perspective. The difference between the two conditions may be accounted for by the large number of "other" devices (i.e., SC, CR) reviewed by subjects in the behavioral condition.

An analysis of the results indicates that regardless of condition, subjects selected technically adequate devices most frequently early in the review process and increased their use of technically inadequate measures as the decision-making process continued. Similarly, decisions for children with academic rather than behavioral problems tended to be based on technically inadequate measures.

Subjects were asked to complete a series of questions after they had read the case description and reviewed their selected assessment information. The initial question addressed the issue of eligibility for special education services. Overall, 51 percent of the professionals declared the student to be eligible for special education services while 49 percent of the subjects indicated either that the student was not likely to be eligible for services or that they were not sure about the student's eligibility. A notable exception to this general trend may be seen in the case of administrators, who were considerably less likely to declare the student eligible for services than were the other professionals. Two of the sixteen referral conditions also ran counter to the general trend. Subjects who reviewed a student in condition 2 (male, unattractive, high SES, academic referral) and in condition 5 (male, attractive, low SES, academic problem) were also considerably less likely to indicate that the student was eligible for services.

Following the determination of eligibility for special education services, subjects were asked to indicate, using a Likert scale (1 = very likely, 5 = very unlikely), the degree to which the child was mentally retarded, emotionally disturbed, and/or learning disabled. A comparison of the overall means for each decision indicated that the subjects rated the child as likely to be learning disabled ($\bar{X} = 2.3$), very unlikely to be mentally retarded ($\bar{X} = 4.7$) and unlikely to be emotionally disturbed ($\bar{X} = 3.5$). The tendency was to find the case study child learning disabled; however, when the presenting problem was behavioral, a diagnosis of emotional disturbance was more likely than when the presenting problem was academic.

Subjects were asked whether they felt the student would be apt to exhibit difficulties in the areas of speech, reading skills acquisition, and mathematics skill acquisition. Very few subjects ($N = 18$) felt that speech would be a problem and less than half felt that difficulties might occur in mathematics. However, almost two-thirds of the subjects indicated that it was quite probable that the student would have difficulty in acquiring reading skills, in spite of test data indicating skill development and performance well within the average range.

Placement recommendations for the case studies used in this investigation indicated that of the six educational placements available (i.e., regular class, regular class with consultation by resource teacher, part time resource room, full time resource room, full time special class, and extra-school setting), regular class with consultation by a resource teacher and part time resource room were the most frequently selected settings. Educational alternatives that involved full time special class or resource room and extra school setting were not seen as likely placements by the subjects in the simulation.

Study participants perceived different kinds of assessment data as affecting their outcome decisions. Overall, scores on achievement tests, scores on measures of intelligence, and the disparity between the two were seen as most useful and influential. However, scores on personality tests and behavioral recording data were perceived as having a greater influence on outcome decisions when the referred student demonstrated behavior problems than when he or she demonstrated academic problems.

The subjects perceived naturally occurring pupil characteristics as influencing the decisions they had made. Socioeconomic status was said to influence decisions more when the student was from a high than from a low socioeconomic status family. Also, sex, socioeconomic status, and reason for referral were indicated to have a greater influence on outcome decisions than did physical appearance, but only when the referral was academic in nature. Participants reported that the reason for referral had a pronounced effect on outcome decisions, having a significantly greater effect on decisions than did sex, appearance, or socioeconomic status.

Following the completion of the simulation activity, the subjects were asked to complete an interview questionnaire addressing the efficacy of the computer simulation. The majority of the comments offered by the subjects indicated that the simulation did not significantly differ from real-life placement decision processes. Some subjects indicated that the simulation did differ from real-life decision-making practices in that they had no contact with other educational personnel and a greater array of assessment data was available for review. Approximately 88 percent of the subjects believed they had sufficient time to complete the simulation. When asked what kinds of information in addition to those provided by the program would be helpful in making their decision, the majority of responses suggested interviews with teachers and/or parents.

DISCUSSION

Data collected in assessment should be functionally useful in educational decision making. In this investigation educational decision makers were presented referral information varied only in terms of the child's sex, socioeconomic status, physical appearance, and type of referral problem. They were given an opportunity to select specific kinds of assessment data (all of which indicated pupil performance and behavior within the average range), were asked to make diagnostic and prognostic decisions, and were asked to report the extent to which specific kinds of test data and naturally occurring pupil information influenced their decisions.

Decision makers did not use different kinds of tests as a function of the sex, socioeconomic status, physical attractiveness, or reason for referral. Rather, across conditions, achievement tests were used most often.

Referral information did affect the outcome decisions made, but only for one of the four independent variables. The referred student's sex, socioeconomic status, and physical appearance had no effect on the diagnostic and prognostic decisions made. Reason for referral did significantly affect the decision. Although all assessment data indicated average or normal performance, students referred for behavior problems were significantly more often diagnosed and labeled as emotionally disturbed than were students referred for academic problems. The statement of referral problem biased outcome decisions.

Decision makers perceive different kinds of assessment data as affecting their outcome decisions. Overall, scores on achievement tests, scores on intelligence tests, and the disparity between the two were perceived as most useful and influential. However, scores on personality tests and behavioral recording data were perceived as having a greater influence on outcome decisions when the referred student demonstrated behavior problems than when he or she demonstrated academic problems.

Decision makers did perceive naturally occurring pupil characteristics as influencing the decisions they made. Specifically, socioeconomic status was said to influence decisions more when the student was from a high than from a low socioeconomic environment. Secondly, sex, socioeconomic status, and reason for referral were said to have a greater influence on outcome decisions than did physical appearance, but only when the reason for referral was academic in nature. Participants reported that reason for referral has a pronounced effect on outcome decisions, having a significantly greater effect on decisions than did sex, appearance, or socioeconomic status.

Referral information biases the decisions made about students. While there was no difference in the kinds of tests used by decision makers, different outcome decisions were reached under different referral conditions. Furthermore, decision makers perceived different kinds of data and pupil characteristics as having influenced their decisions, and these differences were a function of the referral information.

REFERENCES

Algozzine, R. F. "Attractiveness as a Biasing Factor in Teacher-Pupil Interactions." Unpublished doctoral dissertation, Pennsylvania State University, 1975.

Algozzine, B., and Ysseldyke, J. E. *Decision Makers' Prediction of Students' Academic Difficulties as a Function of Referral Information* (Research Report No. 18). Minneapolis: University of Minnesota, Institute for Research on Learning Disabilities, 1979.

Berscheid, E., and Walster, E. "Physical Attractiveness." In *Advances in Experimental Social Psychology*, Vol. 7, edited by L. Berkowitz. New York: Academic Press, 1974.

Coates, B. "White Adult Behavior Toward Black and White Children." *Child Development* 43 (1972):143–54.

Elstein, A. S.; Shulman, L. S.; and Sprafka, S. *Medical Problem Solving: An Analysis of Clinical Reasoning.* Cambridge, Mass.: Harvard University Press, 1978.

Gil, D.; Wagner, C. C.; and Vinsonhaler, J. F. *Simulating the Problem Solving of Reading Clinicians* (Research Series No. 30). East Lansing, Mich.: Michigan State University Institute for Research on Teaching, 1979.

Meyer, W., and Thompson, G. "Sex Differences in the Distribution of Teacher Approval and Disapproval among Sixth Grade Children." *Journal of Educational Psychology* 47 (1956):385–96.

Patriarca, L.; Van Roekel, J.; and Lezotte, L. *Simulated Reading and Learning Disability Cases: Effective Tools for Research and Teacher Education* (Research Series No. 29). East Lansing, Mich.: Michigan State University, Institute for Research on Teaching, 1979.

Ross, M., and Salvia, J. "Attractiveness as a Biasing Factor in Judgments." *American Journal of Mental Deficiency* 80 (1975):96–98.

Rubovitz, P., and Maehr, M. "Pygmalion Black and White." *Journal of Personality and Social Psychology* 25 (1973):210–18.

Schlosser, L., and Algozzine, B. "The Disturbing Child: He or She?" *Alberta Journal of Educational Research* 25 (1979):30–36.

Shulman, L. S., and Elstein, A. S. "Studies of Problem Solving, Judgment, and Decision Making." In *Review of Research in Education*, Vol. 3, edited by F. N. Kerlinger. Itasca, Ill.: Peacock, 1975.

9

Current Status of Research on the Development of a Formative Evaluation System for Learning Disabilities Programs

Stanley Deno, Phyllis Mirkin, Berttram Chiang, Kathryn Kuehnle, Lisa Lowry, Douglas Marston, and Gerald Tyndal

THE research reported here has as its purpose the development of formative evaluation systems for teachers to use in improving learning disabilities service programs. The primary assumptions upon which the research is based are:

1. The success of learning disabilities services is defined primarily by the extent to which those services improve the academic and social behavior goals of the individual students served.

2. Teachers can increase the success of learning disabilities services by systematically measuring student progress toward achievement of program goals and then adjusting student programs to improve that progress.

3. The technology presently available for teachers to use in measuring student progress and adjusting programs based on measured progress is either not sufficient or has not been sufficiently tested.

A first, and critical, question that is raised when developing a formative evaluation system is: what student performance data can be routinely and easily obtained that validly indexes achievement? The question arises because, for several good reasons, commercially prepared standardized tests ordinarily used to assess achievement cannot be routinely used in a formative evaluation system to monitor performance. First, commercially produced standardized tests take too much time to administer. Second, an insufficient number of equivalent forms is available for any test to be used in the repeated measurement of performance required for formative evaluation. Third, the cost of using achievement tests repeatedly is prohibitive. The development of measurement procedures that can be relatively easily incorporated into the daily routine of most teachers working in learning disabilities programs is deemed desirable if intensive monitoring of program effects on student performance is to occur.

The research and development program described here has been designed to systematically construct formative evaluation procedures for learning disabilities programs that specify: (1) What behaviors to measure when improved reading proficiency is an IEP goal; (2) how to repeatedly measure those behaviors reliably; (3) who should administer the measurement procedures; (4) how often measurement should occur; (5) how to obtain data most efficiently; and (6) how to use repeated measurements of student performance to increase intervention effectiveness.

The strategy employed in the present research was first to review available literature to identify behaviors that are commonly used to assess achievement in the academic domains of reading, spelling, and written expression as well as in the area of social adjustment; second, to develop measurement procedures for taking data on those behaviors; third, to determine the reliability and validity of these measures by correlating the scores obtained with scores obtained on standardized measures; and fourth, to use the measures as part of a formative evaluation system to determine whether teachers who collect and use data on student performance can provide more effective instruction to children being served in learning disabilities programs.

To be considered for inclusion in a formative evaluation system, the developed measures had to fulfill the following criteria. (1) They must be *valid* with respect to widely used measures of achievement. (2) They must be immediately *sensitive* to the effects of relatively small adjustments made in (a) instructional methods and materials, (b) motivational techniques, and (c) administrative arrangements (e.g., adjustments in grouping, setting for instruction, teacher/tutor, time of instruction, etc.). (3) They must be *easy to administer* by teachers, parents, and students. (4) They must include many parallel forms that are *frequently administrable* (daily if necessary) to the same student. (5) They must be *time efficient*. (6) They must be *inexpensive* to produce. (7) They must be *unobtrusive* with respect to routine instruction. (8) They must be *simple to teach* to teachers, parents, and children.

The present paper is divided into five sections. The first four sections describe the procedures and results of studies conducted to determine the reliability and validity of procedures designed to measure performance on selected reading, spelling, written expression, and social adjustment behaviors. The final section reports the results of a formative evaluation study comparing the frequency with which performance was measured and two data utilization techniques.

Our hope is that regardless of personal philosophical, theoretical, historical, and current situational constraints, those responsible for ensuring the quality of learning disabilities services will continuously evaluate the impact of those services on the academic and social behaviors of their individual students. The research described here is an important step in the development of such an evaluation system.

THE VALIDATION OF PROCEDURES TO BE USED IN FORMATIVE EVALUATION OF SPELLING

An extensive review of the literature on the assessment of spelling performance revealed word list dictation as the most common procedure used to assess a student's performance.

Formative Measures

Three word lists were developed to be used as measures for isolated word list dictation. The lists were comprised of words selected at random from *Basic Elementary Reading Vocabularies* (Harris and Jacobson 1972). The lists included words from: (1) pre-primer through first grade (PP–1); (2) pre-primer through third grade (PP–3); (3) pre-primer through sixth grade (PP–6). A fourth list was developed comprised of words selected non-randomly from a third grade basal reader. This list simulates an approach teachers would more likely use than randomized lists in their classrooms to develop spelling measures.

Scores were obtained for total number of words spelled correctly and number of letter sequences spelled correctly (White and Haring 1976) from the dictated word lists.

Criterion Measures

Three standardized achievement tests were selected as criteria to determine the concurrent validity of the formative measure. The achievement tests were: (1) Test of Written Spelling (TWS) (Larsen and Hammill 1976); (2) Peabody Individual Achievement Test: Spelling Subtest (PIAT) (Dunn and Markwardt 1970); and (3) Stanford Achievement Test: Primary III, Spelling section (SAT) (Madden, Gardner,

Rudman, Karlsen, and Merwin 1973). These standardized tests have reported technical characteristics that are adequate in terms of norms, reliability, and validity. Tests were scored for number of correct answers.

Subjects

Subjects were 148 children from ten schools in the greater Minneapolis/St. Paul area randomly selected to participate in the study. The children represented grades two through six and ranged in age from seven to thirteen years. Ninety-four children attended regular classes and fifty-four students were receiving learning disabilities services in a school-based resource program.

Procedures

Each student was tested on an individual basis and completed one standardized test and three or four dictated word lists. Students were given fifteen seconds to write each dictated word which the examiner said and then repeated. Sentences were provided for homonyms. Time limits were imposed for each list. Comparisons were made of scores from one-, two-, and three-minute dictations.

Results

Intercorrelational matrices were developed to determine the correlations between the behavioral measures, and the standardized tests. These results indicate very high correlations (.87 to .94) between number of correctly spelled words on the PP–6 grade word list for a three-minute dictation, and the standardized tests. Similar high correlations are revealed for the other lists, including non-randomly selected words, for both number of correct letter sequences (.81 to .94) and words (.83 to .96). Results computed for one- and two-minute samples indicated very high correlations across time limits (.79 to .92). Table 9.1 reveals differences between regular and learning disabled students across grade levels for correct letter sequences and words (PP–6 list)

TABLE 9.1

Mean Number Correct by Grade and Group

(PP-6 List for One-Minute Sample)

		2	3	4	5	6
Letter Sequences	Regular (N = 67)	23.9	33.2	46.3	60.8	53.8
	LD (N = 39)	7.8	21.8	14.4	37.4	25.0
Words	Regular	2.4	3.9	6.2	8.3	7.1
	LD	.4	1.9	1.1	3.9	1.9

for a one-minute dictation. At every grade level, except third grade, regular students wrote significantly more correct letter sequences and words than LD students ($p < .05$). Similar scores were obtained for the other word lists. An increase in scores across grade levels for correct letter sequences and words was also obtained although a slight decrease occurred between fifth and sixth grades and the differences between scores of the two groups for third grade were nonsignificant. However, this may be more the result of unequal numbers of students at each grade level than an indication of insensitivity of the measure to developmental growth. Overall, regular students correctly spelled more words and letter sequences than LD students ($p < .001$).

Conclusions

The results of these analyses suggest that a dictated word list is a highly valid measure of spelling skill in relation to three standardized spelling achievement tests. Variations in list difficulty and time allotted for dictation appear to be equally valid as does scoring using either number of correct letter sequences or words. The dictated word list also indicated developmental differences in students' spelling across all grade levels as well as between regular class students and students receiving learning disabilities service in resource programs.

These formative measures could easily be included in a formative evaluation sytem for spelling. The dictated word lists are easy to administer, inexpensive to produce, time efficient, and easy to record. The word lists can be utilized for both LD and non-LD students from second to sixth grade. By recording correct number of letter sequences or words, teachers could monitor individual students' spelling skills and determine effective materials and instructional interventions.

THE VALIDATION OF PROCEDURES TO BE USED IN
FORMATIVE EVALUATION OF WRITTEN EXPRESSION

An extensive review of the literature related to measurement of written expression led to the selection of five types of measures that appeared to satisfy the specified criteria of a formative evaluation system. Some of these measures are direct applications of procedures developed by other researchers and others were developed by our own group.

Formative Measures

Prominent on the list of potentially useful procedures for a formative evaluation system was Kellogg Hunt's (1966) work on T-units, a measure of syntactic complexity. The concept of minimal T-unit length seemed to fit the criteria and was included for analysis. A second measure of written expression, Mature Word Choice, was adopted from Finn's (1977) Undistinguished Word List. This index is simply a count of the number of words in a compotition that are infrequently used in the English language. A third measure of written expression focused simply on the total number of words written in a composition. Support for this measure has been reported by Myklebust (1965) and confirmed by factor analysis (Slotnick 1972). A pilot study conducted by our research staff and Page's (1968) work evoked interest in a fourth measure of written expression that emphasized the number of large words used in a composition, that is, words with seven or more letters. The last measure focused on the number of words spelled correctly in a composition, as well as the number of letters written in correct sequence, a modification intended to increase the sensitivity of the measure in learning disabled populations (White and Haring 1976).

Criterion Measures

Three standardized achievement tests were selected as criteria to determine the concurrent validity of the formative written expression measures. They were: Hammill and Larsen's (1978) Test of Written Language, the Word Usage subtest from the Intermediate Level of the Stanford Achievement Test (Madden, Gardner, Rudman, Karlsen, and Merwin 1978) and Lee and Canter's (1971) Developmental Sentence Scoring, a measure of grammatical maturity.

Subjects

Subjects were 135 students, 72 males and 63 females ranging in age from seven years to eleven years and from third to sixth grade, randomly selected from Metropolitan Twin City schools. Forty-seven of these children were receiving services in a learning disabilities resource program.

Procedure

Each student was presented with a stimulus to help elicit a written composition and was then given five minutes to write. Stimuli included pictures, story starters, and topic sentences. The compositions were then scored using the six formative measures. Students also were asked to complete an achievement test in the domain of written expression. Intercorrelation matrices were then generated to study the relationship between the dependent and criterion measures.

Results

The results of the correlational analysis may be found in Table 9.2. Correlations of .62–.84 for Total Words Written, .72–.76 for Mature Words, .67–.76 for Words Spelled Correctly, and .75–.86 for Letters in Correct Sequence suggest that these measures are valid indices of written expression performance.

When the range of scores obtained for each measure is considered, Mature Words is ruled out. The range for this measure, for third through sixth grade students, is zero to twenty-seven mature words written on a composition. Compared to Total Words (0 to 103), Words Spelled Correctly (0 to 96), and Letters in Correct Sequence (0 to 458), the Mature Word index does not seem to fit as well into the formative evaluation scheme.

Table 9.3 presents the means and standard deviations for Total Words Written by grade level and educational status. If a measure is a valid index of written expression one would predict increments in performance with grade level and differences between students receiving learning disabilities services in a resource program and students from regular classrooms. The results of a two-way ANOVA using the mean

TABLE 9.2

Validity Coefficients for Correlations Between Formative Evaluation Measures of Written Expression and Criterion Achievement Measures

	Test of Written Language	Stanford Subtest	Developmental Sentence Scoring
Mean T-unit Length	.36*	.32*	.29*
Mature Words Written	.76	.72	.74
Total Words Written	.72	.62	.84
Large Words Written	.63	.68	.47
Words Spelled Correctly	.71	.67	.76
Letters Written in Correct Sequence	.75	M†	.86

All correlations significant at $p < .001$ unless otherwise noted.
*Significant at $p < .05$.
†Not computed.

TABLE 9.3

Means and Standard Deviations for Resource and Regular Students on Total Words Written

	Resource Students			Regular Students		
Grade	N	Mean	SD	N	Mean	SD
3	9	9.0	9.1	11	40.1	15.0
4	10	34.5	13.5	36	51.1	20.4
5	11	39.9	21.6	22	54.9	21.2
6	14	41.6	14.4	17	64.4	23.1

scores obtained from Total Words Written confirmed this hypothesis. Both the main effect for grade level ($F = 10.4$, $p = .001$) and educational status ($F = 23.1$, $p = .001$) were highly significant. Two-way ANOVAs for Words Spelled Correctly and Letters in Correct Sequence yield similar results.

Conclusions

The results of these analyses suggest that Total Words Written, Words Spelled Correctly, and Letters in Correct Sequence are valid indices of written expression performance and may be considered useful data in a formative evaluation system.

THE VALIDATION OF PROCEDURES TO BE USED IN FORMATIVE EVALUATION OF READING

Three studies were conducted to identify student performance data that validly index achievement in reading. The purpose of the first study was to identify those reading behaviors that could be readily measured to obtain reliable and valid indices of students' reading skills. The second two studies were conducted to develop appropriate assessment measures of the reading behaviors, measures that could be used in the classroom setting by the teacher.

Formative Measures

After an extensive review of the literature on assessment of reading performance, five potentially useful formative reading measures were identified for study. The behaviors were: (1) Words in Isolation — student reads a list of words; (2) Words in Context — student reads underlined words in a passage of text; (3) Oral Reading — student reads a passage of text; (4) Cloze Comprehension — student inserts words while reading a passage of text with some words missing; and (5) Word Meaning — student defines underlined words in a passage of text.

Criterion Measures

Three standardized achievement tests were selected as criterion measures. These were: (1) Stanford Diagnostic Reading Test; Reading Comprehension Subtest (Karlsen, Madden, and Gardner 1975); (2)

Woodcock Reading Mastery Test (Woodcock 1973); (3) Peabody Individual Achievement Test, Reading Comprehension Subtest (Dunn and Markwardt 1970).

Subjects

One hundred and forty students in grades one–six from two Minneapolis/St. Paul metropolitan school districts (six individual schools) participated in the research. Eighty-eight students were from regular classes and fifty-six receiving reading instruction in a learning disabilities resource program.

Procedures

Students participating in the first study were tested on the five formative reading measures and on two standardized reading tests (Stanford Diagnostic Reading Test and Woodcock Reading Mastery Tests). Students participating in the second study were tested only on modified versions of the five classroom reading measures. The modifications were made to help identify testing procedures that could be used by teachers but which would remain as reliable as the original measures. Modifications involved changing the time required for the test (from one minute to 30 seconds), or changing the difficulty level of the test. Students participating in the third study were tested on the modified classroom reading measures and on two standardized tests (Peabody Individual Achievement Test, Reading Comprehension Subtest, and Stanford Diagnostic Reading Test).

Results

Results from the first study are shown in Table 9.4. Three of the five formative measures (Words in Isolation, Words in Context, and Oral Reading) provided good indices of the reading level estimated by the standardized measures. Correlations for these measures ranged from .73 to .91 with scores on the standardized measures; most correlations were in the .80s. Scores on the Cloze and Word Meaning formative measures also were significantly correlated with scores on the standardized measures, although at a slightly lower level (.60–.83). In addition, perform-

TABLE 9.4

**Validity Coefficients for Correlations Between Formative
Evaluation Measures of Reading and Criterion
Achievement Measures: Study One**

	Stanford Diagnostic	Woodcock Reading Mastery Word Ident.	Woodcock Reading Mastery Comprehension
Words			
Isolation	.76	.91	.83
Context	.80	.90	.84
Oral Reading	.73	.87	.82
Cloze	.60*	.83	.82
Word Meaning	.66*	.77	.73

All correlations significant at p < .001 unless otherwise noted.
*Significant at p < .005.

ance on the three classroom measures reflected the students' grade levels, with scores increasing as the grade level of students increased.

Results from the second study are reported in Table 9.5 and indicate that the modified measures generally were comparable to the original measures. Thus, scores on third-grade materials correlated highly with scores on sixth-grade materials, and scores on 30-second tests correlated highly with scores on one-minute tests. Most correlations were in the .80s and .90s. The modified Cloze and Word Meaning measures yielded significant, but lower, correlations with the original measures.

Results from the third study confirm the relationship previously found between the modified and original measures and between these measures and the standardized tests. The relationships were somewhat lower for the resource students, possibly due to their generally lower level of functioning (many more were considered non-readers or pre-readers and failed to score on any of the formative and standardized tests).

Conclusions

The formative reading measures investigated can be used by classroom teachers to monitor students' growth so that the effectiveness of instructional interventions can easily be evaluated when in progress, and then modified to improve program success. Considerable evidence for the reliability and validity of the formative reading measures was

TABLE 9.5

Validity Coefficients for Correlations Between Original and Modified Formative Evaluation Measures of Reading: Study Two

	PP-3				PP-6				3rd Grade Pass		6th Grade Pass		
	Isolated		Context		Isolated		Context		Oral Rdg.		Oral Rdg.		Cloze WM
	30	60	30	60	30	60	30	60	30	60	30	60	
PP-3 Words													
Isolation 30 sec.	.93	.78	.80	.94	.91	.85	.80	.85	.89	.86	.90	.83	.53
Isolation 60 sec.		.89	.90	.97	.95	.92	.89	.89	.92	.87	.91	.81	.57
Context 30 sec.			.97	.96			.96	.84	.85	.82	.84	.74	.67
Context 60 sec.				.95			.95	.83	.86	.82	.84	.76	.68
PP-6 Words													
Isolation 30 sec.			.85	.86	.97	.90	.86	.87	.89	.87	.91	.82	.57
Isolation 60 sec.			.86	.86		.91	.89	.85	.87	.85	.91	.82	.62
Context 30 sec.							.93	.89	.90	.87	.90	.82	.64
Context 60 sec.								.78	.84	.83	.82	.76	.74
3rd Grade Passage													
Oral Rdg. 30 sec.									.96	.92	.95	.84	.39*
Oral Rdg. 60 sec.										.96	.97	.85	.48*
6th Grade Passage													
Oral Rdg. 30 sec.											.96	.80	.49*
Oral Rdg. 60 sec.												.85	.47*
Cloze Word Meaning													.44*

All correlations are significant at $p < .001$ unless otherwise noted.
*Significant at $p < .05$.

obtained. The one instance of limited usefulness indicated that the formative measures probably are not appropriate for students not yet receiving systematic reading instruction. Such a limitation is not serious since the classroom measures are meant to be used to monitor progress; if a student is not receiving instruction, the teacher would not be interested in obtaining continuous information on progress in reading.

THE VALIDATION OF PROCEDURES TO BE USED IN FORMATIVE EVALUATION OF SOCIAL SUCCESS

Social behaviors that could be monitored by teachers to index a student's social functioning within the classroom were studied through correlational analyses. Correlations were obtained between teacher sociometric ratings, peer sociometric ratings, and systematic observation of selected social behaviors in the classroom.

Pilot Study

The first study attempted to establish empirical evidence for selected social behaviors as simple and valid measures of students' social status within a classroom setting. The social behaviors, viewed as meeting the requirements for the measurement component of a formative evaluation system, were selected for inclusion in the first investigation from a large pool of behaviors derived from a thorough review of the literature.

Formative Measures

The behaviors selected for observation included: (1) initiations by peers to target; (2) verbal interaction with peers; (3) aversive behavior; (4) ignoring behavior; and (5) inappropriate behavior. Rate and frequency data were calculated for each of the five categories. A complex coding system was designed that coded the initials of peers who initiated and/or interacted with the target. This coding permitted us to calculate the number and frequency with which different peers initiated and interacted with the target. Although the coding system did not meet the requirements for the measurement component of a formative evaluation system, it had utility as a measurement system within the pilot study.

Criterion Measures

The two criterion measures selected to assess social status were the roster and rating inventory and the peer nomination technique (Moreno 1934). Both methods were utilized for maximum discrimination of the isolated child. Two roster and rating scales required each student to rate classmates on a scale of 1–5, in terms of how much he or she like to "play with" that student and in terms of how much he or she liked to "work with" that student. A student's score on this measure was the average rating received from classmates. The peer nomination measure required each student to nominate three classmates with whom they would like to play and three classmates with whom they would like to work. The roster and rating scales and the peer nomination procedure were administered only within sexes and not between sexes, since previous research indicated that children discriminate in their sociometric ratings and nominations of classmates by gender (Asher 1973).

Subjects

Subjects were forty-eight students: fourteen males and ten females in class one, and sixteen males and eight females in class two, from two fourth-grade classes within a suburban Minneapolis public school.

Procedure

Both students and teachers completed the sociometric criterion measures. The measures were administered to students in an area away from the classroom in groups of three. Social interactions in the classroom were assessed using a six-second interval observation system. Two trained observers collected data across both structured and unstructured school settings over a three-week period. Interrater reliability using the Pearson product moment reliability coefficient yielded an interrater agreement of .87. The calculated agreement using a weighted formula (Harris and Lahey 1978) yielded an agreement of .71.

Due to the low incidence of observed behaviors, cluster scores were developed that included several individual categories. Cluster one data included all measures in which peers were directing initiations or verbal interactions to targets. Cluster two data included the different number of peers engaging in each peer to target behavior found in cluster one. For each of these clusters, a composite measure was computed. Cluster three data included target to peer behaviors. A composite measure was not computed for this cluster.

Results

In Class One, moderate to moderately high correlations of .60 to .74 ($ps = .001$) were obtained between the composite scores for the first two clusters and the sociometric criterion measures administered to the students. Low to moderate correlations of .27 to .47 were obtained for the individual behavior scores in cluster three. Moderate to moderately high correlations of .42 to .72 were also obtained in Class One between teacher "play with" and "work with" ratings and the students' sociometric ratings.

In Class Two, the correlations between the composite scores for the first two clusters and the sociometric criterion measures administered to the students were all low and all but one were in the wrong

direction (.01 to −.40). The correlations between the individual behaviors in cluster three and the sociometric measures were consistent
with the findings for the first two cluster composites. Moderate correlations of .31 to .68 were obtained in Class Two between teacher's
sociometric ratings and student's sociometric ratings and were more
consistent with correlations obtained in class one than were the composite score correlations.

Study Two

The second study was a continuation of the attempt to determine
empirically the utility of selected behaviors as simple and valid measures
of a student's social functioning within the classroom.

Formative Measures

As a result of the findings in the pilot study, in which the frequency
of social interactions between peer and target, and the number of different peers talking to target showed moderate to high correlations with
social status criterion measures in Class One, the following behaviors
and their definitions were selected for classroom observation in Study
Two: (1) frequency of verbal interaction by peers to the target (any
instance of the target being talked to, whether an initiation by a peer, a
response by a peer to the target initiation, or as part of an ongoing
exchange), and (2) the number of different peers with whom the target
interacted. Each instance of an interaction with a different peer for that
observation day was tallied. A change was made in the recording procedure to approximate what might actually be used by a classroom teacher.
The observation interval was increased from 6 to 30 seconds and an
event rather than an interval recording system was used.

Criterion Measures

The sociometric criterion measures in Study Two were identical to
those used in the pilot study. Additionally, eight items were selected
from a student behavior rating scale used by the Project Prime Study
(Agard, Veldman, Kaufman, Semmel, and Watkins 1978). These items
included: (1) talks to children, (2) is outgoing and friendly, (3) is too shy

and withdrawn to make friends, (4) other children seem to like, (5) participates in class activities, (6) plays by self most of the time, (7) gets in lots of fights or arguments, (8) has lots of friends.

Subjects

Subjects were fifty-eight students, fifteen males and thirteen females in Class One and nineteen males and eleven females in Class Two, from two third-grade classes within a suburban Minneapolis public school.

Procedure

Both students and teachers completed the sociometric criterion measures. The procedures for administration were identical to those in the pilot study. The teachers were also requested to complete the eight items selected from the Project Prime Rating Scale. Social interactions in the classroom were assessed across both structured and unstructured school periods by two trained observers over a three-week period. Students were observed according to the alphabetical order of their last name, with the initials of the peer interacting with the target recorded during the observation interval. Interrater reliability data were collected by the two observers rotating through the class list at three arbitrarily selected times during the study. A Pearson product moment reliability yielded an interrater agreement mean of .92. The calculated agreement using a weighted agreement (Harris and Lahey 1978) yielded a mean agreement of .75.

To ensure comparability of data across classrooms, data were transformed to z-scores and analyses were performed using the z-score transformation. Intercorrelational matrices were generated to study the relationship between teacher and peer nominations and systematic observation of the identified behaviors.

Results

Moderate correlations of .36 to .48 (*p*s = .001) were obtained between the frequency of verbal interaction by peers to the target and the roster and rating and peer nomination criterion measures administered to the students. Low and unreliable correlations of .16 to .17 were obtained between the number of different peers with whom the target interacted per minute of observation and the sociometric criterion measures administered to the students.

The correlations between the sociometric criterion measure administered to the students and the roster and rating criterion measures administered to the teachers were moderate, ranging from .48 to .50. Low to moderate correlations of .15 to .36 were obtained between the sociometric criterion measures administered to the students and the following Project Prime behavior rated items: talks to children, participates in class activities, and has lots of friends. Correlations between the criterion measures and other Project Prime items (2, 3, 4, 6, 7) were inconsistent and often in the wrong direction, ranging from −.57 to .30. These results are shown in Table 9.6.

Discussion

The results suggest that the frequency with which peers interact with a target child may be a valid measure of that child's social status. However, this conclusion is tentative due to limitations in the present study. Problems existed with respect to failure to control for differences in frequencies of behavior across settings. There was some evidence that the observers were aware of time periods for reliability checks. Additionally, since we seek measures for our formative evaluation system that can be used to continuously evaluate the effect of interventions on a child's social adjustment, measures that consistently account for more than one-half the variance on criterion measures would be desirable.

Current studies on social adjustment at the Minnesota Institute for Research on Learning Disabilities are continuing to investigate measures that teachers can use to index social functioning. Behaviors presently under study include those that occur during structured and unstructured activities, and should provide additional data on whether simple and valid measures of students' social success can be determined.

THE DEVELOPMENT OF DATA UTILIZATION SYSTEMS

The essential aspect of this research was to determine the critical components of an ongoing assessment system in which programs are ad-

TABLE 9.6

Combined Class Correlations of Sociometric and Teacher Prime Item Ratings: Study 2

	Teacher Ratings							
	1	2	3	4	5	6	7	8
Sociometric Roster and Ratings by Students								
Play	.22†	−.01	−.06	−.22†	.33*	−.57*	−.08	.36*
Work	.15	.04	−.03	−.10	.33*	−.54*	−.12	.33*
Peer Nominations								
Play	.27†	.26†	−.16	−.12	.33*	−.52*	−.26†	.34*
Work	.19	.30*	.15	−.10	.28†	−.50*	−.17	.33*

1 = Talks to children
2 = Is outgoing and friendly
3 = Is too shy and withdrawn to make friends
4 = Other children seem to like
5 = Participates in class activities
6 = Plays by self most of time
7 = Gets in lots of fights and arguments
8 = Has lots of friends

*Correlations significant at ≦ .01.
†Correlations significant at ≦ .05.

justed in accordance with student performance. In previous sections of this manuscript, the development of simple, functional, and valid measures of reading, spelling, written expression, and social adjustment was described. The benefits of having such measures include: (1) being able to evaluate instructional programs frequently (daily, if necessary) to determine whether they are appropriate or effective, and (2) being able to use student progress as the basis for program changes. Research is needed, however, to identify the type of information that will be most useful to teachers, how frequently it needs to be collected, how it should be recorded and organized, and, most importantly, how best to utilize this information to increase teacher effectiveness. The present study was designed specifically to answer two questions. (1) Are teachers more effective when they measure student performance every day or once a week? (2) When performance is measured daily, are teachers more effective when program changes are based on their own judgment or when they are based on specific decision rules?

Subjects

Twenty-three teachers providing learning disabilities services to eighty students in Grades two–six in the Minneapolis/St. Paul metropolitan area participated in this study.

Treatments

Three data utilization procedures were compared: (1) teacher judgment with weekly measurement (WMTJ); (2) teacher judgment with daily measurement and graphing (DMTJ); and (3) data decision rules with daily measurement and graphing (DMDB). Each teacher was randomly assigned and rotated through two of the three data utilization conditions.

Dependent Measures

Two types of word lists were developed: (1) a list of 100 words that represented a random sample of words from seven basal readers, Grades Primer–six (Harris and Jacobson 1972); and (2) seven lists of 100 words each that represented a random sample of words from each grade level. Students were pretested on both types of lists and were placed for instruction in grade-level spelling tests where they were spelling at a rate of 15–29 letters in correct sequence/minute. At three weeks and six weeks one three-minute dictation from the primer–grade six master list and three three-minute dictations from the grade-level list were administered to each student as a post test.

Procedures

Once students were placed in a grade-level spelling list, teachers were given the hundred-word list for that grade and asked to teach as many words as they could, in any way they wished, for the next three weeks. During this time, whenever they gave a spelling test (daily or weekly) it was a random sample of twenty-five words from the hundred-word list.

The procedures in the three treatments were as follows.

Weekly Measurement Teacher Judgment (WMTJ)

This group most closely approximated the usual teaching-testing system used to teach spelling in schools today. Teachers taught spelling every day for fifteen minutes. At the end of the week, a three-minute spelling test was given to each student and the teacher corrected it.

Based on the student's performance, it was possible for the teacher to evaluate the instructional strategies used that week and make changes where he or she thought it appropriate. The teacher kept a record of the spelling strategies used and noted changes accordingly.

Daily Measurement Teacher Judgment (DMTJ)

The teachers in this group taught spelling for ten minutes each day and administered a daily spelling test to each student. The teacher corrected the test and plotted the student's score on a graph. Again, the teacher decided whether the student's performance was sufficient to maintain the same instructional strategies or whether to implement a program change. The teacher kept a record of the spelling strategies used and noted changes on the graph.

Daily Measurement Data-Based Decisions (DMDB)

The instruction and measurement procedures for this group were similar to the DMTJ group. However, instead of the teachers making the decision as to when to change their instructional strategies, a set of guidelines was developed for them to follow. Specifically, a three-week aimline was set for each student. The aimline began at the point representing the intersection of the student's median spelling score and Day 2 of the first three days of the program. A 30 percent increase per week in letters spelled correctly over this initial performance was used as the criterion for drawing the aimline. Whenever the student's performance fell below this aimline for three consecutive days, or conversely, was above the aimline for three consecutive days, the teacher was asked to change instructional strategies. In addition, a new aimline was drawn at this time, parallel to the original one and beginning at the point representing the median score of the three scores below (or above) the original aimline. The teacher also kept a record of the spelling strategies used and noted changes on a graph.

Results

The results were analyzed along two dimensions. First, pre-planned between-group comparisons were implemented using t tests to determine whether differences existed between the three treatment groups at either three weeks or six weeks. The first analysis involved between-teacher comparisons. A consistent difference appeared between the frequency of measurement conditions, daily vs. weekly. These results are consistent for rate and accuracy (percent correct), for both letters spelled in correct sequence and whole words spelled correctly from grade level lists, when teachers or students are the unit of analysis. The comparisons between the use of decision rule and teacher judgment revealed no differences.

When the post-test words are comprised of a random sample of all possible words from across the six grades (Grand Master lists), only the rate data show daily measurement to be superior. In other words, it is quite likely that when performance is measured on a daily basis, students will write significantly more words per minute than when they are measured once a week, whether these words are from their grade level or above; however, they will be more accurate only on words from their grade level.

A second analysis of the data involved a within-teacher, within-student comparison. Since each teacher was randomly assigned to rotate through two of the three treatment conditions, some teachers (and their students) participated in DMDB and DMTJ, some in DMDB and WMTJ, and some in DMTJ and WMTJ. Results show that the students of teachers who used decision rules for three weeks and their own judgment for three weeks achieved more when the decision rules were in use. If measurement occurred on a daily basis and decision rules were used, students wrote both more letters in correct sequence and more words per minute, more accurately, than if measurement was on a weekly basis and teachers decided when changes should be made. When the only difference was in data utilization (i.e., all the students were being measured on a daily basis), students wrote more letters in correct sequence per minute when decision rules were used than when teacher judgment was used. However, no differences were found in accuracy (percent correct) of letters spelled correct in sequence or in rate or accuracy of words spelled correct. There also was no difference in student performance when teachers used their own judgment to alter programs regardless of whether the student was measured on a daily or weekly basis.

Discussion

The results of the present study provide clear evidence that teachers are more effective when they measure student performance daily rather than weekly. The results are not as clear with respect to the contrast of a specific decision rule with teacher judgment. While the trend appears to favor the decision rule treatment, sufficient evidence is not provided in this study to categorically rule out or include either component, as presently constituted, in a formative evaluation system. Thus, the present results, while confirming the effects for daily measurement found by Bohannon (1975), are somewhat at variance with previous research findings with respect to the efficacy of the decision rule as a data utilization strategy.

In the present study teachers in the teacher judgment treatment were provided only minimal training in data analysis for the purpose of making program decisions while teachers in the decision rule group were told only to watch the aimline and the daily data points to determine when a program change was needed. The simplicity and ease of implementation of these procedures made them particularly attractive candidates for inclusion in a formative evaluation system. A fruitful area of research with respect to the development of an effective formative evaluation system may be to test alternative data utilization approaches that would include more intensive teacher training and monitoring of performance.

REFERENCES

Agard, J. A.; Veldman, D. J.; Kaufman, M. J.; Semmel, M. I.; and Walters, P. B. *Teacher Rating Scale: An Instrument of the PRIME Instrument Battery.* Baltimore, Md.: University Park Press, 1978.

Asher, S. R. "The Influence of Race and Sex on Children's Sociometric Choices Across the School Year." Unpublished manuscript, University of Illinois, 1973.

Bohannon, R. "Direct and Daily Measurement Procedures in the Identification and Treatment of Reading Behaviors of Children in Special Education." Ph.D. dissertation, University of Washington, 1975.

Dunn, L. M., and Markwardt, F. C. *Peabody Individual Achievement Test.* Circle Pines, Minn.: American Guidance Service, 1970.

Finn, P. "Computer-Aided Description of Mature Word Choices in Writing." In *Evaluating Writing: Describing, Measuring, Judging,* edited by C. Cooper and L. Odell. Urbana, Ill.: National Council of Teachers of English, 1977.

Hammill, D. D., and Larsen, S. C. *The Test of Written Language*. Austin, Tex.: PRO-ED, 1978.

Harris, A. J., and Jacobson, M. D. *Basic Elementary Reading Vocabularies*, New York: Macmillan, 1972.

Harris, F. C., and Lahey, B. B. "A Method for Combining Occurrence and Nonoccurrence Interobserver Agreement Scores." *Behavior Research and Therapy* 11 (1978):523–26.

Hunt, K. W. "Recent Measures in Syntactic Development." *Elementary English* 42 (November 1966):732–39.

Karlsen, B.; Madden, R.; and Gardner, E. F. *Stanford Diagnostic Reading Test* (Green level, Form B). New York: Harcourt Brace Jovanovich, 1975.

Larsen, S. C., and Hammill, D. D. *Test of Written Spelling*. Austin, Tex.: PRO-ED (Empiric Press), 1976.

Lee, L. L., and Canter, S. M. "Developmental Sentence Scoring." *Journal of Speech and Hearing Disorders* 36 (1971):335–40.

Madden, R.; Gardner, E.; Rudman, H.; Karlsen, B.; and Merwin, J. *Stanford Achievement Test* (Primary Level III). New York: Harcourt Brace Jovanovich, 1973.

Madden, R.; Gardner, E. F.; Rudman, H. C.; Karlsen, B.; and Merwin, J. C. *Stanford Achievement Test*. New York: Harcourt Brace Jovanovich, 1978.

Moreno, J. L. *Who Shall Survive? A New Approach to the Problem of Human Interrelations*. Washington, D.C.: Nervous and Mental Disease Publishing Company, 1934.

Myklebust, H. R. *Development and Disorders of Written Language*. New York: Grune & Stratton, 1965.

Page, E. B. "Analyzing Student Essays by Computer." *Internal Review of Education* 14 (1968):216–17.

Slotnick, L. B. "Toward a Theory of Computer Essay Grading." *Journal of Educational Measurement* 9, 4 (1972):253.

White, O. R., and Haring, N. G. *Exceptional Teaching: A Multimedia Training Package*. Columbus, Ohio: Merrill, 1976.

Woodcock, R. W. *Woodcock Reading Mastery Tests* (Form A). Circle Pines, Minn.: American Guidance Service, 1973.

BACKGROUNDS TO EDUCATION

10

Toward the Demystification of the Clinical Electroencephalogram

Drake D. Duane

IT IS BOTH INTERESTING AND ENLIGHTENING to review the origins of the physiologic investigation of electrical activity of the central nervous system. Our story begins in a large London amphitheater. It is August 4, 1875. The Section of Physiology of the British Medical Society is holding its meetings. In the chair, Dr. Burdon Sanderson presides. Surrounded by his contemporaries, who lean forward in their seats, a young British physician steps forward to explain his work involving the so-called galvanic currents that he has recorded from the brains of animals. Applying one electrode to the skull and the other to the surface (cortex or gray matter) of the brain of rabbits and monkeys, he relates that to his delight he is able to record variations in the galvanic currents, and this suggests that electrical activity emanates from the surface of the brains of these animals. He shows his colleagues that as the animal rotates its head and chews, brain activity can be recorded. Furthermore, in the brain area said to be involved with the control of the eyelids, when the opposite eye is stimulated with light, the response is altered.

This young physician from Liverpool, Dr. Richard Caton (1875) has, for the first time, reported on the successful recording of electrical activity from the surface of the brain in animals. This marks the beginning of the recording of electrical activity of the central nervous system. Before that time, the Italian physiologists Volta and Galvani had noted that electrical activity could be recorded from the nerves of the extremities in animals.

Fifty years were to elapse before these rudimentary studies on animals were to be replicated in the intact human nervous system. In this instance, the place is the laboratory of a German psychiatrist who is intrigued with the possibility of recording the predominant electrical activity of the brain through the intact skull without injuring the patient. The psychiatrist was Hans Berger, and his patient was his son Klaus,

My thanks to Drs. F. W. Sharbrough, B. F. Westmoreland, J. J. Stockard, and J. D. Grabow of the Mayo Clinic EEG Laboratory for their kind assistance in the preparation of this manuscript.

aged fifteen years. A single pair of electrodes were attached over the central part of the head, and a rhythmic activity of approximately 10 cycles per second was recorded. The original recording was performed in 1924, but it was five years later before the cautious Dr. Berger (1929) would publish this material. His report, which was greeted with skepticism by some, was followed by a flurry of studies in the 1930s investigating the nature of the so-called Berger rhythms of the brain. These confirmed the validity of the Berger study.

Soon it became necessary to apply specific terms to describe these background rhythmic and semirhythmic activities as recorded by the instruments available in that day. Adrian and Matthews (1934) subsequently designated the Berger rhythm as the "alpha" rhythm and noted that it was maximal at the back part of the brain where visual activity was known to be localized.

Here, surely, was the description of a link between a person's central nervous system and the external environment. What was all of this to signify? Berger, as a psychiatrist who believed that mind and brain were one, hoped that in persons with mental derangement or various psychiatric disorders the pattern of the electroencephalogram, as he chose to call this recording, would shed light on their personality characteristics. Since that time, the hope that a link could be drawn between recordable electrical events of the brain and behavior has repeatedly been expressed, and experiment after experiment has been conducted in this pursuit. As we shall see, over the years various alterations have taken place in the technique of electroencephalography and in the variety of rhythms and patterns of discharges described and types of responses to stimuli obtained. These changes stirred controversy and speculation over whether they would lend themselves to a description of the behavioral characteristics, traits, or innate capabilities of the individual from whom the recording was being obtained.

Dr. Grey Walter, like Adrian and Caton also from Great Britain, found that in the presence of structural disease of the brain (brain tumors), slow-wave activity could be seen that was much slower than the alpha rhythm. Alpha rhythms had been found to have a rate of 8 to 13 cycles per second, and for these slower frequencies — 1 to 3 cycles per second — he chose the term "delta" rhythm. Walter was also instrumental in the decision that frequencies that were slightly faster than the delta rhythms and slower than the alpha rhythms — ranging from 4 to 7 cycles per second — would be referred to as "theta" rhythms. Walter (1936) was the first to record and localize brain tumors by using the electroencephalogram or EEG. This was the first hint of what was to become a recurring pattern in the history of the EEG. What would be advanced as being potentially useful for a description of human behavior would prove to be of value in the diagnosis of known structural and physiologic disturbances of the nervous system.

Figure 10.1 compares the appearances of the basic rhythms observed on the EEG. There are four, the fastest, or beta rhythm (more than 13 cycles per second), having been added to the original three—the alpha (8 to 13 cycles per second), the theta (4 to 7 cycles per second), and the delta (1 to 3 cycles per second).

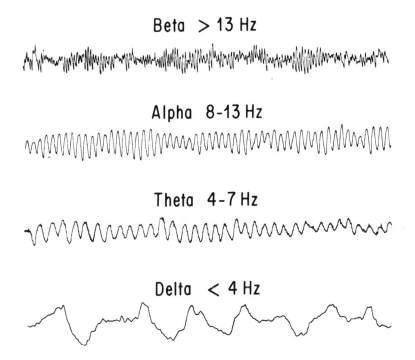

FIGURE 10.1. The four major rhythms observed in the resting electroencephalogram as denoted by their frequency or cycles per second (hertz, Hz). From J. R. Daube, B. A. Sandok, T. J. Reagan, and B. F. Westmoreland, "Integrated Neuroscience for the Clinician: Systems and Levels," in *Medical Neurosciences: An Approach to Anatomy, Pathology, and Physiology by Systems and Levels,* edited by B. A. Sandork and J. R. Daube. (Boston: Little, Brown, 1977); by permission.

We must bear in mind, as we review how the EEG is used, that within each age group, patterns emerge that are seen in asymptomatic persons. Also, these basic rhythm patterns vary considerably within each age group. Some patterns may even appear somewhat peculiar when contrasted with those seen in age-matched controls, but these unusual patterns are not necessarily associated with any definite pathology. They are simply the idiosyncrasies of that individual's EEG and fall onto those edges of the spectrum of recorded activity within the somewhat arbitrarily defined "normal range." Figure 10.2 gives an example of some of the basic background activities seen from birth through adulthood, with an analysis of the amplitude, or height, of these wave forms and their predominance in the tracing within each age group (Corbin and Bickford 1955).

Since these beginnings, it can be stated that there is a range of electroencephalographically recorded activity that can be construed as normal. That is, it has a very low probability of being associated with any underlying disease of the nervous system. Then there are other types of

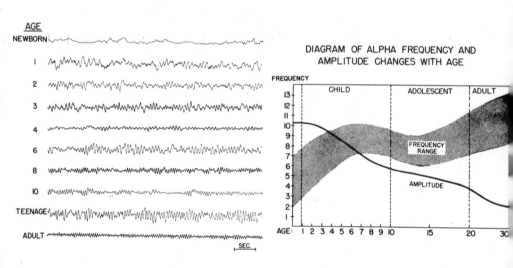

FIGURE 10.2. Basic background activity, or alpha activity, as typified at various ages, appears on the left half of the illustration. Note that with time there is a change in the appearance of both height and frequency (cycles per second) and the regularity of the rhythm in the resting electroencephalogram. On the right, the dark stippled area illustrates the predominant frequency range observed at each age; the line indicates the relative amplitude, or height, of these wave forms in the electroencephalogram, again related to age. Modified from R. G. Bickford and H. M. Keith, "Electroencephalography in Pediatrics," *Quarterly Review of Pediatrics* 10 (1955): 69–78.

activity that are clearly beyond the limits of normal, and for these one can rightfully use the term "abnormal." That is, there is a relatively high probability that something is wrong clinically with the nervous system.

As a tool, the EEG can thus be used for diagnostic purposes to determine the presence of either structural derangement of the nervous system that has secondarily affected its physiology or primary physiologic disturbance of the nervous system, as in the case with the epilepsies. In the epilepsies or, as they are commonly called, seizure disorders, the EEG becomes very important in defining the nature of the seizure disorder. The EEG in the seizure-prone patient determines for the physician whether it is necessary to carry out other diagnostic studies in order to define the cause of the abnormality, and it assists the clinician in selecting the most appropriate medication in helping his or her patient maintain good health.

In addition to this diagnostic aspect, we must separate out the other aspect of EEG, that of investigation. In many instances, investigative EEG is utilized for research purposes, and in many instances it is based on the premise that by more careful inspection of the EEG — if not by the naked eye then with the help of contemporary electronic devices — one may be better able to approximate the physiologic basis of behavior.

Beginning in the 1930s and progressing rapidly through the 1940s and into the 1950s, it became clear that sharply contoured wave forms, which are called spikes or sharp waves, suggest that the affected person has a high probability of experiencing clinical seizures. These seizures have been classified into two major varieties on the basis of the pattern of the EEG, namely, generalized or localized (focal) (Ajmone Marsan 1965; Commission on Terminology 1964). When the epileptiform discharge is generalized (Figure 10.3), this implies that from the very outset the abnormal wave forms appear simultaneously on both sides of the brain. The clinical manifestation — the behavior of the patient — might be a brief arrest of activity, which is referred to as petit mal or absence, or it might be in the form of a grand mal or generalized convulsion. The other type of abnormality, referred to as localized or focal or, in the official nomenclature, partial, suggests that one area of the nervous system is physiologically altered and that this produces a stereotyped form of spell (Figure 10.4). These types of alterations may have various manifestations, depending on where in the brain the seizure focus is located. Hallucinations may occur involving smell, taste, formed or unformed visual experiences, sounds, voices, re-enactment of prior experiences, the conjuring up of emotions, and the like. All of these are subjective experiences reminiscent of activities that are part of conscious thought. These loci of abnormal electrical activity have provided insights into the basic functioning or underlying activities of certain regions of the central nervous system. These experiments of nature — as well as those of man, such as exploring by stimulation the surface of the brain as was done by Penfield and Jasper (1954) in the late 1940s and throughout the 1950s — were important in the evolution of knowledge of brain function.

It was the existence of the secondarily generalized seizure patterns that led to the surgical procedures carried out in the 1950s and 1960s in which the great commissure between the two hemispheres of the brain, called the corpus callosum, was severed in an effort to suppress seizure activity. These operations provided man-made experiments of the bisected human brain (Sperry, Gazzaniga, and Bogen 1969). Studies of patients who have had this operation have led to much information about right and left brain function and also to much speculation regarding its

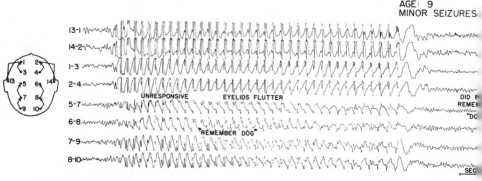

FIGURE 10.3. Electroencephalographic pattern of a true, or classic, petit mal seizure — that is, a generalized seizure, caused here by overbreathing — as documented by the electroencephalogram. The predominant clinical manifestation is that of a brief detachment from the environment. Note that the child is unresponsive during the appearance of the three-per-second spike-and-wave form. The eyelids are noted to flutter and a technician says "Remember the word dog"; after the spell is over electrographically, the child cannot recall what had been said. The line drawing on the left shows what the various numbers refer to with regard to brain areas; the odd numbers represent the left half of the brain and each channel then alternates left-right, left-right, and so on from front to back. From R. G. Bickford and H. M. Keith, "Electroencephalography in Pediatrics," *Quarterly Review of Pediatrics* 10 (1955): 69–78; by permission of J. B. Lippincott Company.

relevance to individual learning style. That is, some persons may be more dependent on processes that have been associated with left-hemispheric function, such as behaviors that are well ordered and sequential, as opposed to the less well-ordered and "freer" activity that has been associated with right-brain function. These studies have also told us much about the language capacities, in the adult, of the two sides of the brain (Zaidel 1978).

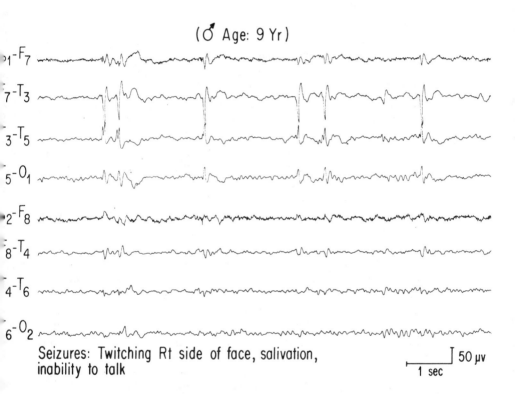

(♂ Age: 9 Yr)

Seizures: Twitching Rt side of face, salivation, inability to talk

50 μν
1 sec

FIGURE 10.4. Spike or potentially epileptiform discharge emanating from the left temporal region. During the episode, muscle twitching was noted about the opposite side of the body in the area of the face, associated with salivation and inability to talk. This type of seizure discharge represents some acquired dysfunction of the brain, whereas that in the preceding figure is apt to be under hereditary influence. Note that the top four channels use odd numbers; they represent areas in the left side of the head in the frontal and temporal regions and then extending to the back or occipital region. The lower four channels represent homologous areas on the right.

APPLICATION OF EEG TO BEHAVIORAL STUDIES

Because of its ease of use, the EEG became part of the clinical neurologist's armamentarium in evaluating youngsters who are not succeeding in school. An EEG might be done to ascertain whether a focal or generalized seizure disorder is present. For example, if the student was experiencing recurrent absence spells, these spells might interfere with the acquisition of new learning and in this way contribute to academic underachievement.

Conventionally, routine EEG is carried out when the subject is awake. However, the person may be fatigued and spontaneously fall asleep; the clinician may also choose to have the patient become fatigued by sleep deprivation so that spontaneous sleep is apt to occur, or he may provide a sedative compound. This is done because some seizure patterns are more apt to be manifest in the tracing during sleep. Other maneuvers are also commonly carried out during routine EEG, such as the performance of mental arithmetic, to observe its effect on the background rhythms, which should be suppressed in their amplitude; over-breathing, which in many persons, particularly if they have been fasting, causes an increase in the overall amplitude and a slowing of the background activity, and in some instances may precipitate certain types of seizure discharges; and the use of flashing lights while the subject is awake, which may precipitate what is known as a stimulus-sensitive seizure.

In some persons being investigated because of selective academic underachievement, one may particularly wish to have the subject read, write, or perform calculations. In rare instances, the EEG may, under such circumstances, show a stimulus-sensitive seizure pattern that appears to be under genetic influence. In these cases unequivocal abnormalities occur, as illustrated in Figures 10.5 through 10.7. Such specific seizures would limit the individual's capability of learning to read, of expressing himself or herself in writing, or of performing calculations. However, these types of seizures are extremely rare. Furthermore, even as a group, seizures are not that common: the probability in the population of the occurrence of a seizure at least once in a person's life is estimated to be 1 in 200 (Robb 1965).

The EEG reveals more than the basic alpha activity described by Berger and Adrian, the slow-wave delta and theta rhythms described by Walter, and the sharply contoured waves of seizure discharges, whether generalized or focal. Variations of the above patterns occur, and their significance in clinical medicine is also of interest. In the period from the mid-1930s to the early 1960s, the Gibbses (1941, 1950, 1952), who re-

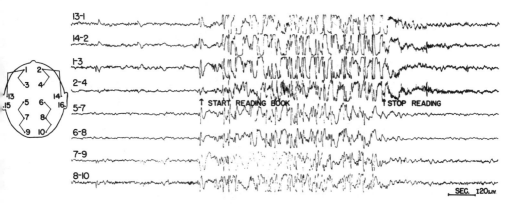

FIGURE 10.5. Seizure discharge induced by reading. This is a generalized sharp-wave discharge that is precipitated by the act of reading and disappears when reading stops. Each channel alternates between left and right, from the front to the back of the head. Seizures precipitated by reading are very uncommon.

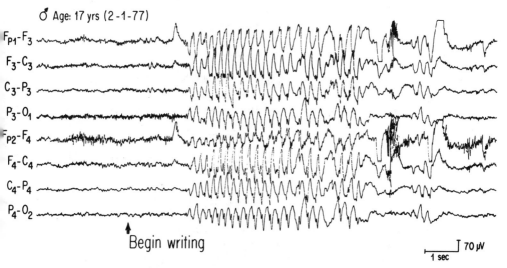

FIGURE 10.6. Seizure disorder precipitated by the act of writing. Note that there is a latency between the onset of the act of writing and the appearance of the seizure discharge. This type of seizure, like the reading seizure discharge previously illustrated, represents reflex forms of seizure disorders. The top four channels represent the left half of the brain, the bottom four channels the right half of the brain. From F. W. Sharbrough, unpublished data.

corded thousands of EEGs, noted a wide variety of patterns, for which they provided numerous terms and accurate descriptions.

Again the question is, however, what is the significance of these findings? Do these variations in the EEG reflect some personality trait or physical symptom affecting the individual? This was what the Gibbses suspected, for they noted that in association with some irregular patterns, the patients complained of abdominal cramps or headache. At other times such records were obtained from persons who had been involved in unusual behavior, at times antisocial or at least socially inappropriate (Gibbs and Gibbs 1964). One of the variations obtained on the resting EEG, called the psychomotor variant, is illustrated in Figure 10.8. These wave forms in the theta range, which have a notched,

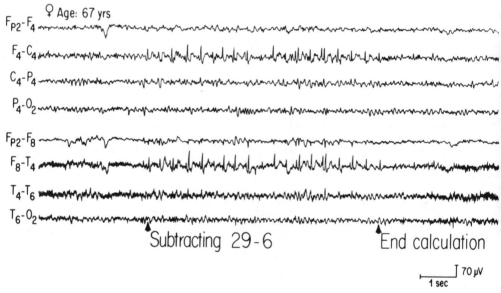

FIGURE 10.7. Electroencephalogram of a sixty-seven-year-old woman in whom seizure discharges (spikes) developed during the act of mental calculation. These originated in the right frontal area. Note that the numbers on the left are all even numbers; thus this tracing represents a selection of recorded electrodes (montage) entirely from the right half of the brain. Previous recordings had shown that there was no similar activity on the left. This too is an unusual type of seizure discharge and is unlikely to be of hereditary origin. From D. O. Wiebers, B. F. Westmoreland, and D. W. Klass, "EEG Activation and Mathematical Calculation," *Neurology* (Minneapolis), in press; by permission of Harcourt Brace Jovanovich, Inc.

somewhat sharply contoured, semirhythmic appearance, were noted by the Gibbses in a number of patients' EEGs but not examined by them personally.

Thus, the question was raised, "Do these wave patterns tell us why these symtoms have occurred?" The answer is not clear. Although Jack Ruby, the man who killed Lee Harvey Oswald, the alleged assassin of the late President Kennedy, had this wave pattern in his EEG, it is not clear whether this was related in any way to his behavior. The problem with these variations from the norm — a term that usually indicates that

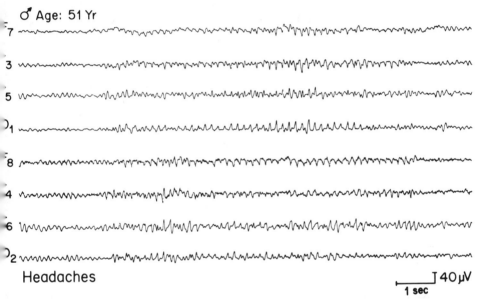

FIGURE 10.8. Electroencephalogram demonstrating the so-called psychomotor variant pattern, as described by Gibbs and Gibbs, in a fifty-one-year-old man who complained of headaches. The predominant feature is periodic bursts of somewhat sharply contoured semirhythmic medium-amplitude wave forms of six to seven cycles per second seen throughout the tracing but most commonly in the temporal area (designated by T). The upper four channels refer to the left half of the brain from front to back; the bottom four represent the right half of the brain, also from front to back. Some have claimed that this type of electroencephalographic pattern may be associated with behavioral disturbance. This appears not to be the case (see text). From B. F. Westmoreland, "EEG in the Evaluation of Headaches," in *Current Practice of Clinical Electroencephalography*, edited by D. W. Klass and D. D. Daly (New York: Raven Press, 1975), pp. 381–94; by permission.

the wave pattern occurs in less than 50 percent of the general population — is that they lack diagnostic specificity. Many EEGs may show these patterns, and a large number of persons who have such patterns may be described as having some of the traits mentioned above, but this does not necessarily mean that the wave form is causally related to the behavior. Before the EEG can be called "diagnostic," one must have the sense that there is virtually a one-to-one correlation between the EEG pattern and a specific behavior.

Other patterns that have been regarded as suspect include the so-called phantom spike-and-wave pattern, which we have found is not associated with any clinical seizure problem (Thomas and Klass 1968), and the small sharp spikes that occur in a number of asymptomatic persons (Reiher and Klass 1968). Indeed, my own sleeping EEG shows these small sharp spikes, and to the best of my knowledge I have never experienced a clinical seizure.

Of all the variations from the norm observed on the resting EEG, two patterns have been thought to occur more often in children who demonstrate academic underachievement despite adequate intelligence. They are the 14 and 6 positive spikes and occipital slow waves. The first of these two patterns tends to arise from the back, or posterior, temporal region of the brain and with asymmetric amplitude — that is, they are higher on one side than on the other (Figure 10.9). Studies by Hughes (1968) with statistical treatment of the data from borderline and unequivocal learning disabled students (using their learning quotient parameter) suggested a higher frequency of occurrence of these 14 and 6 positive spike patterns in that population. However, the real question is whether the pattern is predictive of that disorder. The answer with regard to this profile is that it is not, for at least 30 to 35 percent of the general young adult population may demonstrate occasional bursts of these 14 and 6 positive spikes and have no apparent problem in educability (Reiher and Klass 1968). Similarly, no differential frequency of occurrence of this EEG pattern is noted when delinquent and nondelinquent populations are compared (Wiener, Delano, and Klass 1966). Thus, although the pattern and its frequency of occurrence may reinforce the suspicion in a given person that there is a physiologic basis or concomitant to learning underachievement, these findings do not prove a causal relationship.

Hughes (1971) also inspected periodic slow waves in the delta range — that is, 1 to 3 cycles per second — in the same population of youngsters. These waves are most prominent in the back portion of the brain, and they vary in the consistency with which they occur on the resting EEG. This pattern, too, was thought to occur more frequently in learning disabled children. However, one must also take into account maturational changes, for these same periodic slow-wave patterns occur not uncommonly in children between the ages of ten and fourteen years and are signs neither of disease nor of any dysfunction in cognitive ability or learning skill. Once more, the EEG pattern fails the test of being able to predict learning underachievement and therefore cannot be

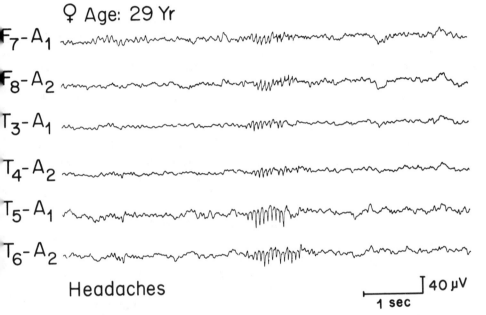

FIGURE 10.9. Appearance of fourteen and six positive spikes in the electroencephalogram of a twenty-nine-year-old woman whose chief complaint was headaches. The arrangement of the electrodes is from frontal to temporal, alternating left and right, with the reference being to the ipsilateral ear (A_1 being the left ear, A_2 being the right ear). Note that the pattern is seen best in the bottom two channels. It consists of a frequency of fourteen cycles per second but may occur in slower frequencies such as six per second. They are downward-deflecting forms or have a positive deflection. Because of their somewhat sharp contour they have been referred to as spikes, but they are not to be confused with spikes associated with seizures. Some have claimed that this EEG pattern may be more common in persons who have educational problems, but this appears not to be the case (see text). From B. F. Westmoreland, "EEG in the Evaluation of Headaches." In *Current Practice of Clinical Electroencephalography*, edited by D. W. Klass and D. D. Daly (New York: Raven Press, 1975), pp. 381–94; by permission.

called diagnostic. That is, of course, important. If I bring my child to a neurologist or you bring yours, and an EEG is performed, we want to know what the test will tell us is wrong or different about our child and what treatment that particular specialist can offer us. On the basis of data from routine resting EEGs, thus far nothing can be said is of diagnostic significance pertaining to the area of learning disability other than the presence or absence of structural or physiologic disease of the nervous system. This is not to say that such information is not valuable, *but it means that any other pattern on the EEG does not permit a diagnosis with respect to educability; nor does it provide a physician any basis for prescribing medication.* Of course, this fact does not exclude physicians from being an important part of the evaluation team. Not only can physicians be quite sensitive in their own right, but some physicians themselves have children with learning disabilities and in that respect become even more sensitive to the needs of children who are under-achieving academically.

But even in the routine clinical setting the EEG has other uses than the ones already described. Two applications in particular have gained ascendance since the mid-1950s. One is referred to as averaged evoked responses and the other, frequency or spectral analysis.

AVERAGE EVOKED RESPONSES

The term "average" here implies that several samples are taken, from which the mean or average response is obtained. The number of stimuli may range from a few dozen to a few thousand. The term "evoked response" suggests that something has stimulated the central nervous system and that there is an electrophysiologic concomitant. Although various stimuli may be employed, the two most common involve the visual or the auditory apparatus. Responses to touch, or somatosensory responses, are increasing in use. In visual studies, some form of light—white or colored, steady or flashing, or patterned—is used and the responses are simultaneously recorded on magnetic tape. On replay, the response to the signal, which might have eluded the naked eye, can now be seen as standing out against the background, which fluctuates and becomes erased; and an averaged pattern may be seen on an oscilloscope screen or on a computer write-out. When the visual system is being used, the term "visual evoked response" is applied, and when sound is used, "auditory evoked response" is the term commonly employed. Both of these are long-latency responses—that is, they occur several milliseconds after the stimulus (flash or click) — and they are thought to represent the response of the surface of the brain to the stimuli. They are, however, dependent on the intactness of the peripheral receptors — that is, the eyes and ears.

Various studies of hyperactive and of reading disabled children have been carried out with the use of these visual and auditory evoked responses. Although some have been suggestive of a correlation, none has given consistent results, particularly when one study is contrasted with another (Conners 1970; Preston, Guthrie, and Childs 1974; Symann-Louett, Gascon, Matsumiya, and Lombroso 1977; Weber and Omenn 1977). Several difficulties are encountered with such studies: (1) when light is used, a minor shift of the eye by the subject can alter the response recorded by the EEG; (2) variations occur on the basis of age; and (3) data gathered from a group of subjects may show an "abnormality" that actually represents the results from a few persons in the group who are beyond the normal limits but that is not representative of all members of the group. Although the results of these studies are somewhat better in their predictive value and in their correlation with, in particular, reading underachievement, they are not diagnostic.

Here again, in the course of attempting to make behavioral inferences from a physiologic response, it was found that known structural or physiologic disease of the nervous system could be better defined with these methods. Visual evoked responses have proved to be of immeasurable value in clarifying the presence of the demyelinating condition known as multiple sclerosis. The response obtained is referred to as the P-100, meaning that it is positive and that it occurs 100 milliseconds after the stimulus. It may show prolonged latency, and this suggests that something has happened to the optic nerve apparatus (Figure 10.10). Pattern stimuli provide a far more stable response than the response to a flash of light.

Auditory evoked responses have gained importance in the early detection of peripheral hearing loss, which is known to delay the acquisition of speech and higher forms of language such as reading and writing (Cody and Bickford 1965). In this instance, early identification permits intervention, such as amplifying the sound or providing special educational services for the young child. The stimuli that are used vary from laboratory to laboratory, but short clicks usually provide a response that is reproducible within the same individual and from which norms may be established for various age ranges. The value of these averaging techniques (visual and auditory) is that, when properly performed, they provide a stable response — that is, it does not become degraded, and it can be inspected readily and repeatedly. As a result of studies on normal individuals, normative data have now been firmly established; thus, when a variation of the norm occurs in a given individual, unequivocal dysfunction of the nervous system can be defined.

Analysis of auditory evoked responses in recent years has been extended to very minute impulses that originate in the lower part of the brain, or brainstem, and ascend upward. These short- or early-latency responses (observed shortly after the stimulus of sound, usually a click) or brainstem auditory evoked responses tell us of the functioning of the auditory pathways in this region of the nervous system (Picton, Hillyard, Krausz, and Galambos 1974). Figure 10.11 illustrates the components of the brainstem auditory evoked responses and the regions from

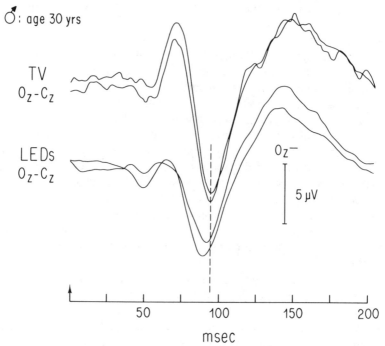

FIGURE 10.10. Visual evoked response showing a positive downward-deflecting wave form recorded from the back midline region of the head to the center midline region from both a television stimulus (TV) and a light-emitting diode stimulus (LEDs). The positive wave form is seen at approximately 100 milliseconds and has been referred to as the P-100. This response is commonly used in assessing the function of the optic nerve, which could be altered in multiple sclerosis, trauma, tumor, or similar physical dysfunction of this nerve for vision. In contrast to the pattern demonstrated in the preceding figure, well-established normative data can be provided, so that specific abnormalities may be defined.

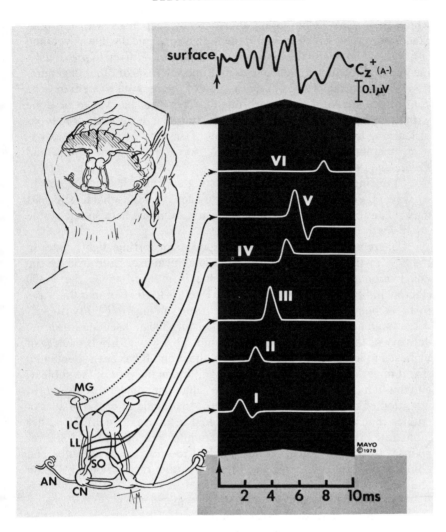

FIGURE 10.11. Minute potentials of short latency from sound stimuli in the form of clicks delivered to the ear. These reflect lower brain or brain stem physiology. Each of the compound wave forms reflects a given level of the auditory system in the brainstem. This study has been useful in the definition of physiologic dysfunction at the level of the brainstem. AN = auditory nerve; CN = cochlear nucleus; SO = superior olive; LL = lateral lemniscus; IC = inferior colliculis; MG = medial geniculate. From J. J. Stockard, J. E. Stockard, and F. W. Sharbrough, "Nonpathologic Factors Influencing Brainstem Auditory Evoked Potentials," *American Journal of Electroencephalographic Technology* 18 (1978): 177–209; by permission of Raven Press.

which they occur. Comparing short-latency responses with the mid-range responses, which are not thought to be of clinical value as yet, and contrasting them with the long-latency responses referred to previously, the presence of such conditions as multiple sclerosis or other degenerative or structural diseases in that region of the nervous system may be confirmed (Stockard and Sharbrough 1978). What has yet to be done with these early-latency responses is to study the thesis that some types of learning disabilities may depend on brainstem mechanisms, as has been postulated by de Quirós (1976), Ayres (1972), and Frank and Levinson (1973).

Yingling (1979) described interesting asymmetries in somatosensory average evoked responses among dyslexic persons that he suggests may relate to disturbances in transmission from one hemisphere to the other via the corpus callosum.

There are two types of these responses occurring slightly later in the EEG, which, although not in general clinical use, have aroused the imagination of neurophysiologists. One is referred to as the P-300 (Picton and Hillyard 1974). Again, the P refers to the fact that the wave form is positive (which, by convention, means it is downward-deflecting), and the 300 indicates that it occurs 300 milliseconds after the delivery of the stimulus of light or sound. This wave form is usually of highest amplitude in the parietal area of the brain. It has been speculated that it might represent conscious recognition on the part of the subject, and thus it has come to be known as the "aha" phenomenon. The level of attention of the subject is another factor that could alter the results of studies that make use of average evoked responses. Figure 10.12 demonstrates that there need not be a stimulus preceding the P-300 response; thus, it is not necessarily linked to an external stimulus and could instead reflect something going on within the individual (Picton and Hillyard 1974).

An even later-occurring wave form, which deflects slowly upward (DC shift) and occurs over several entire seconds after the stimulus (and thus subsequent to the P-300 response), is the contingent negative variation or CNV (Walter, Cooper, Aldridge, McCallum, and Winter 1964). Some investigators have called this the expectancy or E wave. The supposition is that this represents a reflection on the EEG of some expectancy on the part of the individual with regard to a coming event. Figure 10.13 demonstrates the CNV. However, its importance and true meaning, both physiologically and behaviorly, is in dispute. Some have suggested that the length of time for the occurrence of the various evoked responses (most commonly the visual evoked response) or the pattern of the P-300 or the CNV response may be an index of intelligence that is independent of cultural factors and thus represents a pure physiologic test of basic intelligence (Ertl and Schafer 1969; John, Karmel, Corning, Easton, Brown, Ahn, John, Harmony, Prichep, Toro, Gerson, Bartlett, Thatcher, Kaye, Valdes, and Schwartz 1977). However, the use of these derivatives of the EEG as so-called neurometric devices is at this juncture premature. These data are not only held in dispute, but if the study were being done on my child, I would not allow the results obtained to replace the more conventional tests of academic potential or my own clinical impression as to the intelligence of the child. Although I am a neurologist and am interested in the functioning of the

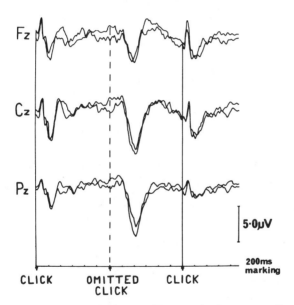

FIGURE 10.12. Three channels show auditory evoked responses from the front midline, center, and back midline portions of the head. Clicks were presented regularly every 1.1 second, and occasionally the click was omitted. The subject was asked to count the number of omissions. The deeply contoured wave form has been referred to as the P-300 because it is positive and occurs 300 milliseconds after the stimulus. The presence of that response without there having been a preceding click illustrates that the anticipation of the click is enough to produce the response and that it need not be a direct response to sound. From T. W. Picton and S. A. Hillyard, "Human Auditory Evoked Potentials. II. Effects of Attention," *Electroencephalography and Clinical Neurophysiology* 36 (1974): 191–200; by permission of Elsevier/North Holland.

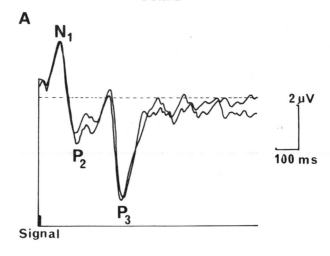

A

N₁

P₂

P₃

2 µV

100 ms

Signal

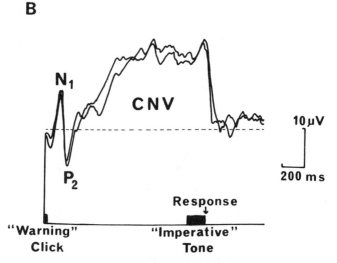

B

N₁

C N V

P₂

Response

10 µV

200 ms

"Warning"   "Imperative"
Click   Tone

FIGURE 10.13. In A, following a signal, a P-300 response is observed. In B, following the P_2, there is a slow, positive build-up (upward deflection) of the wave forms labeled CNV, which refers to contingent negative variation or, as some have called it, the E or expectancy wave. This is thought to represent the fact that the subject, who has been warned by the preceding click that there will be a tone appearing to which a response must be given, makes a cerebral electrical response in anticipation of the next stimulus. The true significance of this wave form, however, is in debate. It is not a technique used in routine electroencephalography. From T. W. Picton and R. F. Hink, "Evoked Potentials: How? What? and Why? *American Journal of Electroencephalographic Technology* 14 (1974): 9–44; by permission of Raven Press.

nervous system and in recording its activities, I believe the judgment of an experienced clinician is more sensitive in this regard than any test, whether it be a paper and pencil test or an electrical test.

The mixed results regarding prediction of learning disability from auditory and visual evoked responses may in part be a reflection of technical differences in how the study was carried out and of intrinsic differences among the individuals being tested. All of us who have seen children with learning disabilities know that they are not all the same, and so even if we refine the population to the segment of children with reading disabilities, we recognize that these children, too, are a heterogeneous group. Thus, it should not surprise us that a single type of physiologic assessment and, one must add, a rather primitive physiologic assessment, is not fully predictive. Whether or not better correlation with an auditory or a visual reading impairment will be obtained with the use of these two types of average evoked responses remains to be further delineated. My suspicion is that we will have to be more clever in carrying out these studies and to improve the techniques themselves before a more definitive statement concerning their value can be made.

FREQUENCY ANALYSIS

Another derivative of the EEG, which may be obtained with the resting record or under a variety of testing circumstances, including stimulus responses, is referred to as frequency analysis (Picton and Hillyard 1974). Frequency analysis is an attempt to discern all the wave-form patterns present on the EEG (Kooi, Tucker, and Marshall 1978). It has been used to determine whether there are differences within a given individual under certain circumstances or between persons in one or more selected populations. These so-called power spectral analyses (some have substituted the word *energy* for *power,* but either term refers simply to how much of a given frequency of wave form is present) are based on principles that were devised in physics by Fourier and that were initially used to analyze heat waves. They fit best the analysis of the harmonics of music. In brief, one may describe any pattern in terms of sine waves (that is, something which has a sinusoidal configuration at a given periodicity or frequency), and the underlying EEG can be represented with any number, and up to an infinite number, of these sine-wave patterns. This derivative of the tracing can then be visualized by the naked eye or transformed by a computer or analyzer, and, in brief, it states the amplitude of each sine wave necessary for replicating (or, more accurately, counterfeiting) the original wave form seen on the EEG. The advantage of this tool is that it allows the electroencephalographer to look at the EEG in a manner heretofore not possible with the naked eyes (Figure 10.14). The difficulty is that one runs the risk that various artifacts may interfere with what the computer is analyzing. For no computer is as good as a trained electroencephalographer in sorting out eye movement or other artifacts that cause deflections of the EEG pens and thus may introduce error in what the computer reports as true activity generated solely from the brain. Indeed, the best means of obtaining a relatively artifact-free spectral frequency analysis is for the trained electroencephalographer to select the periods of time that are to be subjected to computer analysis. The trained human eye rejects those records that are contaminated by artifact; then, after the computer has performed the task of revisualization, the human operator directs the computer to resynthesize the original record. If the resynthesized record looks like the original tracing, then the computer did the job accurately.

In contrast to the average evoked responses, power spectral analysis is not part of routine clinical EEG. It is a research tool. Its application to reading-disabled youngsters has been investigated by Sklar, Hanley, and Simmons (1972). Their studies suggested that there were differences between the right and left hemispheres in reading-impaired boys and that this finding correlated well with the clinical diagnosis. However, groups of individuals may be called abnormal when only a few persons have unusually deviant results on the test.

Similarly, in this era of trying to comprehend right and left brain function, attempts have been made to correlate shifts, as recorded in spectral analyses, between the two hemispheres when selected mental tasks are performed that have been ascribed to left or right brain function, such as language activities on the left and musical or so-called spatial tasks on the right (Butler and Glass 1974; McAdam and Whitaker 1971; McKee, Humphrey and McAdam 1973). The thesis is that when one half of the brain is engaged in a specific activity, a reduction in overall brain activity occurs, which might escape detection by the naked eye but which can be retrieved with the use of this computer-assisted technique. However, correlation of specific hemispheric functions with power spectral analysis has not been universally successful (Gevins, Zeitlin, Doyle, Yingling, Schaffer, Callaway, and Yeager 1979; Grabow, Aronson, Greene, and Offord 1979). Whether this technique will prove of definitive service in any form of learning disability has yet to be determined. It would prove very valuable if it could be used to determine

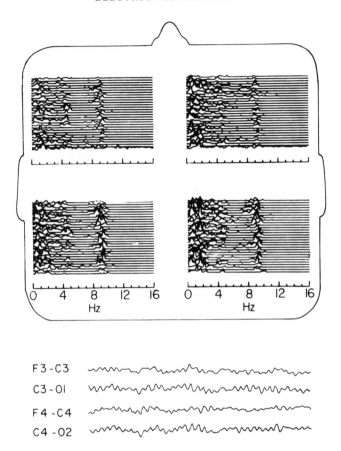

F3-C3

C3-OI

F4-C4

C4-O2

FIGURE 10.14. Conversion of a routine electroencephalogram in the lower part of the picture into a compressed spectral array seen at the upper part and represented in the four quadrants of the schematic head as seen from the top. The upward deflections demonstrate the amount of activity at given frequencies or cycles per second. In each instance, thirty four-second periods from each channel have been subjected to computer analysis. The first channel, F_3 to C_3, represents the left upper quadrant, C_3 to O_1 the left lower quadrant, F_4 to C_4 the right upper quadrant, and C_4 to O_2 the right lower quadrant. This is not a routine electroencephalographic technique but one that requires computer assistance and is used in research laboratories (see text). From J. J. Stockard, R. G. Bickford, R. R. Myers, M. H. Aung, R. B. Dilley, and J. F. Schauble, "Hypotension-Induced Changes in Cerebral Function During Cardiac Surgery," *Stroke* 5 (1974): 730–46; by permission of the American Heart Association.

which hemisphere is the language-dominant hemisphere. Such information is important in doing brain surgery for the removal of a growth or to eliminate a focus of seizures that has not responded to medicine. Such a "noninvasive" technique would be useful. For the present, the clinician must rely on the Wada test, which requires injection of a barbiturate drug into the main artery supplying half of the brain (Ramussen and Milner 1977). This "invasive" technique is cumbersome and is not without hazard. A power spectral analysis technique, if reliable, would reduce the risk and provide useful information. It could be complemented by so-called dichotic listening tests, which are based on the concept of right ear, left brain superiority in function with respect to language tasks, as opposed to left ear, right brain superiority for nonlanguage tasks such as music. Additionally, if reliable, spectral analysis could be useful in further studies of right and left brain function.

CONCLUSIONS

Do any of the above statements suggest that electroencephalography is not a useful tool? Certainly not. The EEG is an important clinical tool, which is helpful to the clinical neurologist in a variety of settings. In the evaluation of the child for a potential learning disability, the EEG is of value whenever a question is raised whether there might be an underlying seizure disorder or some disease of the brain. In these circumstances the EEG is highly reliable and it may readily affect the course of therapy to be undertaken. However, as a tool for the diagnosis of learning disability, one must say that this instrument is not yet sophisticated enough to provide sufficient data with which to ascertain the diagnosis as accurately as is possible with tests of intelligence and academic competence, not to mention the clinical impression of experienced observers, including parents.

Does this mean that electroencephalography will never play a role in the definitive diagnosis of various types of learning disabilities? The answer to that question is not yet available. Some day it may very well play such a role. In the last six years we have seen dramatic changes in our ability to understand brain structure as a result of the development of computed tomography (Figure 10.15), which allows us to visualize the structure of the central nervous system. Recently, some investigators have suggested that with the use of computed tomography it may be possible to associate asymmetries of the brain with reading disability (Hier, LeMay, Rosenberger, and Perlo 1978). Who knows which variations of the electroencephalographic techniques described here or techniques not yet mentioned may allow us to define with greater precision areas of the nervous system whose alteration in function are related to learning disabilities?

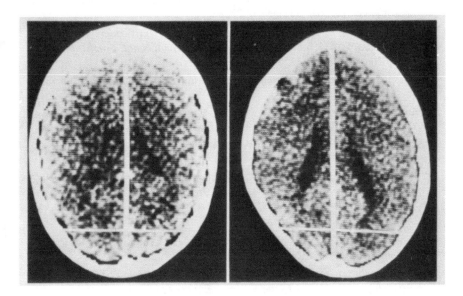

FIGURE 10.15. Computed tomograms of the brain of two dyslexic patients. The outer white circle represents the skull. The heavy bar running vertically divides the right and left halves of the brain of each person. The thinner horizontal line toward the bottom of the figure illustrates the fact that the usual pattern as demonstrated on the left is that of a slightly widened parietal-occipital region on the left side compared with the right side. In the case on the right part of the figure, the person's right parietal-occipital region is wider than the left; this is referred to as reversal of asymmetry. This reversal of asymmetry was seen in a higher portion of dyslexic patients in the study than would be expected by chance. From D. B. Hier, M. LeMay, P. B. Rosenberger and V. P. Perlo, "Developmental Dyslexia: Evidence for a Subgroup With a Reversal of Cerebral Asymmetry," *Archives of Neurology* 35 (1978): 90–92; by permission of the American Medical Association.

REFERENCES

Adrian, E. D., and Matthews, B. H. C. "The Berger Rhythm: Potential Changes From the Occipital Lobe in Man." *Brain* 57 (1934):355–85.

Ajmone Marsan, C. "A Newly Proposed Classification of Epileptic Seizures: Neurophysiological Basis." *Epilepsia* 6 (1965):275–96.

Ayres, A. J. *Sensory Integration and Learning Disorders.* Los Angeles: Western Psychological Services, 1972.

Butler, S. R., and Glass, A. "Asymmetries in the Electroencephalogram Associated With Cerebral Dominance." *Electroencephalography and Clinical Neurophysiology* 36 (1974):481–91.

Caton, R. "The Electric Currents of the Brain." *British Medical Journal* 2 (1875):278.

Commission on Terminology (H. Gastaut, Chairman). "A Proposed International Classification of Epileptic Seizures." *Epilepsia* 5 (1964):297–306.

Conners, C. K. "Cortical Visual Evoked Response in Children With Learning Disorders." *Psychophysiology* 7 (1970):418–28.

Corbin, H. P. F., and Bickford, R. G. "Studies of the Electroencephalogram of Normal Children: Comparison of Visual and Automatic Frequency Analyses." *Electroencephalography and Clinical Neurophysiology* 7 (1955):15–28.

De Quirós, J. B. "Diagnosis of Vestibular Disorders in the Learning Disabled." *Journal of Learning Disabilities* 9 (1976):39–47.

Ertl, J. P., and Schafer, E. W. P. "Brain Response Correlates of Psychometric Intelligence" (Letter to the Editor). *Nature* 223 (1969):421–22.

Frank, J., and Levinson, H. "Dysmetric Dyslexia and Dyspraxia: Hypothesis and Study." *Journal of the American Academy of Child Psychiatry* 12 (1973):690–701.

Gevins, A. S.; Zeitlin, G. M.; Doyle, J. C.; Yingling, C. D.; Schaffer, R. E.; Callaway, E.; and Yeager, C. L. "Electroencephalogram Correlates of Higher Cortical Functions." *Science* 203 (1979):665–68.

Gibbs, F. A., and Gibbs, E. L. *Atlas of electroencephalography.* Cambridge, Mass.: Cummings, 1941.

———. *Atlas of Electroencephalography.* Vol. 1, 2nd ed. Cambridge, Mass.: Addison-Wesley, 1950.

———. *Atlas of Electroencephalography.* Vol. 2. 2nd ed. Cambridge, Mass.: Addison-Wesley, 1952.

———. *Atlas of Electroencephalography.* Vol. 3. Reading, Mass.: Addison-Wesley, 1964.

Grabow, J. D.; Aronson, A. E.; Greene, K. L.; and Offord, K. P. "A Comparison of EEG Activity in the Left and Right Cerebral Hemispheres by Power-Spectrum Analysis During Language and Non-language Tasks." *Electroencephalography and Clinical Neurophysiology* 47 (1979):460–72.

Hier, D. B.; LeMay, M.; Rosenberger, P. B.; and Perlo, V. P. "Developmental Dyslexia: Evidence for a Subgroup With a Reversal of Cerebral Asymmetry." *Archives of Neurology* 35 (1978):90–92.

Hughes, J. R. "Electroencephalography and Learning." *Progress in Learning Disabilities* 1 (1968):113–46.

———. "Electroencephalography and Learning Disabilities." *Progress in Learning Disabilities* 2 (1971):18–55.

John, E. R.; Karmel, B. Z.; Corning, W. C.; Easton, P.; Brown, D.; Ahn, H.; John, M.; Harmony, T.; Prichep, L.; Toro, A.; Gerson, I.; Bartlett, F.; Thatcher, R.; Kaye, H.; Valdes, P.; and Schwartz, E. "Neurometrics." *Science* 196 (1977):1393–410.

Kooi, K. A.; Tucker, R. P.; and Marshall, R. E. *Fundamentals of Electroencephalography.* 2nd ed. Hagerstown, Md.: Harper & Row, 1978, pp. 9–21.

McAdam, D. W., and Whitaker, H. A. "Language Production: Electroencephalographic Localization in the Normal Human Brain." *Science* 172 (1971):499–502.

McKee, G.; Humphrey, B.; and McAdam, D. W. "Scaled Lateralization of Alpha Activity During Linguistic and Musical Tasks." *Psychophysiology* 10 (1973):441–43.

Penfield, W., and Jasper, H. *Epilepsy and the Functional Anatomy of the Human Brain.* Boston: Little, Brown, 1954.

Picton, T. W., and Hillyard, S. A. "Human Auditory Evoked Potentials. II. Effects of Attention." *Electroencephalography and Clinical Neurophysiology* 36 (1974):191–200.

Picton, T. W.; Hillyard, S. A.; Krausz, H. I.; and Galambos, R. "Human Auditory Evoked Potentials. I. Evaluation of Components." *Electroencephalography and Clinical Neurophysiology* 36 (1974):179–90.

Preston, M. S.; Guthrie, J. T.; and Childs, B. "Visual Evoked Responses (VERs) in Normal and Disabled Readers." *Psychophysiology* 11 (1974):452–57.

Rasmussen, T., and Milner, B. "The Role of Early Left-Brain Injury in Determining Lateralization of Cerebral Speech Functions." *Annals of the New York Academy of Sciences* 299 (1977):355–69.

Reiher, J., and Klass, D. W. "Two Common EEG Patterns of Doubtful Clinical Significance. *Medical Clinics of North America* 52 (1968):933–40.

Robb, P. *Epilepsy: A Review of Basic and Clinical Research (NINDB monograph no. 1).* Washington, D.C.: USGPO, 1965.

Sklar, B.; Hanley, J.; and Simmons, W. W. "An EEG Experiment Aimed Toward Identifying Dyslexic Children" (Letter to the Editor). *Nature* 240 (1972):414–16.

Sperry, R. W.; Gazzaniga, M. S.; and Bogen, J. E. "Interhemispheric Relationships: The Neocortical Commissures; Syndromes of Hemispheric Disconnection." In *Handbook of Clinical Neurology*, vol. 4, edited by P. J. Vinken and G. W. Bruyn. New York: Wiley, 1969.

Stockard, J. J., and Sharbrough, F. W. "Unique Contributions of Short-Latency Auditory and Somatosensory Evoked Potentials to Neurologic Diagnosis." *Progress in Clinical Neurophysiology* 7 (1978):77–123.

Studdert-Kennedy, M. "Dichotic Studies. II. Two Questions." *Brain and Language* 2 (1975):123–30.

Symann-Louett, N.; Gascon, G. G.; Matsumiya, Y.; and Lombroso, C. T. "Wave Form Difference in Visual Evoked Responses Between Normal and Reading Disabled Children." *Neurology* (Minneapolis) 27 (1977):156–59.

Thomas, J. E., and Klass, D. W. "Six-per-Second Spike-and-Wave Pattern in the Electroencephalogram: A Reappraisal of Its Clinical Significance." *Neurology* (Minneapolis) 18 (1968):587–93.

Walter, W. G. "The Location of Cerebral Tumours by Electroencephalography." *Lancet* 2 (1936):305–308.

Walter, W. G.; Cooper, R.; Aldridge, V. J.; McCallum, W. C.; and Winter, A. L. "Contingent Negative Variation: An Electric Sign of Sensorimotor Association and Expectancy in the Human Brain." *Nature* 203 (1964): 380–84.

Weber, B. A., and Omenn, G. S. "Auditory and Visual Evoked Responses in Children With Familial Reading Disabilities." *Journal of Learning Disabilities* 10 (1977):153–58.

Wiener, J. M.; Delano, J. G.; and Klass, D. W. "An EEG Study of Delinquent and Nondelinquent Adolescents." *Archives of General Psychiatry* 15 (1966):144–50.

Yingling, C. D. "EEG Research and Learning Disabilities." Paper read at the International Conference of the Association for Children with Learning Disabilities, San Francisco, February 28–March 3, 1979.

Zaidel, E. "Lexical Organization in the Right Hemisphere." In *International Symposium on Cerebral Correlates of Conscious Experience*, edited by P. A. Buser and A. Rougeul-Buser. Amsterdam: Elsevier/North-Holland, 1978.

11

An Illustrated Review of Normal Brain Anatomy and Physiology

Howell I. Runion and Sandra L. McNett-McGowan

AT THE 1979 ACLD CONFERENCE held in San Francisco, a great deal of interest was expressed in our illustrated materials presented under the title, "a review of normal brain anatomy and physiology." This response was extremely gratifying. The acceptance of our drawing and the correspondence that it generated signals an apparent need for a brief primer that might be useful to individuals recently entering the field of learning disabilities and, at the same time, serve as a review for the already sophisticated student. We have in this presentation divided the paper in two parts with the hope of meeting some of the needs that were expressed by those kind enough to review our work. First we revised and expanded the original thirteen drawings to seventeen and added descriptive statements. In the second section additions were made to include diagnostic methodology. In this section two new exciting clinical techniques currently being applied to evaluate nervous system pathophysiology along with two older, but reliable, techniques are illustrated. However, we feel compelled to caution the reader that it is beyond the scope of these illustrations to be any more than a simplistic pictorial reference source, and as such we have taken extensive artistic license to highlight the major concepts. Therefore, we must refer you the reader to the literature for a definitive discussion of neuroanatomy, pathology, and clinical instrumentation.

ANATOMY AND PHYSIOLOGY OF THE BRAIN

Central Nervous System

The central nervous system (CNS) is divided into two major component parts as seen in Figure 11.1. The upper central nervous system or upper motor neuron, consists of two paired-cerebral hemispheres: the brain

179

stem and cerebellum. The lower central nervous system, or lower motor neuron, is represented by the spinal cord. The entire CNS is differentiated from the peripheral nervous system by its being encased in bone. Thus, the peripheral nerve system by definition begins with the cranial and spinal nerve roots once they leave the protective environment of the bony cranium and vertebral column.

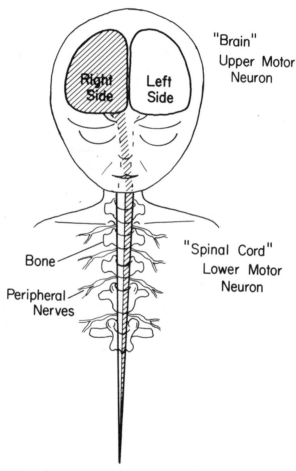

NERVOUS SYSTEM CROSSOVER

FIGURE 11.1. General organization of the central nervous system illustrating the distinct upper motor neuron and lower motor neuron divisions

In the organization of the brain, or "upper motor neuron" portion of the CNS, the right cerebral hemisphere exerts control over the left side of the body while the left cerebral hemisphere controls the right side. Decussation or crossover of efferent motor tracts occurs in the brainstem while afferent or sensory pathways crossover occurs from the body to the cerebral cortex either in the spinal cord or in discrete regions of the medulla.

Spinal Cord

The spinal cord (Figure 11.2) composes the lower central nervous system and may be referred to as the "lower motor neuron." The spinal cord is anatomically characterized by four distinct regions: the cervical, comprising nerve root C2–C8, thoracic T1–T12, lumbar L1–L5, and sacral S1–S6. The nerve roots emanating from the spinal cord do so via the foramen or openings in the boney vertebral column. These nerves now become the peripheral nervous system. Each nerve root subserves a specific region of the body termed a dermatome. For example, dermatome C4 encompasses the lower dorsal aspect of the trapezius muscle from the midline of the neck down to the dorsal aspect of the deltoid muscle. The nerves serving dermatome C4 innervate respective muscle fibers and report sensory modalities in this region via the dorsal root of the spinal cord (Figure 2B) to the brain. The dorsal roots are exclusively sensory while the ventral roots are exclusively motor.

Transection of the spinal cord at any level will result in all functions below the area of insult expressing paralysis and anesthesia. One may see a wide range of pathology including paralysis and anesthesia always dependent, however, upon the degree of damage to the cord or the peripheral nerves.

Cereberal Hemispheres—Organization

While the brain is one of the most important structures in the body, it is the specialization of its cerebral hemispheres that bring to conscious awareness our appreciation of existence. Lying within the cortex of the cerebral hemisphere are the neurons that not only provide voluntary control of the body, but also permit conscious cognitive reasoning, rational behavior, and evaluation of internal and external sensory input.

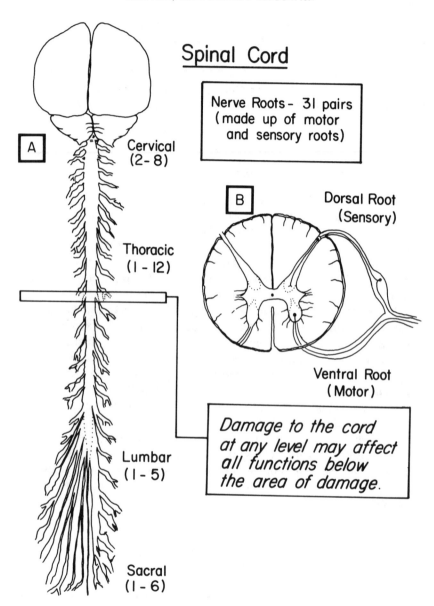

FIGURE 11.2. Organization of the spinal cord

The cerebral hemispheres are highly structured as indicated in Figures 11.3, 11.4, and 11.5. Anatomically, the hemispheres and their cortex surfaces are organized into four distinct regions, consisting of the frontal lobes, parietal, occipital, and temporal lobes.

The frontal lobes are associated with personality and intellectual functions that include imagination, creative and conscious thought, and some aspects of memory. Lesions to this area may result in behavior changes ranging from stupor to uncontrolled violence. The range between these two behavioral extremes includes intelligence to dementia; good to poor judgment; instant fact recall to loss of memory for even the most simple facts such as one's name; loss of appreciation for society; irritability; childish behavior and high idealism; abstract thought to inappropriate antisocial thoughts. Contained also in the anatomical margins of the frontal lobe, and located on the left hemisphere in 90 percent of the population is Broca's speech area. Damage or destruction to this area results in a total loss of or impaired speech in which the individual must labor to articulate a simple request like "Could — I — have — some — water."

The parietal lobes of the cerebral hemisphere contain the motor association cortex, the primary motor cortex, primary sensory cortex, and sensory association cortex. The primary motor cortex (Figure 11.4) is concerned with voluntary willed motor control such as picking up a pencil, scratching your ear, or walking. While the primary sensory cortex (Figure 11.5) provides an uninterpreted but conscious awareness of the body and its respective parts, the association areas adjacent to both the sensory and motor cortexes are involved in the integrative organization of willed motor commands for a specific body movement and the simultaneous cognitive sensory evaluation of receptors input relating to willed or passive movements of body muscles. Destruction of neurons in the primary motor cortex results in weakness or paralysis on the opposite side of the body, while lesions in the primary sensory cortex and associative sensory areas result in anesthesia or parapsis and paraesthesine of body parts.

Posterior to the parietal lobes is the occipital lobe, composed of the primary visual cortex and visual associative cortex. The primary visual cortex is the posterior portion of the occipital lobe and is concerned with the projection of sensory data from the retina of the eye (see Figure 11.17). Visual association and interpretation of an image is accomplished in part by the visual association cortex and memory in the frontal and temporal lobe regions. Damage to the primary visual or associative cortex results in varying degrees of blindness. Bilateral destruction of cells in these two cortex regions results in total blindness.

The temporal lobe contains areas for primary audition and hearing association. In Figure 11.3 only the hearing associative cortex is illustrated. The primary auditory cortex lies obscured from view by the lateral fissure. The primary auditory cortex is in juxtaposition to the insula (a portion of the frontal lobe hidden from view by the temporal lobe). Bilateral destruction of the primary auditory cortex results in deafness. However, destruction of the associative areas may produce receptive aphasia or result in impaired language comprehension.

FUNCTIONAL ANATOMY

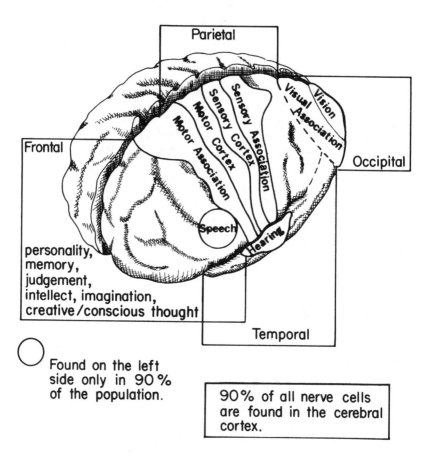

FIGURE 11.3. Organization and functional anatomy of the cerebral hemisphere

It should be apparent from the discussion of Figure 11.3 and the four distinct regions of the cortex that a considerable amount of cortex tissue is yet unspecified as to its exact physiologic function. No doubt these unspecified cells are a part of the total integrative activity of conscious awareness, conscious thought, willed behavior, and sensory appreciation. Future research involving average evoked potential recording techniques (see Figures 11.16, 17) may provide us with significant insight as to the exact function of these heretofore unmapped cortical areas and insight as to how data is processed by the brain.

In Figure 11.6 the frontal section of the brain, with its two cerebral hemispheres, is shown along with the corpus callosum. The corpus callosum contains myelinated axons that interconnect the two cerebral

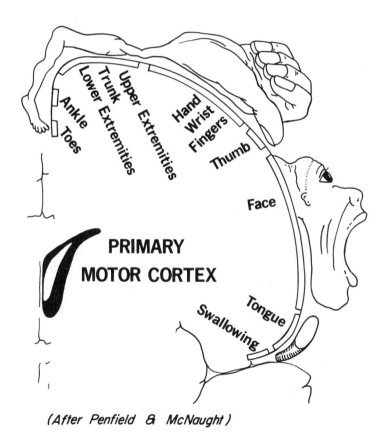

(After Penfield & McNaught)

FIGURE 11.4. Spatial organization of body limbs as seen in the primary motor cortex of man enabling voluntary motor control

hemispheres enabling information sharing between the two cerebral cortexes. The corpus callosum is also seen in the longitudinal brain section. It runs anterior/posterior over the surface of the two lateral ventricals forming a roof over the brainstem.

The brainstem is phylogenetically the older part of the brain. It is composed of the thalamus, midbrain, hypothalamus, pons, and medulla. The thalamus subserves the critical functions of sorting afferent sensory information ascending to the brain from somesthetic, auditory, and visual receptors of the body. It further acts as an integrative structure for complex functions in pain perception and is involved in level setting of the reticular activating system (Figure 11.8). The integrated sensory data passing through the thalamus is thus appropriately directed to the

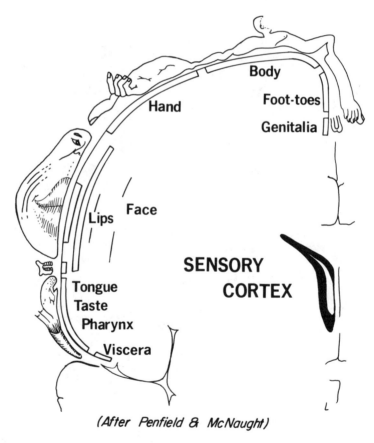

(After Penfield & McNaught)

FIGURE 11.5. Organization and body relationship to the primary sensory cortex involved in conscious awareness of somatic tissue

respective regions of the cortex for conscious awareness, e.g., sensory apperception of a pin prick in dermatome C-7 (Figure 11.5). In addition, the thalamus serves important functions in efferent control of somatic motor commands initiated by the primary motor cortex as seen in Figures 11.3 and 11.4.

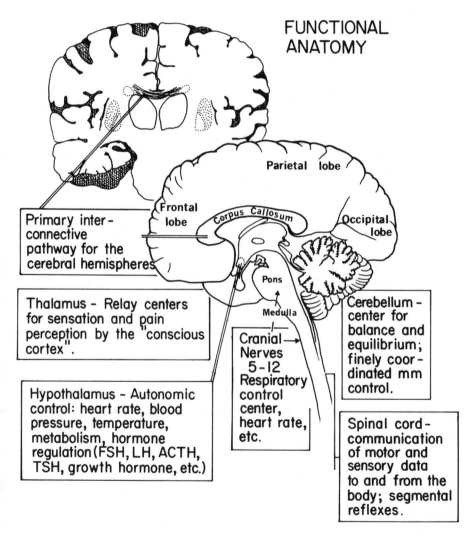

FIGURE 11.6. Functional anatomy and organization of the brain in frontal section and hemisection demonstrating the brainstem

Located anterior to the pons and below the thalamus or diencephalon is the hypothalamus. The hypothalamus is a small structure, but one with numerous regulatory mechanisms. The hypothalamus is responsible for temperature regulation, neuroendocrine control of the production of catecholamines, vasopressin, oxytocin, thyroid stimulating hormone (TSH), adrenocorticotropic hormone (ACTH), follicle stimulating hormone (FSH), luteinizing hormone (LH), prolactin, and growth hormone. In addition, the hypothalamus regulates "appetite" behaviour such as thirst, hunger, and sex drive and participates in the emotional reactions of rage and fear. It also controls various endocrine and activity rhythms of the body.

The midbrain, pons, the medulla contain the nuclei of cranial nerves 3 to 12, i.e., occular motor, trochlea, trigrominal, abducens, facial, vestibular/cochlear, glossopharyngeal, vagus, accessory, and hypoglossal. In addition, centers for respiratory, vasomotor, and heart rate are to be found in the pons and medulla. The medulla continues on to become the spinal cord after passing through the foramen magnum of the skull. The medulla contains both efferent and afferent tracts leading to and from the body, thus enabling the brain to control the entire organism.

The Cerebellum

Adjacent to the pons and connected by cerebellar peduncles are the lobes of the cerebellum. The primary function of the cerebellum is fine coordination of all motor activity in the body (Figure 11.7). The cerebellum performs a major role as the efferent modulator of balance and anti-gravity control. Sensory data coming in from proprioceptors in the body musculature are integrated by the cerebellum along with primary efferent activity originating in the primary motor cortex and learned patterns stored in nuclei of the internal capsule. Thus one can say that while the primary motor cortex (Figures 11.3, 11.4) decides what movements are to be made, the cerebellum ultimately dictates how those movements will be directed. Reference to Figure 11.7 clearly indicates the complexity of cerebellar integrative functions.

As already noted, the cerebellum is intimately concerned with fine coordination of musculature contractions and the maintenance of body posture. Any lesions which occur in brainstem tracts leading to the cerebellum or in the cortex of the cerebellum result in a deficit of muscle coordination, such as ataxia, seen as a loss of coordinated muscle control in walking. Lesions of the cerebellum also lead to tremor of the

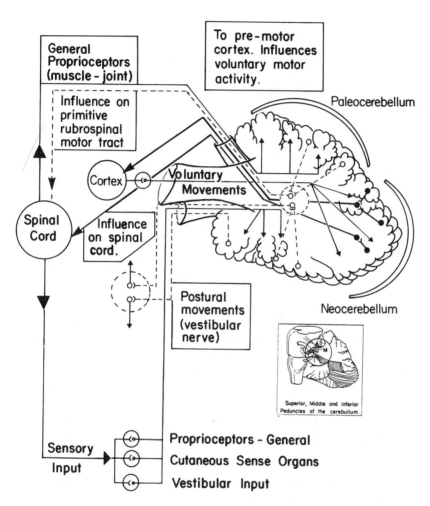

General Proprioceptors (muscle - joint)

To pre-motor cortex. Influences voluntary motor activity.

Influence on primitive rubrospinal motor tract

Paleocerebellum

Cortex

Voluntary Movements

Spinal Cord

Influence on spinal cord.

Postural movements (vestibular nerve)

Neocerebellum

Superior, Middle and Inferior Peduncles of the cerebellum.

Sensory Input

Proprioceptors - General

Cutaneous Sense Organs

Vestibular Input

CEREBELLUM - Afferent / Efferent Control on Fine Motor Movements

FIGURE 11.7. Efferent-afferent pathways in cerebellar control of fine motor movements

intention type (not to be confused with the essential benign tumor) and "cerebellar speech," which is characterized by slow scanning of the syllables and vowels in a word: the word *coordination* would be spoken as co...or...din...ation. One also sees patients with cerebellar lesion dyssynergia, or the inability to perform movements smoothly because of the loss of normal synergistic action between agonists and antagonistic muscle groups normally controlled by intact cerebellar tracts.

Reticular Activating System

The reticular activating system (RAS) presented in Figure 11.8 is not easily described anatomically. The RAS does not exist as a discrete nucleus that can be identified like the putamen, substantia nigra of the basal ganglia, or the thalamus. Rather it is composed of a myriad of small neurons arranged in a complex intertwining net that extends from the medulla through the pons midbrain into the thalamus. However, located within this reticular net of neurons formed by the RAS are centers associated with respiration, blood pressure, heart rate, and other vegetative functions. Simplistically, one can say that the RAS is responsible for our levels of consciousness ranging from coma through all four stages of sleep (stage 1 to stage 4 including the REM and non-REM components of sleep), to total conscious awareness. The RAS in turn is responsible to a large extent for the level of attention to be given to sensory input processed by the thalamus and projected to the primary sensory cortex. Conversely the RAS level of consciousness will affect the outflow of efferent motor commands to the body. There is little argument among neurobiologists as to the interplay of somatic sensory receptor to activation of muscle tissue as a correlate of conscious cortical processing. This relationship has long been established by conventional electroencephalographic (EEG) recording techniques, and has led to the clear understanding of the differences in EEG recordings seen in coma, sleep, drowsy awareness, and critical analytical thought. Undoubtedly, the functions of the RAS to peripheral sensory stimulation and cortically recorded EEG potential will be further clarified by the techniques of average evoked potential recordings as described in Figure 11.14.

The Neuron, Neurotransmitters, and Membrane Potentials

Thus far in our discussion, we have dealt with the physiology of specific brain areas and have totally ignored the functional unit, the neuron. All of the efferent or afferent processing accomplished by

The Reticular Activating System

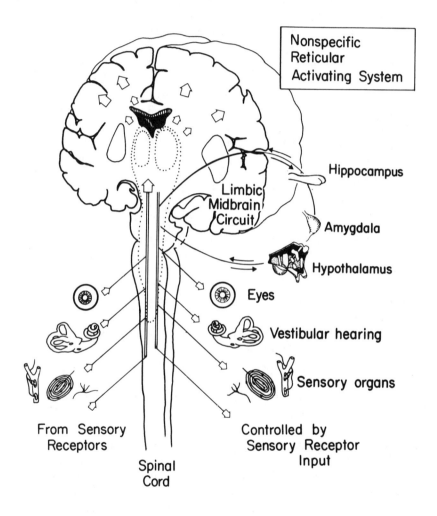

Nonspecific Reticular Activating System

Hippocampus

Limbic Midbrain Circuit

Amygdala

Hypothalamus

Eyes

Vestibular hearing

Sensory organs

From Sensory Receptors

Controlled by Sensory Receptor Input

Spinal Cord

FIGURE 11.8. The reticular activating system and its relationship to sensory receptors, the brainstem, and cortex

various component divisions of the brain would be impossible without the neuron (Figure 11.9). A highly diagramatic composite neuron is presented. It is important to stress that Figure 11.9 illustrates a number of physiological and anatomical features found among neurons, but in no way should the illustration be considered to represent all neurons found in the brain. For example, the structure of a neuron found in the cerebellum is considerably different from that found in the occipital cortex. However, in both cases their physiological functions are similar. Simply stated, the physiological functions of the neuron are (1) to receive information, (2) to integrate and in some instances store information, and (3) to process an appropriate response in the form of an action potential (Figure 11.11). Anatomically, all neurons are appropriately structured to carry out these three basic functions.

The transmission of one neuron to a second is accomplished at the synaptic junctions (Figures 11.9 and 11.10). The synaptic junctions may occur on specialized structures designed to receive information called dendrites. The neuron may also receive information directly on its soma at appropriate receptor sites. Transfer of information occurs on the liberation of a neurotransmitter substance from the pre-synaptic bouton or junction of the communicating neuron. The receptor sites on the post synaptic membrane will respond to the neurotransmitter released either at the dendrite or on the soma. The transmitter will cause the membrane potential of the second neuron (Figure 11.11) to depolarize and shift toward zero (excitation) or hyperpolarize and move in a more negative direction (inhibition).

The integrative function of the cell membrane will sum the excitatory potentials, thus moving the membrane toward its critical threshold, enabling an action potential to be generated, or it will integrate the inhibitory potentials, lowering the membrane potential, i.e., becoming more negative or hyperpolarized. Typically, a neuron will exhibit a resting potential of -65 to -70 millivolts. The membrane potential can be measured by a glass microelectrode inserted intracellularly into the soma of the cell as seen in Figure 11.11A. The integrative activity of the membrane in response to excitatory transmission is seen in Figure 11.11B. Note that one isolated excitatory impulse did not move the membrane towards the critical threshold value of -30 MV, but that two impulses integrated by the membrane delivered in close succession resulted in an action potential being generated, i.e., the critical threshold point had been crossed and an action potential generated. In Figure 11.11C, the membrane response to an inhibitory neural transmitter is seen. The hyperpolarization of the membrane is in a negative direction, i.e., away from the critical -30 MV threshold; thus an action potential was not generated in the neuron.

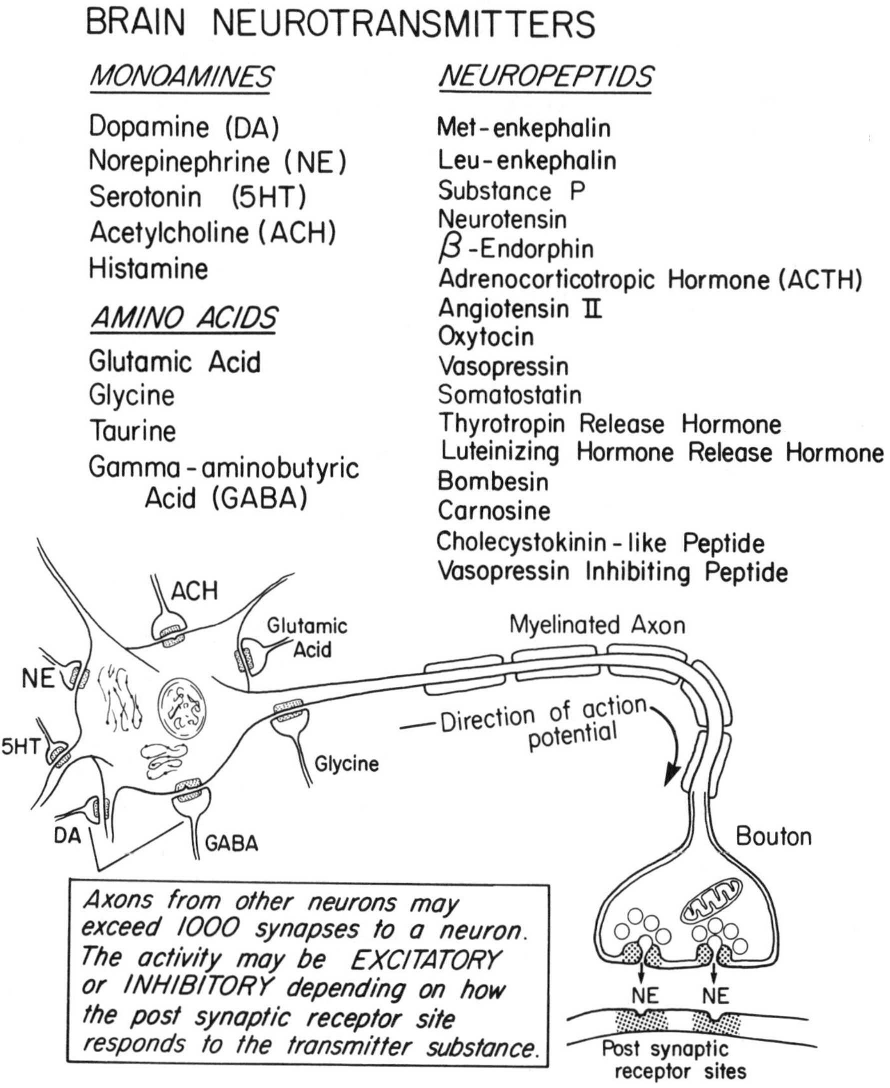

BRAIN NEUROTRANSMITTERS

MONOAMINES

Dopamine (DA)
Norepinephrine (NE)
Serotonin (5HT)
Acetylcholine (ACH)
Histamine

AMINO ACIDS

Glutamic Acid
Glycine
Taurine
Gamma-aminobutyric
Acid (GABA)

NEUROPEPTIDS

Met-enkephalin
Leu-enkephalin
Substance P
Neurotensin
β-Endorphin
Adrenocorticotropic Hormone (ACTH)
Angiotensin II
Oxytocin
Vasopressin
Somatostatin
Thyrotropin Release Hormone
Luteinizing Hormone Release Hormone
Bombesin
Carnosine
Cholecystokinin-like Peptide
Vasopressin Inhibiting Peptide

ACH
Glutamic Acid
NE
5HT
Glycine
DA
GABA
Myelinated Axon
—Direction of action potential
Bouton
NE   NE
Post synaptic receptor sites

Axons from other neurons may exceed 1000 synapses to a neuron. The activity may be EXCITATORY or INHIBITORY depending on how the post synaptic receptor site responds to the transmitter substance.

FIGURE 11.9. The "idealized" neuron and neurotransmitters affecting function

DISRUPTION OF SYNAPTIC ACTIVITY AS SEEN IN A NORADRENERGIC SYNAPSE.

Examples of Active Compounds:

① α Methyltyrosine   ⑥ Phenylephrine
② Disulfram   ⑦ Phenoxybenzamine
③ Reserpine   ⑧ Imipramine
④ Amphetamine   ⑨ Tropolone
⑤ Bretylium   ⑩ Iproniazid

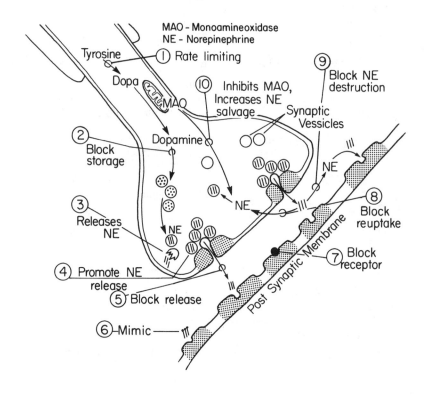

FIGURE 11.10. Synaptic activity in the noradrenergic neuron and external modification by drug interaction presynaptically and post synaptically

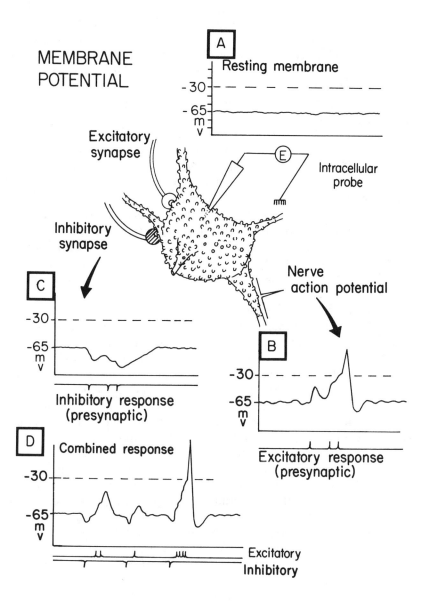

FIGURE 11.11. The electrophysiological correlates of excitation and inhibition in the neuron

Under normal physiologic conditions, a neuron will receive input from a wide variety of other neurons, some attempting to excite the post-synaptic membranes, others attempting to inhibit. This interplay is seen in Figure 11.11D. Basically, a neuron has two states: it is either silent or it is actively producing an action potential. Thus excitation facilitates production of the "on-state," and an inhibition actively insures an "off-state."

Once excitation has occurred, the generated action potential is conducted down the neuron's axon to the terminal endings or synaptic bouton. Neuronal axons may be myelinated or non-myelinated in both the central nervous system (CNS) or peripheral nervous system. Myelination is of major significance. It speeds the conduction of nerve impulses by several orders of magnitude over that seen in non-myelinated axons of the same cross-sectional diameter. Its physiological evolution may well have been derived as a result of sequence timing needs. For example, an action potential occurring in one part of the brain may need to be replicated or providing information in a second part of the central nervous system within a few milliseconds in order to facilitate a coordinated response. Thus the myelinated axons facilitate the speedy delivery and assures correct timing of neuronal messages as compared with non-myelinated, slower conducting axons.

On arrival of the action potential in the terminal or synaptic bouton region, a series of biochemical events occurs that results in the release of the neutral transmitter substance. Generally, the neurotransmitter will not be released by the presynaptic membrane in the absence of an action potential. Once an action potential has reached the bouton, a "quantum" of neurotransmitter substance is released; it diffuses across the synaptic cleft, complexes on the post-synaptic receptor site, and either initiates excitation or inhibition of the post-synaptic membrane.

It is important to recognize that a neuron may respond to a wide variety of chemical transmitter substances, i.e., excitatory or inhibitory. However, it is the receptor site on the post-synaptic membrane that determines whether the membrane will respond in an inhibitory or an excitatory fashion. Thus, throughout the CNS it is possible for a chemical transmitter like norepinephrine to excite one neuron while acting as an inhibitory transmitter to a second neuron. This variability of receptor sites is illustrated in the composite neuron of Figure 11.9. Note that while a wide variety of chemical transmitter substances are known to be active as shown in this illustration, it is important to state that a single neuron can produce only one kind of chemical transmitter substance for release at its synaptic bouton, although it may respond to several different types of chemical transmitters on its dendritic receptor site or somal membrane receptors.

In recent years our appreciation of the number of neurotransmitter substances active in the brain has grown immensely. For a long period of time we assumed that there were only a few neural transmitter substances. Classically, receptors of neural transmitters included acetylcholine, norepinephrine, 5-hydroxy-tryptamine (also known as serotonin), and dopamine. Recently the list has been expanded to include twenty-one other compounds, mostly polypeptides. These substances have been shown to have biochemical activity in a variety of various neurons studied to date. This expanded list has led to a clearer understanding of mental disease states and the improved explanations for observed neuronal behavior and interneuronal communications, including memory and aspects of the learning process.

Our understanding of the neuronal synapses coupled with the disciplines of electrophysiology-pharmacology has given us powerful tools for modifying, adjusting, terminating, or inducing neuronal behavior. In Figure 11.10 an example of the various ways in which synaptic transmission may be facilitated, blocked, potentiated, inhibited, or mimicked is presented. We have chosen nonrepinephrine (NE) as an example; it is perhaps the best understood of all chemical transmitters known in the brain to date. The activities of some of the drugs listed in Figure 11.10 are seen to act a variety of ways, i.e., post-synaptically, or pre-synaptically. For example: (1) in interference with biochemical synthesis processes producing NE; (2) in the conversion of its precursor dopamine to NE; (3) by disruption of any storage in the pre-synaptic membrane; (4) blockade of transmitter release even though an action potential may have been successfully transmitted to the synaptic bouton; (5) through interference post-synaptically at the receptor site by drugs which compete for receptor site binding surfaces; (6) via interference of enzyme systems that normally degrade NE and would generally allow NE re-uptake into the pre-synaptic bouton for conservation and re-encapsulation; (7) and finally mainly by conserving NE through inhibiting monoamine oxidase (MAO) in the bouton form, destroying the recently recovered NE before it can be encapsulated in a synaptic vessicle and stored for release.

Localization of Language Function in the Cortex

Returning our attention to the cortex once more, we should now see that if individual neurons or groups of neurons fail to communicate, cortical functions will inevitably fail, followed by disruption of function. Some of the more common dysfunctions that can be related to neuron failures of the cortex are illustrated in Figure 11.12. The etiology for these types of failures are difficult to assess in many instances. However, some of the more obvious causes for cortical failures other than congenital malformations or birth injury are: trauma, vascular insufficiency or accident, high fever, meningitis and tumors. However, one must also consider metabolic and systemic toxins such as lead, mercury, and arsenic as contributors to the loss of cerebellar function. Unfortunately, neurological damage may not always be as easy to pinpoint as suggested in the simplistic illustrated approach of Figure 11.12. Further, it should be pointed out that maps like Figure 11.12 are derived correlates of observed pathology made from autopsy material and thus can only represent a potential pattern as each individual case of brain dysfunction must be evaluated on its own merit. The reader must be duly warned that such lesion maps are useful only in forming generalizations about disrupted brain function and that reliance on a complete medical workup and standard testing will be required in each case to adequately explain the observed neurologic deficit.

The Final Common Pathway

The ultimate act of behavior in man or animal is expressed through activation of skeletal or somatic muscles. Therefore, much of the organization of our brain is directed toward one final expression, overt behavior. Behavior always results in some form of motor activity, be it somatic or visceral. For the sake of simplicity let us consider somatic motor behavior. The control of any skeletal muscle in the body is ultimately channeled through the final common pathway as illustrated in Figure 11.13. Located in the ventral horn of the spinal cord is the giant motor neuron on final common pathway; when the motor neuron (MN) is excited it produces an action potential which is then propagated down the myelinated axon to the neuromuscular junction on the skeletal muscle fiber. At the neuromuscular junction or synapse, acetylcholine is released, which depolarizes the post-synaptic membrane of the muscle, thus initiating the sequence of steps that ultimately results in a contraction of the muscle. One motor neuron may synapse with 10 or 1,000 or more muscle fibers. Motor neurons that communicate with a few muscle fibers are reserved for those muscle groups that require extensive neuronal control, leading to fine control behavior, for example, the muscle controlling eye movement or the muscle involved in finger control. This is in contrast with the course control exerted by a motor

Localization of Language Functions

*Dysfunction of these areas results in
aphasia, e.g. agraphia, motor aphasia,
word deafness and word blindness.*

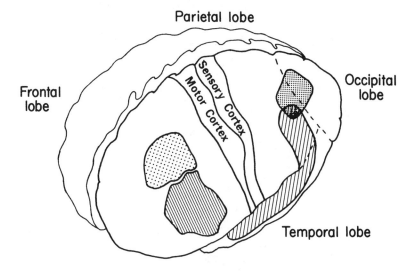

Difficulty in:

- ⊙ *expressing ideas in writing*
- ⊕ *expressing ideas orally (Broca's Speech Area)*
- ⊘ *understanding spoken words*
- ⊛ *understanding written words*

Adapted from Ruch & Patton (1965) <u>Physiology and Biophysics</u>
19th edition, Saunders.

FIGURE 11.12. Cerebral hemispheric disruption as a key to the localization of
language function and pathology

MOTOR UNIT (Final Common Pathway)

● Spinal cord interneurons
   forming reflex arcs

⊗ Cortico-spinal tract   ⊖ Reticulo spinal tract
☉ Rubro-spinal tract   ◎ Ventro vestibular spinal tract
◍ Dorso-vestibular-spinal tract   ⦶ Tecto spinal tract
⊛ Olivo-spinal tract   O Primary afferent input

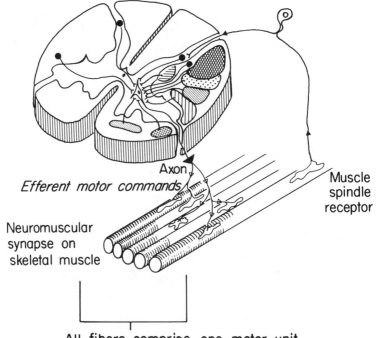

Axon

Efferent motor commands

Muscle spindle receptor

Neuromuscular synapse on skeletal muscle

All fibers comprise one motor unit
under one motor neuron's control,
thus the FINAL COMMON PATHWAY.

FIGURE 11.13. The final common pathway and neuromotor control of skeletal muscle tissue

neuron that will innervate 1,000 or more muscle fibers, such as the gastrochemius muscle of the leg. This muscle is capable of rather limited activity. It is mainly responsible for extension of the foot, thus it does not require large number of motor neurons for control as do the muscles of the hand or eye.

Synapsing on the motor neurons in the spinal cord are several behavior-controlling neurons. Some of these neuronal influences involve segmental sensory input from both ipsilateral and contralateral sides of the spinal cord. In addition, there are direct influences from the "upper motor neurons" of the primary motor cortex, the cerebellum, and extrapyramidal tracts of the basal ganglion. All of these upper motor neuron influences communicate with the lower motor neuron in highly organized nerve tracts. The end result of these nerve tracts are synapses on the final common pathway enabling CNS control of motor behavior. Damage to any of these special nerve tracts or their upper central nervous system nuclei will result in impairment or loss of peripheral motor control. For example, loss of primary proprioceptive input from the muscle spindles via the dorsal root results in impaired segmental muscle reflexes as well as a loss of proprioceptive input to the cerebellum. For example, destruction of the corticospinal tract leads to paralysis of voluntary motor movements initiated from the primary motor cortex; interruption of the dorso-vestibular and olivo-spinal tracts incurs losses of reflex and proprioceptive evaluations of reflex activity in both the spinal cord and the upper central nervous system. Following involvement of the reticulospinal tract, one sees gross modifications of muscle tone, while disturbance to the ventro vestibular spinal tract alters postural balance and anti-gravity movements. In addition, the tecto spinal tract is involved in our audiovisual responses to sound location as well as visual clues for horizon positioning judgments. It is important to indicate that the above descriptions are gross oversimplification of the variety of pathology that one may see on clinical evaluation of nerve tract disruption to the lower motor neuron. Finally, it should be noted that the lower motor neuron itself may suffer damage either by disease or through trauma. If the motor neuron dies or is disabled, the final outcome is always absolute paralysis of those muscle fibers innervated by the affected neuron. Obviously, it is far beyond the scope of this paper to discuss the ramifications of cord lesions caused by disease, compression, or trauma. Thus the reader is referred to more definitive medical literature for a discussion of pathology.

DIAGNOSTIC TECHNIQUES

The obvious rationale for the study of normal anatomy and physiology is that it leads to an understanding of abnormal functioning. Methodology for demonstrating the existence of pathology is rapidly changing and improving. We felt it to be of interest to describe three new diagnostic techniques that are just now coming to the medical marketplace. These techniques are : (1) Xenon 133 chromatographic blood flow measurements pioneered by Lassen, Ingvar, and Skinhoi; (2) computerized transaxial tomography for visualization of brain structure; and (3) average evoked potential recordings of visual, auditory, and sensory information processing by the brain.

Arteriography and Xenon 133 Chromatographic Blood Flow Studies

To fully appreciate the significance of the Xenon 133 chromatographic blood flow studies, one must first recall the basic anatomy of arterial supply to the brain and its visualization by the traditional method of X-ray, i.e., the arteriogram. In Figure 11.14, the arterial supply is reviewed. By cross referencing the arterial supply distribution of Figure 11.14 to the topographical maps of Figure 11.3, 11.4, 11.5, and 11.12, one can make a gross interpretation of functional loss that generally occurs following regional arterial insufficiency or localized ischemia. The traditional method used to verify arterial blood flow in the brain involves injection of radio opaque dye into the carotid artery and rapid multiple X-ray photography. This technique is certainly well established, has a high reliability, and is of major diagnostic importance. However, it is not without certain risks to the patient and is rarely done without careful consideration of the risk versus diagnostic gain that the procedure might produce. In Figure 11.14-1 the arteriogram of a nine-month-old female child is presented. In this instance, standard arteriograms were the definitive diagnostic choice. The arteriogram in this case clearly defines the appearance of the cerebral blood supply and delineates those areas of the cortex that are deficient in arterial investment. The significance of adequate cerebral profusion of blood to normal brain function is obvious and thus in this case its absence provides the correlative data that would explain the clinical symptoms seen in the presenting child.

The Xenon 133 chromatographic computer assisted display technique for blood flow analysis (Figure 11.14-2) will, in our opinion, serve an important diagnostic role in the evaluation of minimal brain

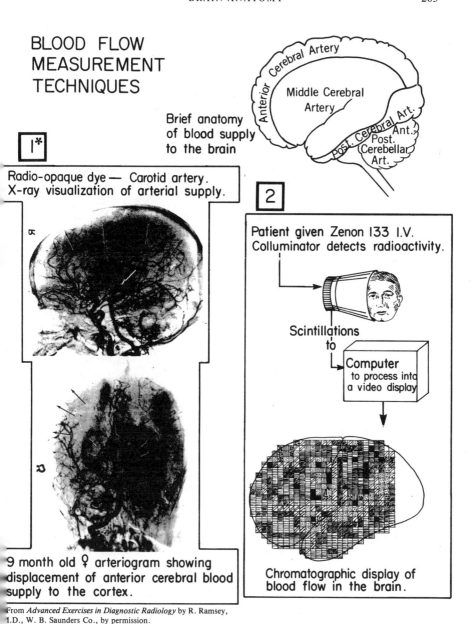

BLOOD FLOW MEASUREMENT TECHNIQUES

Brief anatomy of blood supply to the brain

Anterior Cerebral Artery

Middle Cerebral Artery

Post. Cerebral Art.

Post. Cerebellar Art. Ant.

1*

Radio-opaque dye — Carotid artery. X-ray visualization of arterial supply.

2

Patient given Zenon 133 I.V. Colluminator detects radioactivity.

Scintillations to

Computer to process into a video display

9 month old ♀ arteriogram showing displacement of anterior cerebral blood supply to the cortex.

Chromatographic display of blood flow in the brain.

From *Advanced Exercises in Diagnostic Radiology* by R. Ramsey, I.D., W. B. Saunders Co., by permission.

FIGURE 11.14. Evaluative techniques for determining cerebral blood flow using arteriographic and chromatographic measurements

dysfunction, but it will not substitute for arteriogram studies. This technique allows for evaluative procedures classed as "physiological" rather than anatomical as in arteriographic studies. Essentially the Xenon 133 technique examines the microcirculation of the cortex by scintillation of the decomposing radioactive Xenon 133. The patient is given an injection of saline containing the Xenon 133 radioactive isotope. The saline and isotope circulate to the brain where a colluminator (gamma-ray camera) consisting of 254 individual scintillation detectors is pressed to one side of the head as illustrated in Figure 11.14-2. The gamma radiation emitted by the Xenon 133 is then detected by each of the 254 scintillation detectors, that data is sent to a microcomputor for storage and processing. The radiation intensity seen at any individual scintillation detector is an accurate index of blood flow for a specific instant of time. The computer translates the 254 detectors information into color such that the spectrum from blue to red correlates with blood flow volumes, i.e., mean flow is presented in green, flows 20 percent lower are in blue, while those 20 percent higher than the mean are red. The significance of this technique is that it provides for a visualization of cerebral blood flow and a method of correlating real time cortex processing such as one would encounter in reading, speaking, thinking, or math manipulations. The implications of this innovative technique are enormous and will undoubtedly add significantly to our basic understanding of cerebral flow and neuronal processing not only in the normal brain, but in the damaged brain as well.

Computerized Transaxial Tomography

Perhaps no single advance in medical instrumentation has contributed more to the physicians' ability to diagnose brain tumors, abscess, structural abnormalies, and ventricular pathology than the computerized transaxial tomography or CT scanner (Figure 11.15). This noninvasive technique combines X-ray technology with computer analysis to produce clear "slices" of brain tissue that can be visualized without surgical procedures. Essentially the system works as follows: an X-ray tube mounted on a trackway is opposed by a photomultiplier/scintillation tube (Figure 11.15A) also mounted on a track. The two devices move in tandem left to right in 1.5mm incremental steps. The X-ray tube is pulsed, producing short discrete emissions that are detected by the photomultiplier/scintillation tube AB. The data is stored in a computer that dignitizes the information for density on a 0–10 scale

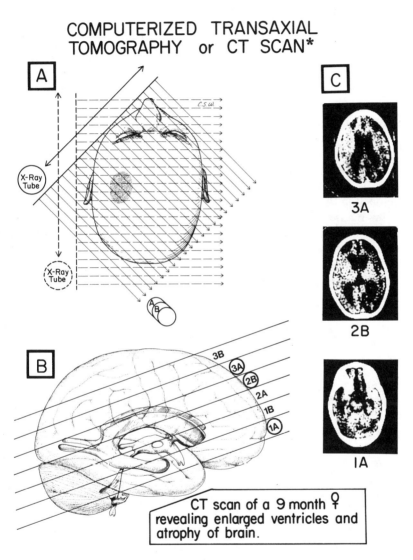

COMPUTERIZED TRANSAXIAL TOMOGRAPHY or CT SCAN*

CT scan of a 9 month ♀ revealing enlarged ventricles and atrophy of brain.

*Adapted from: *Advanced Exercises in Diagnostic Radiology* by R. Ramsey, M.D., W. B. Saunders Co., by permission.

FIGURE 11.15. Computerized transaxial tomography of a nine-month-old female demonstrating enlarged ventricles and severe atrophy of the cerebral hemispheres

along with exact position address of the X-ray tube. The brain is scanned left to right, then the entire trackway X-ray tube and photomultiplier tubes are rotated 90° and the process again repeated. The computer is programmed to take the data obtained from the two scan sequences, recombined, and presents a pictoral display similar to those seen in Figure 11.15C. As noted above, the CT scan can take "slices" of the brain (Figure 11.15B) thus providing a complete picture of the brain from the base of the skull to the dorsum. The entire process takes approximately 4–6 minutes to complete the standard cuts or "slices" and is thus of minimal irritation to the patient. The computer can also accommodate programs for enhancing the scan data, or it can be used in conjunction with radio opaque dyes to further delineate structural features, thus making it one of the most important diagnostic tools to have been developed in the past 100 years of contemporary medicine.

In Figures 11.15A and 11.15B, the CT scan cuts for the nine-month-old female child as presented. Note the enlarged ventricles and atrophy of brain tissue; this is compatible with the findings in the angiography records from the same child seen in Figure 11.14-1. The standard "slices" 1A, 2B, and 3A correlate with the scans 3A, 2B, 1A.

Average Evoked Potential Recordings

In our opinion, a major breakthrough in technology for electroencephalographic (EEG) evaluation has been made that enables us to interpret cortical information processing by the brain using computer assisted average evoked potential recordings in response to repetitive stimulation. This relatively new technology is being extensively employed in the fields of vision, audition, and tactile sensory processing in man. It is currently being used routinely in the diagnosis of multiple sclerosis, i.e., auditory and visual responses are indicative of the plaquing seen in the neuron axons and soma. More recently it has been used by investigators to study information processing such as brain dysfunction in the severely retarded; as a measure of quantifying cortical dysfunction; in the evaluations of schizophrenia; as a technique to describe affective disorders; in the mapping and distribution of olfactory input; in assessment of alterations in brain functions of the alcoholic, to mention but a few of the important questions on neural processing now being studied by this technology.

Simplistically, the concept of average evoked brain potential recording is illustrated in Figure 11.16. In this illustration the stimulus is a flash of light. The initiation of the flash is under computer control which also simultaneously opens a window permitting EEG potentials re-corded at occipital electrode position $0_1 0_2$ to be digitized by the 8080 microcomputer and stored in memory. A second stimulus is given, and again the computer selects a sample of 350 msec duration for digitiza-tion; it is stored in memory and added to the first sample. This process may be repeated up to 200 or more times depending on the study needs,

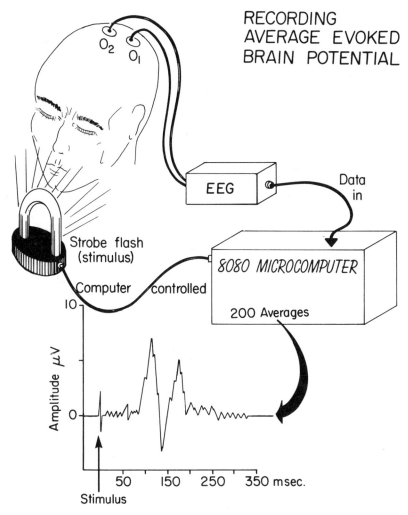

FIGURE 11.16. Average evoked visual potential brain recording techniques utilizing computer assisted analysis of EEG potential

type of stimulus, and level of EEG potentials recorded (typically these potentials are in a range of 1–10 microvolts in amplitude). Arithmetic operations are then accomplished as part of the computer program and the final average evoked potentials displayed either on an oscilloscope or a plotter. The data derived presents a picture of how the stimulus is processed by the brain: this is described by its latency from the initiation of the stimulus, the amplitude of the response, and the wave shape. This technique exploits the traditional EEG recording by averaging out extraneous data that does not directly relate to the processing of a specific stimulus.

In Figure 11.17, an explanation of the electrophysiological basis for the average evoked brain potential recording technique is presented. In this illustration we elected to explore the rationale behind visual evoked potential recordings as they are perhaps the best understood and most widely described in the literature; however, the principles of visual stimulation can be applied to other modalities of brain processing currently being investigated.

Initially it is useful to review the interneuronal processing of visual images detected by the retina of the eye. In Figure 11.17 the initial process of vision begins with (1) the retina transducing visual image into action potentials that are conducted via the optic nerve to the lateral geniculate bodies; (2) here the first synapse of visual data occurs in the brain. Note that the retina (1) of the left eye shares its information with the lateral geniculate body (2) of the right hemisphere and conversely for the right eye to the left hemisphere. The crossover occurs outside the brain at the optichasma. Next the lateral geniculate bodies project their axons onto the occipital lobe (3) where thousands of cortex synapses occur and bring to consciousness visualization of the original images transduced by the retina. Recording electrodes 0_1 and 0_2 detect the visually evoked EEG activity from the occipital region; this data is processed by the computer for averaging as previously described in Figure 11.16.

Essentially, the visual system can be simplified by stating that the eye represents a peripheral receptor (it is outside the bond encasement of the brain) that communicates with the brain; the brain in turn must process the peripheral data through two clearly defined synaptic regions, the lateral geniculate bodies and occipital lobes. This processing ultimately gives rise to cortex activation known as vision. It is this activation that is recorded and averaged. Again, examining the typical display of a visually average evoked potential study in Figure 11.17, we see that (4) represents the stimulus starting point, (5) the initiation of a large wave occurring slightly before or around 90 msec post stimulation

THE ELECTROPHYSIOLOGICAL BASIS FOR AVERAGE EVOKED BRAIN POTENTIAL.

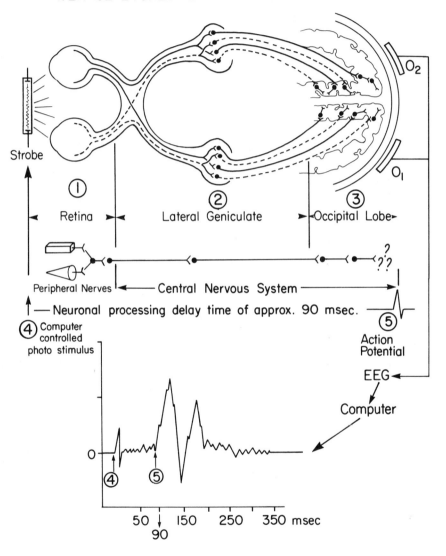

FIGURE 11.17. The electrophysiological basis for average evoked visual potential recording in humans

of the retina. The appearance of this wave correlates with the excitation of thousands of cortical neurons. The 90 msec delay indicates a normal visual response to the flash stimulus. Delay beyond the 90 msec range is indicative of slowed conduction and impaired processing of neutral data and would be compatible with the degenerative changes seen in multiple sclerosis. In addition, the amplitude of the initial response might be reduced over normal values, suggesting a loss of cortical neurons available for processing the evoked response. Thus the average evoked potentials in studies of the human brain add a new dimension for which quantification without subjective evaluation can be made. As stated earlier, in our opinion this technology opens entirely new avenues of research for understanding the neuronal process of information processing in the normal or the abnormal brain.

To be of assistance to those whose curiosity is raised by these procedures, we have assembled a limited bibliography that will open the literature. We feel it is important to stress that all technical advances that lead to a better understanding of human brain behavior must be explored to the maximum, be it traditional testing or exotic neurometrics in our never-ending quest to understanding our wonderful gift of the human brain.

REFERENCES

Anatomy: Williams and Warwick. *Functional Neuroanatomy of Man,* Philadelphia: Saunders, 1975.

Developmental Anatomy: Moore, K. L. *The Developing Human,* Philadephia: Saunders, 1977.

Neurology: Chusid, J. G. *Correlative Neuroanatomy and Functional Neurology,* 16th ed. Lang, 1976.

Gardner, E. *Fundamentals of Neurology,* Philadelphia: Saunders, 1975.

Ramsey, R. *Advanced Exercises in Diagnostic Radiology: Computed Tomography of the Brain,* Philadelphia: Saunders, 1977.

Spillane, J. D. *An Atlas of Clinical Neurology,* 2nd ed. New York: Oxford University Press, 1975.

Evoked Potentials: Begleiter, H. *Evoked Brain Potentials and Behavior.* Proceedings of the Downstate Medical Symposia, New York, New York on evoked potentials. New York: Plenum Press, 1979.

Lehman, D. and Callaway, E. *Human Evoked Potentials Applications and Problems,* Proceedings of the NATO Conference on Evoked Potentials held at Konstanz, West Germany. New York: Plenum Press, 1979.

General Reading: "The Brain," *Scientific American* (September 1979). San Francisco: Freeman.

12

Learning Disabilities and the Child-Care Physician

Janet W. Lerner and Susan L. Cohn

T HE PURPOSE OF THIS PAPER is to examine what role the physician who works with children *should* play with the learning disabled child, the teacher, and the school and to contrast that ideal role with what physicians *actually know* and *do* about learning disabilities. Some of this field data has been recently collected by the American Academy of Pediatrics.

The medical profession played a key role in the historical development of the field of learning disabilities. They take an active part in today's research, diagnosis, and treatment. Yet a critical question relates to the extent of the relationship between the physician and the school in caring for the learning disabled child. This paper examines the following areas: changing role of the child-care physician, the need for improved communication between the doctor and the school, the implications of Public Law 94-142 for the child-care physician, the training of child-care medical specialists and educators, and current research indicating the status of pediatricians and educators on these matters.

CHANGING ROLE OF THE CHILD-CARE PHYSICIAN

Today, the physician who accepts responsibility for the treatment of a child's bodily illness must also be responsible for the totality of the child's care. It is not longer enough to simply give children immunization shots, treat ear infections, and give school physicals. A physician today must be able to care for ailments that extend beyond physical illness. Recognizing parent neglect and home-life difficulties is part of the doctor's job today. Diagnosing behavioral delays and learning disabilities is now a skill every child-care physician should acquire. Furthermore, the physician should be able to realize when a patient could benefit from the special education services that are offered in our schools. To be able to carry out these new responsibilities effectively

213

physicians will need to know precisely what these school services entail so that their patients will be able to attain proper and complete care. Knowledge of federal legislation, PL 94-142, as well as state laws, should also be among the competencies of today's physician.

Physicians are in a unique position in that they are able to detect and exclude the treatable medical conditions which could explain a child's learning or behavior problems. These medical conditions can include seizure disorders, progressive neurologic disease, psychiatric disorders of emotional or conduct type, visual or auditory impairments at sensory or perceptual levels, metabolic imbalance, and endocrine abnormalities. For example, many children who are labeled "hyperactive" or behavior problems by their teachers because of excessive acting out in class have been found to be hyperthyroid on a simple blood screening test. Once treated medically or surgically for the physical disability, the hyperactivity disappears and the child generally does well academically and socially.

Of course many children who display learning and behavior problems have no medically detectable abnormalities. However, the physician can play an important role in this situation as well. Often the doctor may be the first person to identify the preschool child's need for special educational services. It is imperative, therefore, for the physician to be fully aware of normal childhood development so that slow maturation and behavioral problems can be recognized and the proper treatment can be initiated. Physicians must accept this expanded responsibility for the total health of the child if their patients are to receive the benefits of full health care.

NEED FOR IMPROVED COMMUNICATION

Medical specialists must be knowledgeable about new laws concerning special education and services available through the school which would benefit their patients. This will occur only if good communication is established between the medical and educational worlds. It is therefore essential for physicians to be able to communicate their evaluation to school professionals.

On the other hand, it is also essential for teachers to know something of the nature of the medical treatment procedure. Teachers should be aware of possible side effects of any treatment so they can be consulted to provide invaluable information of the impact of the treatment procedure. Teachers may be asked by the physician to make adjustments in the curriculum, length of the school day, or testing procedures. If teachers understand what and why, such accommodations can be made more easily and effectively.

The teacher and the physician must integrate disciplines to manage and treat the handicapped child successfully. Together they can supervise the growth and development of the child through the utilization of medical and educational resources giving the child an optimal opportunity to achieve maximal potential.

To enable better communication between educators and physicians terms must be used which have the same meaning and significance for all. Historically a child of normal intelligence with a disorder of behavior and/or learning may have been described as "brain damaged," a "Strauss syndrome child," "hyperactive," or "minimally brain dysfunctioned." These labels did not carry universal meanings which made it difficult for primary physicians who had to diagnose and treat these children, for educators who had to evaluate and participate in the treatment, and for parents who had to deal with their impaired youngsters each day. A generally accepted nomenclature would help abolish some of the ambiguities which are inherent to these disorders, and it would hopefully encourage more meaningful interaction between the professionals needed to properly diagnose and treat these disabled children.

An editorial in the *Journal of Pediatrics,* November 1979, advocates the term "attentional deficit disorder." This term was designated in the Diagnostic and Statistical *Manual* of the American Psychiatric Association to refer to the behavior and/or learning disabled child of normal intelligence. There is good reason to believe that such a designation has merit. We know little about the etiology and pathogenesis of most neuropsychiatric disorders and are therefore, unable to gather external validation of the malady. External validation is an external test such as a blood culture which can be used to help diagnose pneumonia in a child with an infiltrate on a chest X-ray for example. This type of external measurement is used for most pediatric disorders. However, external validation cannot be effectively used when evaluating learning disabled children. An alternate system is therefore necessary to obtain information when diagnosing neuropsychiatric disorders. This alternate system is internal validation, in which the information needed to evaluate a child is obtained to a great degree from history and observation of behavior. It is in this light that the term *attentional deficit disorder* is suggested for communication purposes. Attentional deficit disorder designates the clinical prominence of attentional disorders in this group of children, and it can, therefore, be easily subdivided into categories with and without hyperactivity. It is hoped that with the help of consistently defined terms a unified approach to the diagnosis and management of affected children will now be possible.

The ultimate value of the term depends upon the physician's ability to evaluate the patient with internal validation and recognize the behavioral and/or learning deficit. The *Manual* will then give the criteria to provide a structure and rationale for synthesizing the clinical information. Finally, the pediatrician will be able to orchestrate the treatment that would most benefit his or her patient through open communication with the educators and family.

IMPLICATIONS OF PL 94-142 FOR THE CHILD-CARE PHYSICIAN

Special education is in the midst of a remarkable change as a result of a far-reaching law known as Public Law 94-142, the Education for All Handicapped Children Act. The law resulted from a fortuitous and timely coalition of a number of somewhat disparate groups which included: (1) parents of handicapped children with various maladies, such as parents of the deaf, parents of the mentally retarded, and parents of the learning disabled; (2) special education professional organizations such as the Council for Exceptional Children; and (3) civil rights attorneys who extended their interests from the civil rights of minorities to that of the handicapped. These diverse interest groups were supported and encouraged to combine their efforts by the Bureau of Education for the Handicapped. The passage of PL 94-142 in 1975 was due in large measure to the work of these groups who elicted support of important congressional committees (Martin, 1978).

PL 94-142 is based upon the premise that handicapped children have a right to a free appropriate public education. Under the provisions of the act, state and local education agencies are required to arrange yearly evaluations of handicapped children and to develop and administer individualized educational programs (IEP) for these youngsters.

Federal law does not state explicitly the manner or degree to which the physician should participate in the diagnosis or treatment for the handicapped child. However, PL 94-142, Section 121a.13(4) mentions medical services as a related service: " 'Medical Services' means services provided by licensed physicians to determine a child's medically related handicapping condition which results in the child's need for special education and related services." The implication is that medical services can be used for the diagnostic or evaluation process. State laws may state more specifically the degree to which the physician will be involved with these processes. Therefore, medical specialists should refer to their individual state laws.

Traditionally, physicians have played a major part in the management of handicapped children; hence, they must now acquaint themselves with the new special education process because many of their patients will be affected by the educational innovations imbedded in PL 94-142. It is important for physicians to familiarize themselves with many trends in teacher education such as infant stimulation, behavior modification, the IEP, and least restrictive environment so that they can discuss these knowledgeably with parents and work with school personnel effectively.

The mandates and implications of PL 94-142 will have wide-ranging effects on the education of handicapped, as well as nonhandicapped children, and on the ways in which citizens and professionals perceive handicapped children. The law will also affect physicians' management of handicapped children. In addition the law will affect the preparation of both teachers and physicians in special education.

THE TRAINING OF CHILD-CARE SPECIALISTS AND EDUCATORS

The need for inservice training was recognized by the designers of Public Law 94-142. Built into the law is a section outlining the plan of a *comprehensive system of personnel development.* According to this plan, each state must include in its state plan those procedures and programs intended to train all personnel — regular teachers, special teachers, and support personnel including physicians, to update their skills and attitudes and to acquire information on new instructional procedures and practices. The law seeks "innovative and experimental inservice programs." Moreover, it suggests the use of "incentives which insure participation by teachers such as released time, payment for participation, options for academic credit, salary step credit, certification renewal, or updating of professional skills." The American Academy of Pediatrics is currently developing inservice modules for pediatricians through a USOE grant entitled "In-Service Training for Physicians Serving Handicapped Children."

Training is needed for child-care physicians because of their changing roles, the need for communication with the schools, and the necessity of knowledge of the new federal and state legislation. Teachers also need special training for these same reasons. Moreover many of the children designated as handicapped with whom the teachers will work, will be under the care and treatment of a physician.

There are two ways of viewing training with special reference to the mandate of PL 94-142: preservice training and continuing education training. *Preservice* refers to the curriculum and training of prospective teachers and physicians. *Continuing education* refers to the updating of knowledge, skills, and attitudes of on-the-job teachers and physicians.

The American Academy of Pediatrics recognized this need for pediatricians to carry out these new roles. Today many pediatric residency programs include specialty clerkships designed to acquaint pediatricians with problems of learning and behavioral disorders. In addition to training during a residency period, child-care physicians need continuing education to update their skills and knowledge continually. The American Academy of Pediatrics Committee on Children with Handicaps suggest that training should be acquired through participation in formally designated fellowships or training programs or through several years of clinical experience working with a multidisciplinary team. What is being suggested is a consultant pediatrician whose subspecialty is child development.

Preservice and continuing service education is also being provided for teachers. The leaders of teacher education have recognized the need of training for working with the handicapped. The American Association of Colleges for Teacher Education (AACTE) stated their position in *Beyond the Mandate:* "All graduates of professional education programs who enter the field are knowledgeable about the rights of all children including the handicapped and are prepared to assume their professional role in implementing the process procedures evolving from legislation."

One force designed to make changes and to integrate regular education with special education is the *Dean's Grants*. The Bureau of Education for the Handicapped funded approximately eighty Dean's Grants in teacher preparation programs throughout the country. The goal of the Deans' Grants projects is to increase the knowledge and skills of regular education personnel to more effectively meet the challenge of education for the handicapped.

Continuing on-the-job education or inservice training is needed for teachers. Adult education must be very different from that of preservice education. The needs of the participant are of primary import. Time is the professionals' most valuable commodity, and they must see the need for the training being received. In addition the methods used for preservice training are not suitable for adult education. Methods and materials that take into account the professional experience, the perceived needs, and the interest of the student must be used.

CURRENT RESEARCH

Now that we have examined what ought to occur in regard to the changing role of physicians, communication, knowledge of new laws and school services, and training requirements, what in fact does exist? While available research and data in these areas are sparse, there are a few studies being conducted (Okolo et al. 1979; American Academy of Pediatrics 1980).

The American Academy of Pediatrics, as part of a BEH inservice personnel training project, collected data from sixty randomly selected pediatricians from fourteen states. The questionnaires were mailed to each pediatrician and subsequently each doctor was contacted by telephone to obtain responses. The respondents ranged from relatively new graduates to those who graduated from medical school more than thirty years ago. About 90 percent of the physicians had graduated more than ten years ago. The physicians reported seeing children of all areas of handicapping conditions; 100 percent reported seeing children who were learning disabled.

The most frequently used screening instrument (58 percent) is the Denver Developmental Screening Test, but 7 percent used PPVT, 3 percent Vineland Social Maturity Scale, 3 percent Bender, and 30 percent DQ.

About 70 percent of the respondents reported regular contact with special education departments in local schools. Only 38 percent reported that they had participated in educational planning teams. About 73 percent reported familiarity with PL 94-142. Only 27 percent reported that they had received adequate training in medical school or residency training to adequately prepare them to work with handicapped children and with families. About 73 percent reported the need for more training in issues involving handicapped children.

RESEARCH FROM TEACHERS

A study of teachers concerning the involvement of school personnel in the administration of medical for the hyperactive child was conducted by Okolo et al (1979). Questionnaires dealing with the initiation and monitoring of drug therapy were completed by 138 teachers and nurses. Teachers were rarely contacted while nurses were contacted 66–89 percent of the time.

Teacher opinion regarding therapy for hyperactive children demonstrates that while 91 percent of the teachers thought they had important information to contribute, only 31 percent were satisfied with their involvement.

SUMMARY

Child-care physicians must make changes in their training procedures so that they will be able to develop better diagnostic and evaluative skills in working with handicapped children. Furthermore, it is imperative for doctors to be familiar with the applications of the new laws in special education so that their care for handicapped children will be complete. Educational and medical personnel must join forces to provide appropriate care for handicapped children. Only when the physician and school willingly participate in a joint effort to understand the handicapped child will we succeed in reaching this goal.

REFERENCES

American Academy of Pediatrics. "In-Service Training for Physicians Serving Handicapped Children," Bureau for Education of the Handicapped In-Service Personnel Training Project, Evanston, Ill.: American Academy of Pediatrics; unpublished paper, 1980.

Okolo, C.; Bartlett, S.; Shaw, S., "Communication between Professionals Concerning Medication for the Hyperactive Child." *Journal of Learning Disabilities* 11 (1978):647–50.

13

The Prediction of Reading Failure
A Review and Critique

Archie A. Silver and Rosa A. Hagin

T HIS chapter is concerned with the early identification of and intervention with children with reading problems, here taken as a paradigm of learning problems. Early identification has as its purpose the detection of those children we predict will have difficulty learning to read in the primary grades. Early identification is the first part of a three-part preventive program which involves early identification or scanning, diagnosis, and intervention.

Two general questions immediately arise: (1) what causes this difficulty, and (2) how can we recognize it before it reveals itself in reading failure? The definition used here implies that reading difficulty is but a symptom, the result of many forces acting upon the child and many forces from within him or her. These forces may be biological, psychological, social, and educational, in any and all combinations. The causes of reading difficulty may be found in prenatal, perinatal, or neonatal stress; they may be genetically determined; some may suffer from inappropriate stimulation at critical ages for language development; others may have their cause in inadequate or inappropriate education. In some children the specific cause cannot be determined, and these children we say, have "specific developmental disabilities."

The importance of this diversity in etiology is two-fold.

1. To identify and remove the causes of reading disability is not a simple matter, encompassing as it may the control of prenatal, perinatal and postnatal organic defects, modifying the emotional, perceptual and language environment of the first three years of life, and changing the educational curriculum in kindergarten and in first grade. Overwhelming as these tasks of primary prevention appear, they are not to be dismissed as unrealistic. For example, data from the Collaborative Perinatal Project, designed in 1955 by the National Institute of Neurological Diseases and Blindness as a prospective study of pregnancy and pregnancy complications, is seeping into the literature. These data confirm earlier studies on "reproductive casualties" and identify specific elements in prenatal nutrition, medication and drugs; in obstetrical complications,

medications, and procedures which contribute to such behavioral defects such as short attention span, low intelligence, hyperactivity and reading disability. The field of behavioral teratology has received great stimulus from these studies. Amniocentesis to detect chromosomal abnormalities is now an established procedure as is metabolic screening of neonates to detect inborn metabolic areas. Reducing the incidence of these organic defects is a contribution to the primary prevention of reading disability. Just how many children with reading problems suffer from such organically determined defects is unknown. Silver and Hagin (1972) found that in the sample of the entire first grades of the Lower East Side of Manhattan, 20 percent of the children with reading problems had neurological signs.

The importance of social position of the mothers is emphasized in another study of the Collaborative Perinatal Project. Modest attempts to alter the effects of poverty and of maternal style have been made in Head Start and in early education programs such as those of Bereiter (1972). Highlights of validated programs funded by the U. S. Office of Education's Early Education Project may be obtained from Handicapped Children's Early Education, Bureau of Education for the Handicapped (1975). We are still for the most part limited to secondary prevention, to detect independently of cause those children likely to fail in reading and to intervene before failure occurs.

2. The second implication of heterogeneity in etiology is that we cannot expect a scanning instrument for early identification of reading disability to be able to detect all of the etiological factors. Scanning, therefore, is not diagnosis. It does not tell us the cause of the child's problem. It is not primary prevention. At best, it is a component of secondary prevention of preventing the development of failure even though the causative factors in that potential failure are not removed. This leads to the sceond question raised above. How can we recognize the potential for reading failure before it *becomes* reading failure? This question has been approached in three ways.

1. Retrospective studies: Here the attempt is to define the neuro-psychological correlates of children who have already failed in reading and use this knowledge in testing children at age 4 and 5.

2. Prospective studies: To attempt to define those skills necessary for reading and to test predictive instruments based on these findings. Some of these studies are based on a comprehensive theory and some are not.

3. Combinations of each: That is, defining the neuropsychological correlates of reading failure, from these developing a theory of reading and, from that theory, postulate the antecedents which will predict failure.

Certain warnings are in order. Just as children with reading problems differ as to the cause of their problems, so will they also differ in symptomatology. Within a group of children designated as reading disabled there are marked individual differences in function and a wide range and distribution of assets and deficits. These may appear in all aspects of receptive, associative, and emissive language function, in all aspects of dysgnosias, dyspraxias, and dysphasias. The importance of these variations is that in a statistical survey of large numbers of children, individual differences may well cancel each other out. The investigator may dismiss as unimportant some variables which may be crucially important to some children in the sample. As a further caveat, comparisons between children with and without reading problems must be made in groups matched for age, sex, socioeconomic status, educational opportunities, functional intelligence, and for the presence or absence of organic and psychiatric factors (Parsons and Prigatano 1978). Such information concerning population studied is frequently lacking in neuropsychological investigations, rendering their interpretation most difficult.

With the above caveats, review of retrospective studies indicates that "positive association of a modest degree has been found between reading retardation and deviant performance on a variety of tests making demands on perceptual, linguistic, sequencing and intersensory integrative abilities" (Rourke 1978; and Doehring 1978). But just as frequently the literature has reported no significant differences in these functions when good and poor readers are compared. It is understandable that because of the heterogeneity in etiology and in symptoms, and because the picture of reading disability varies with so many factors as age, sex, socioeconomic status, educational support, findings in even multivariate studies may yield different results.

Retrospectively as far back as 1928, Nila Banton Smith found in two hundred children that letter matching tested in the first week of first grade yielded a correlation of .87 with the Detroit Word Recognition Test 12 weeks later. Visual discrimination of letter size and shape and visual discrimination and knowledge of letter names were found of value as predictors. While auditory discrimination of beginning sounds was emphasized, auditory discrimination, auditory memory blending, and audiovisual integration were not useful in predicting reading ability. Bond and Dykstra (1969), in a review of the Cooperative Research Program in first grade reading instruction, concluded that auditory or visual discrimination and intelligence are related to success in learning to read. The presence of language defects are used as predictors of reading failure. Linguistic theory suggests that reading is a form of linguistic processing dependent upon the reader's psycholinguistic background.

Farr (1969) has suggested that skills related to beginning reading are those which center about the ability to decode written symbols, develop a sight vocabulary, and to use word attack skills. Content analysis of readiness test reveals a striking similarity to the components which Monroe used in 1935 and, in general, conform to Farr's admonition. Specifically the readiness tests cover a wide range of skills involving visual letter and word discrimination and knowledge, visual-motor function, auditory discrimination and recall, sequencing and comprehension, vocabulary, articulation, emissive speech, intermodal integration, concept development, and gross and fine motor abilities.

What is obviously needed is a unifying hypothesis that brings together the diverse findings of both prospective and retrospective studies. The validity of such a hypothesis would enable the building of an instrument which would predict no later than kindergarten which child was to fail and which child was to succeed in reading.

Satz has postulated that in children who will fail in reading there is a lag in the development of those skills, which he presumes to be critical to early phases of reading, namely perceptual discrimination and analysis. They subsume these skills under the term "sensory-perceptual-motor-mnemonic abilities." These variables clustered into a single factor account for 31 percent of the total variance. With three additional factors (socioeconomic status 16 percent, conceptual-verbal 13 percent, motor dominance and laterality 8 percent), 68 percent of the total variance was accounted for. They further state that these kindergarten children will "eventually catch up in those earlier developing skills, but will subsequently lag in the conceptual linguistic skills which have a slower and later ontogenetic development." What Satz has postulated is a specific lag in development, but as maturation overcomes one set of lagging skills, the next hierarchal set will also lag. Accordingly, a cross-sectional study at different ages will of necessity yield different areas of deficit. The perceptual skills described by Satz et al. (1978), namely finger localization, alphabet recognition and discrimination, together correctly classified 77 percent of the children into adequate and inadequate readers, with finger localization itself accounting for 70.5 percent of the correct classification. Unfortunately, the 75 percent correct prediction at the end of first and second grade falls to 57 percent in fifth grade.

Jansky and deHirsch (1972) stressed the importance of the ability to retrieve stored verbal symbols, to comprehend, and to use oral language as predictive of success in reading. Their prediction battery is composed of nineteen test items which include such measures as auditory discrimination and recall, sound blending, oral language level, category names, picture and letter naming, and the Bender Gestalt. Of these, the five tests best predicting reading success or failure were letter naming, picture naming, word matching, the Bender, and sentence repetition (Binet). Jansky and deHirsch state that "three of these activities, letter naming, copying the Bender designs, and word matching can be considered hardy perennials" (p. 57). This battery, administered in the spring of the kindergarten year, correctly predicted 75 percent of failing readers in second grade.

Neither the Satz battery nor the Jansky-deHirsch screening index are listed in the Lee Cross Kenneth Goin 1977 Guide to case finding, screening, diagnosis, assessment and evaluation of handicapped children. Of the 98 tests listed by Cross-Goin, sixteen are considered as scanning instruments. Some of these are designed for children to age eight and can hardly be designated as predictive batteries. Others are designed for specific handicaps, i.e. auditory acuity. Others include testing of fine and gross motor performance. Those batteries testing language and/or perception, and specifically standardized for the kindergarten-age child, number only four, and include the ABC Inventory, the Eliot-Pearson Screening Profile, the Meeting School Screening Test, and Search and Teach.

The Meeting Street Screening Test has as its theoretical base the psycholinguistic processing model of Osgood and Miron (1963). It examines not only visual-perceptive-motor skills but also language functions and gross and fine motor skills.

In their efforts to understand the diverse symptoms presented by children with reading disabilities, Silver and Hagin have attempted to unify their symptoms as all related to orientation as space and organization in time. This means that immaturities may appear in the visual discrimination and recall of asymmetric figures, in specific spatial distortions, in visual motor function, in temporal sequencing of auditory stimuli, and in the orientation of the body and space as seen in finger gnosis, praxis and right-left discrimination, and in those postural responses relating to orientation in space. The perceptual defects seen, regardless of modality, have a common denominator: namely spatial and temporal organization. With this theoretical base and with data obtained from intensive evaluation over two successive years of all children (N = 171), in the first grade of a school on the east side of Manhattan, a test battery of ten items was constructed. These items include three of visual perception (discrimination, recall, visual motor), two auditory (discrimination, sequencing), three of body image (right-left discrimination, praxis, finger gnosis), two intermodal (articulation and intermodal dictation). Administered in the kindergarten year, Search is an individual test which is designed to predict which children will fail and who will succeed in reading by the end of their second grade.

Scanning instruments, however, must have additional attributes to a theoretical base. Ideally, a scanning instrument must be able to serve a large number of children quickly and economically, to predict with validity which child will fail and which will succeed in reading, that the incidence of false positives is negligible and of false negatives is minimal, that it is statistically acceptable from standardization through interpretation, that it is appropriate for the population to be studied, that the administration of the test and the interpretation of the results can be done skillfully by school personnel after brief training, that is able to locate children who need more detailed and extensive diagnostic procedures, and it provides the teacher with a basis for intervention. Again it must be stressed that scanning is not diagnosis. All scanning does is identify those children who, with respect to their peers, perform poorly on the test given. Scanning is not intended to be an all or none phenomenon, a pass-fail decree. It should not therefore be used negatively as evidence for withholding service, for categorizing, non-promotion or non-admission to school. It is intended for positive action, to locate children in need of clinical services and educational intervention, to support and supplement classroom instruction.

Scanning becomes the first step in a program for the prevention of reading problems, enlisting support and involvement from parents, teachers, and school administrators.

Certain of the attributes of the ideal scanning instrument need amplification. The importance of negligible false positives and minimal false negatives is emphasized. In daily practice within the schools, the incidence of false negatives, that is, the test says "will succeed" but the child does not succeed, is not difficult to ascertain. As has been stressed in this chapter, so varied are the causes and the symptoms of reading failure that we could hardly expect a rapid scanning instrument to identify all children who will fail. Empirically, we may place an acceptable incidence of false negatives at about 10 percent of all children scanned. False positives, on the other hand, are potentially more serious and more difficult to determine. Here the test says "will fail," and the child does not fail. To determine the validity of this prediction, specific intervention procedures which may be introduced in the preventive program must be withheld, and the child permitted only the regular classroom instruction. Paradoxically an effective intervention will prevent the vulnerable child from failing and so will increase the percentage of false positives. On the other hand, to withhold remediation within the school in which a preventive program is introduced is a difficult task, and possibly an unethical task. One way or another, teachers will insist that their child receive special help. Fortuitous circumstances, however, sometimes do permit control groups of vulnerable children and some studies are specifically designed only for the predictive aspects of the program and preventive intervention is not part of the experiment. Where control studies are done, we estimate a false positive percentage in the 1–3 percent permissible range.

To cite these percentages however, may be misleading. To understand their significance one needs to know how vulnerability is determined in the particular scanning test. A higher cut-off point means that more children will be considered vulnerable to reading failure and conversely there will be fewer false negatives. A lower cut-off point will mean fewer false positives but greater false negatives. Our experience has suggested that the cut-off point be determined by the actual prevalence of reading retardation within the particular school system. If as we have found, one-third of the fifth grade in a school district is functioning below expectancy in reading, we set the cut-off point at the lowest one-third of the distribution of scores in each subtest of the scanning battery. This maneuver suggests that in each school we are dealing with a continuum of function, that there is no absolute pass and fail but a distribution of skills along a normal curve. Diagnostic labeling is thus avoided and the scanning instrument becomes appropriate for the school population studied.

There is one other factor important in determination of "hit rates" and of false positives and negatives. That is the criterion used to measure reading success and failure. Satz and his associates use teaching rating ± the IOTA Word Recognition Test. Keogh and Becker (1973) suggest that "other measures than teacher ratings are needed to monitor aspects of children's performance and competence." Guidelines for the use of achievement tests as criterion measures are discussed in Farr (1969) and in *A Practical Guide to Measuring Project Impact on Student Achievement* (1975). Our own preference is to use a test of oral reading (Wide Range) word identification, letter identification, and word attack sections of the Woodcock Reading Mastery Tests (1973) at the end of first grade and a comprehension mastery test at the end of second grade (with permission of SRA selected items from levels A–F of mastery tests which accompany the SRA basic series).

Not only are the criterion tests important, but so also is the level of the competence used. Do we use national norms, grade expectancy scores, median scores for the class? Each criterion will yield different results so that the reporting of false positives and false negatives will depend in part on the statistical manipulation. Obviously each test and the criterion used must carefully be considered and documented in evaluation reports.

Even when the content of the early identification battery has been decided and statistical constraints satisfied, do the tests contribute to our understanding of the nature of the reading process? It appears hazardous to interpret the tests in neuropsychological terms. For example, the Metropolitan Reading Test used by one-third of ninety-three school districts sampled by Maitland et al. (1974) consists of six sections in which the child records his or her responses by circling the correct answer on a record blank. Section I is called "word meaning." In this section, the examiner names an object which the child must circle in a three-picture array. Is this really "word meaning?" Is it a test of auditory discrimination, of picture recognition, of figure-background perception, of attention? Other sections are more complex. Another example: Many scanning batteries use a visual-motor test. Is this a test of visual perception, of visual-motor association, of fine motor coordination, or praxis? It is clear that the name which the authors supply to a given subtest does not reveal the underlying neuropsychological mechanisms. The functions studied may not be discreet functions at all, but in fact segments of the same basic function. Certainly the relationship between test and specific neurological function must be viewed with caution.

Most tests do not pretend to add knowledge of the reading process. Those with a very definite theoretical posture and experimental design, however, have supported the contention that beginning reading requires an intact perceptual apparatus, and conversely where specific immaturities are present, word discrimination will be difficult. Our own bias, of course, sees the specific perceptual immaturities as those relating to orientation in space and organization in time.

From a practical point of view, however, readiness tests administered at the beginning of first grade do have a modest relationship with first grade reading. At the end of first grade, for example, the Metropolitan Readiness Test has a product-moment correlation of .52 to .73 with subtests of the Metropolitan Achievement Tests and .52 to .75 with the primary subtests of the Stanford Achievement Tests. The scanning instruments given in the kindergarten grade also have modest predictive value. The Meeting Street School Screening Test correlates .63 with reading achievement at the end of first grade; the Jansky-deHirsch Screening Index identified 75 percent of the children who failed in reading at the end of second grade; Satz reports correct predictions in the 75 percent range at the end of first and second grades but 57 percent in the fifth grade; Silver and Hagin report Search's prediction capability of 1 percent false positives and 10 percent false negatives at the end of second, third, and fourth grade. In terms of false positives, Satz finds 17 percent at the end of grade one, 20 percent at the end of grade 3, and 4.6 percent at the end of grade 5.

With few exceptions, hard data with respect to standardization, population studied, reliability, and validity are not available for most screening tests. Satz et al. (1978) have repeatedly pointed out the weakness of most studies, not only for their statistical lacunae but also for their lack of longitudinal follow-up and cross-validation. In spite of these limitations, the prevention of reading disability is a vital issue and scanning in the kindergarten grade to identify children who have potential for reading failure is becoming an accepted procedure.

As repeatedly emphasized, however, scanning is only the first stage of a program for the secondary prevention of reading problems. Diagnosis and intervention are the remaining components of such a program. By diagnosis we mean the individual examination of the child, to determine if possible the cause of the findings revealed by the scanning instrument, to evaluate his or her physical, including neurological, psychiatric, psychological, social, and educational status, and the influence of each of these components in the child's capacity to learn. Because diagnosis is expensive and professional time scarce, complete diagnosis is reserved for those children vulnerable to learning failure who may score at the lowest end of the scanning battery or for those who are not responsive to intervention. For the majority of vulnerable children, educational intervention alone will be sufficient. In our experience, approximately 25 percent of the entire kindergarten class has the perceptual and neurological immaturities we have come to associate with reading failure. Two-thirds of this 25 percent may immediately be placed in educational intervention. For the remaining one-third educational intervention is also needed but it may not be sufficient. These children may require pediatric neurological, psychiatric, or psychological help for a complete program.

In this paper, we have focused on the identification in the kindergarten grade of children vulnerable to reading failure. This is not too late for secondary prevention. Attempts to identify developmental disabilities in the pre-nursery ages have arisen in large measure from the impetus of the Early Periodic Screening Diagnosis and Treatment Program (EPSDT) mandated by Public Law 90-248, which requires that all states participating in the Medicaid program provide EPSDT services for all persons under twenty-one years of age eligible for Medicaid. Many of these screening devices are a combination of pediatric neurological examination, psychological testing, and the Gesell Developmental schedules.

These screening devices suffer from the same limitations as do the kindergarten scanning tests and in addition, because they attempt to find a much broader range of developmental problems, have increasing difficulty in validity and reliability, and most seriously do not yet have a strong intervention component. They really are trying to do too much for too many with too little.

It has been said, however, that EPSDT "promises to be a giant step in developing and improving child rearing" (Rojcewitz and Aaronson 1976). Certainly the development of programs to prevent reading failure, starting in kindergarten, can be an equally giant step forward in education.

REFERENCES

Bereiter, C. "An Academic Preschool for Disadvantaged Children: Conclusions from Evaluation Studies." *Preschool Programs for the Disadvantaged,* edited by J. Stanley. Baltimore: Johns Hopkins Press, 1972.

Bond, G. L., and Dykstra, R. "The Cooperative Research Program in First Grade Reading Instruction." *Reading Research Quarterly* 2 (1967): 5–142.

Doehring, D. G. "The Tangled Webb of Behavioral Research on Developmental Dyslexia." *Dyslexia,* edited by A. L. Denton and D. Pearl. New York: Oxford University Press, 1978.

Farr, R. "Reading What can be Measured?" *Eric/Crier, Reading Review Series,* Newark, Del.: International Reading Association, p. 10.

Jansky, J., and deHirsch, K. *Preventing Reading Failure,* New York: Harper and Row, 1972.

Keogh, B., and Becker, L. "Early Detection of Learning Problems, Cautions and Guidelines," *Exceptional Children* 40 (1973):5–11.

Maitland, S.; Nadeau, J. B. E.; and Nadeau, G. "Early School Screening Practices." *Journal of Learning Disabilities* 7 (1974):55–59.

Osgood, C. E., and Miron, M. S. *Approaches to the Study of Aphasia,* Urbana, Ill.: University of Illinois Press, 1963.

Parson, O. A., and Prigatano, G. P. "Methodological Consideration in Clinical Neuropsychological Research." *Journal of Consulting and Clinical Psychology* 46 (1978):608–619.

Rojcewicz, S. J., and Aaronson, M. "Mental Health and the Medicaid Screening Program," *Intervention Strategies for High Risk Infants and Young Children,* edited by T. D. Tjossem. Baltimore: University Park Press, 1976.

Rourke, Byron P. "Neuropsychological Research in Reading Retardation: A Review," *Dyslexia*, edited by A. L. Benton and D. Pearl. New York: Oxford University Press, 1978.

Satz, P.; Taylor, H. G.; Friel, J.; Fletcher, J. "Some Developmental and Predictive Precursors of Reading Disabilities: A Six Year Followup," *Ibid.*

Silver, A., and Hagin, R. "Profile of a First Grade: A Basis for Preventive Psychiatry." *American Academy of Child Psychiatry* 11 (1972):645–74.

BRIDGES TO TOMORROW

was composed in 10-point Mergenthaler VIP Times Roman and leaded two points,
with display type in Times Roman, by Partners Composition;
printed offset on 55-pound Warren acid-free Antique Cream paper,
adhesive bound with 10-point Carolina cover,
by Maple-Vail Book Manufacturing Group, Inc.;
and published by

SYRACUSE UNIVERSITY PRESS
SYRACUSE, NEW YORK 13210